TOILETRIVIA ™

THIS DATE IN HISTORY

**The only trivia book that caters
to your everyday bathroom needs**

by Jeremy Klaff & Harry Klaff

This book might contain product names, trademarks, or registered trade-marks. All trademarks in this book are property of their respective owners. If used, they are for non-biased use, and we do not encourage or discourage use of said product or service. Any term suspected of being a trademark will be properly capitalized.

Cover art by Stephanie Strack

About the Authors

Harry Klaff covered the NHL for *The Hockey News* and *Hockey Pictorial*, and reported for both the Associated Press and United Press International. He has written three books, *All Time Greatest Super Bowl*, *All Time Greatest Stanley Cup*, and *Computer Literacy and Use*.

Today, he is a retired Social Studies teacher from Brooklyn. Because he never went on a date in his adolescence, Harry had plenty of time to research useless facts and figures on everything ranging from history to pop culture. Moonlighting as a hockey scoreboard operator and baseball beer vendor, Harry had ample time to collect data.

Yet somehow, he got married. In 1977, Jeremy was born. Rather than being raised on a steady diet of carrots and peas, baby Jeremy was forced to learn facts from textbooks. His first word was "Uzbekistan." Throughout his childhood, Jeremy had a hard time making friends. When other kids wanted to play baseball, he wanted to instruct them about Henry VIII's six wives. After a failed career as a standup comic and broadcaster, in 2000 Jeremy fittingly became a Social Studies teacher. Today he brings trivia to the next generation.

Collect All Toiletrivia Titles

US History

World History

Pop Culture

Sports

Baseball

The 1980s

and more!

Get the full list of titles at
www.toiletrivia.com

Acknowledgements

We at Toiletrivia would like to thank all of the people who made this possible.

- •The ancient cities of Harappa and Mohenjo Daro for engineering advances in plumbing.

- •Sir John Harrington for inventing the modern flush toilet.

- •Seth Wheeler for his patent of perforated toilet paper.

- •Jeffrey Gunderson for inventing the plunger.

We would like to thank our families for suffering through nights of endless trivia.

We would also like to thank the friendly commuters at the Grand Central Station restroom facility for field testing these editions.

Introduction

Here at *Toiletrivia* we do extensive research on what you, the bathroom user, wish to see in your reading material. Sure, there are plenty of fine books out there to pass the time, but none of them cater to your competitive needs. That's why *Toiletrivia* is here to provide captivating trivia that allows you to interact with fellow bathroom users.

Each day of the year enables you to keep score so you can evaluate your progress if you choose to go through the book multiple times. Or, you may wish to leave the book behind for others to play and keep score against you. Perhaps you just want to make it look like you are a genius, and leave a perfect scorecard for all to see. We hope you leave one in every bathroom of the house.

The rules of *Toiletrivia* are simple. Each date has 3 questions for One Roll, Two Rolls, or Three Rolls. The One Rolls are easiest and worth one point. Two Rolls are a bit harder and are worth two points. And of course, Three Rolls are the hardest, and are worth three points. You will tabulate your progress on the scorecard near the end of the book.

The questions we have selected are meant for dinner conversation, or impressing people you want to date. With few exceptions, our queries are geared for the uncomfortable situations that life throws at you, like when you have nothing in common with someone, and need to offer some clever banter. We hope that the facts you learn in the restroom make it easier to meet your future in-laws, or deal with that hairdresser who just won't stop talking to you.

Remember, *Toiletrivia* is a game. No joysticks, no computer keyboards…just you, your toilet, and a pen; the way nature intended it. So good luck. We hope you are triumphant.

Directions

Each set of questions has an answer sheet opposite it. Write your answers in the first available column to the right. When you are done with a three-day set of questions, *fold* your answer column underneath so the next restroom user doesn't see your answers. *Special note to restroom users 2 and 3: No cheating! And the previous person's answers might be wrong!*

Then check your responses with the answer key on the following page. Mark your right answers with a check, and your wrong answers with an "x." Then go to the scorecard on pages 253-255 and tabulate your results. These totals will be the standard for other users to compare.

Be sure to look online for other Toiletrivia titles
Visit us at www.toiletrivia.com

January 1

🧻 One Roll

Flip to pg. 11 for answers

This author of *The Catcher in the Rye* was born on this date in 1919.

🧻🧻 Two Rolls

In 1863, what document signed by Abraham Lincoln went into effect?

🧻🧻🧻 Three Rolls

In 1971, what disappeared from television forever?

January 2

🧻 One Roll

In 1974, President Nixon signed a bill to conserve gas and make interstate travel safer. What did this new law create?

🧻🧻 Two Rolls

In 1900, Secretary of State John Hay announced what new foreign policy concerning trade in China?

🧻🧻🧻 Three Rolls

In 1923, Albert Fall "took the fall" for what scandal?

January 3

🧻 One Roll

Today in 1961, it became a lot harder to get cigars from Cuba. Why?

🧻🧻 Two Rolls

Who was excommunicated from the Church on this date in 1521?

🧻🧻🧻 Three Rolls

Within $10,000, how much money did the New York Yankees pay the Boston Red Sox for Babe Ruth's contract? The deal was completed on this date in 1920.

Answer Sheet | Answer Sheet | Answer Sheet

Name_____ | Name_____ | Name_____

January 1 | January 1 | January 1

January 1	January 1	January 1
1 Roll	1 Roll	1 Roll
2 Rolls	2 Rolls	2 Rolls
3 Rolls	3 Rolls	3 Rolls

January 2 | January 2 | January 2

January 2	January 2	January 2
1 Roll	1 Roll	1 Roll
2 Rolls	2 Rolls	2 Rolls
3 Rolls	3 Rolls	3 Rolls

January 3 | January 3 | January 3

January 3	January 3	January 3
1 Roll	1 Roll	1 Roll
2 Rolls	2 Rolls	2 Rolls
3 Rolls	3 Rolls	3 Rolls

After you have filled out the sheet, fold your column underneath along the dashed line so the next restroom user won't see your answers. *The first player uses the far right column.*

January 4

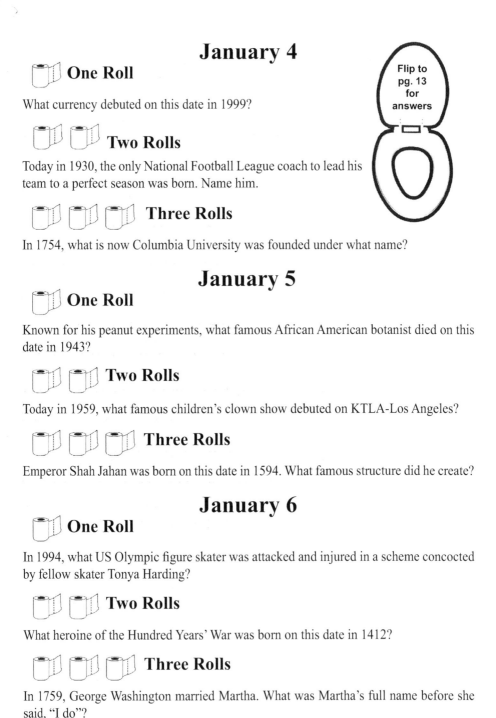

One Roll

What currency debuted on this date in 1999?

Two Rolls

Today in 1930, the only National Football League coach to lead his team to a perfect season was born. Name him.

Three Rolls

In 1754, what is now Columbia University was founded under what name?

Flip to pg. 13 for answers

January 5

One Roll

Known for his peanut experiments, what famous African American botanist died on this date in 1943?

Two Rolls

Today in 1959, what famous children's clown show debuted on KTLA-Los Angeles?

Three Rolls

Emperor Shah Jahan was born on this date in 1594. What famous structure did he create?

January 6

One Roll

In 1994, what US Olympic figure skater was attacked and injured in a scheme concocted by fellow skater Tonya Harding?

Two Rolls

What heroine of the Hundred Years' War was born on this date in 1412?

Three Rolls

In 1759, George Washington married Martha. What was Martha's full name before she said, "I do"?

Answer Sheet | Answer Sheet | Answer Sheet

Name_____ | Name_____ | Name_____

January 4 | January 4 | January 4

1 Roll	1 Roll	1 Roll
2 Rolls	2 Rolls	2 Rolls
3 Rolls	3 Rolls	3 Rolls

January 5 | January 5 | January 5

1 Roll	1 Roll	1 Roll
2 Rolls	2 Rolls	2 Rolls
3 Rolls	3 Rolls	3 Rolls

January 6 | January 6 | January 6

1 Roll	1 Roll	1 Roll
2 Rolls	2 Rolls	2 Rolls
3 Rolls	3 Rolls	3 Rolls

After you have filled out the sheet, fold your column underneath along the dashed line so the next restroom user won't see your answers. *The first player uses the far right column.*

Answers - January 1-3

Jan. 1, 1 Roll: J.D. Salinger
Jan. 1, 2 Rolls: The Emancipation Proclamation. Unfortunately, it only freed the slaves in the places that weren't listening to federal laws. Nonetheless, Lincoln became known as "The Great Emancipator."
Jan. 1, 3 Rolls: Cigarette commercials. The last one was for Virginia Slims, shortly before midnight during *The Johnny Carson Show*.

Jan. 2, 1 Roll: A 55 mph speed limit
Jan. 2, 2 Rolls: The Open Door Policy
Jan. 2, 3 Rolls: The Teapot Dome Scandal

Jan. 3, 1 Roll: The United States cut off diplomacy with Fidel Castro's Cuba
Jan. 3, 2 Rolls: Martin Luther. Four years prior, he hammered the 95 Theses to a church door in Wittenberg, Germany.
Jan. 3, 3 Rolls: $125,000. Red Sox owner Harry Frazee used some of this to finance his Broadway show, *No No Nanette*.

January 7

One Roll

What jungle-centric comic strip debuted in 1929?

Two Rolls

What Axis leader died almost 50 years after World War II ended?

Three Rolls

What dictator of the Khmer Rouge was overthrown in 1979?

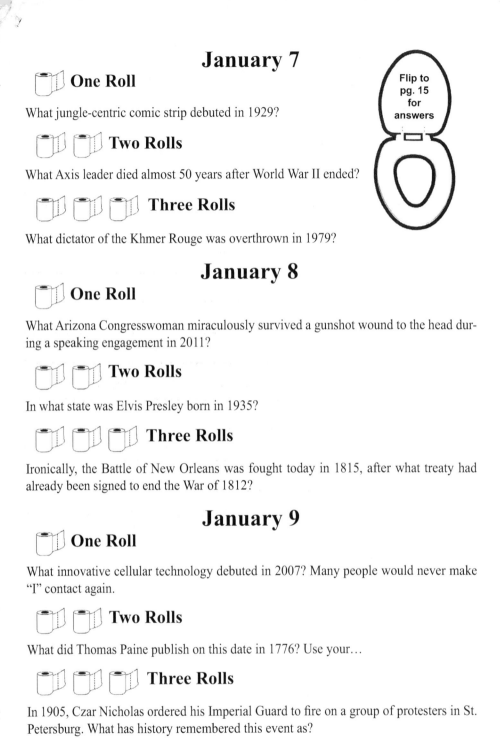

Flip to pg. 15 for answers

January 8

One Roll

What Arizona Congresswoman miraculously survived a gunshot wound to the head during a speaking engagement in 2011?

Two Rolls

In what state was Elvis Presley born in 1935?

Three Rolls

Ironically, the Battle of New Orleans was fought today in 1815, after what treaty had already been signed to end the War of 1812?

January 9

One Roll

What innovative cellular technology debuted in 2007? Many people would never make "I" contact again.

Two Rolls

What did Thomas Paine publish on this date in 1776? Use your...

Three Rolls

In 1905, Czar Nicholas ordered his Imperial Guard to fire on a group of protesters in St. Petersburg. What has history remembered this event as?

Answer Sheet | Answer Sheet | Answer Sheet

Name_____ | Name_____ | Name_____

January 7 | January 7 | January 7

January 7	January 7	January 7
1 Roll	1 Roll	1 Roll
2 Rolls	2 Rolls	2 Rolls
3 Rolls	3 Rolls	3 Rolls

January 8 | January 8 | January 8

January 8	January 8	January 8
1 Roll	1 Roll	1 Roll
2 Rolls	2 Rolls	2 Rolls
3 Rolls	3 Rolls	3 Rolls

January 9 | January 9 | January 9

January 9	January 9	January 9
1 Roll	1 Roll	1 Roll
2 Rolls	2 Rolls	2 Rolls
3 Rolls	3 Rolls	3 Rolls

After you have filled out the sheet, fold your column underneath along the dashed line so the next restroom user won't see your answers. *The first player uses the far right column.*

Answers - January 4-6
Jan. 4, 1 Roll: The Euro
Jan. 4, 2 Rolls: Don Shula
Jan. 4, 3 Rolls: King's College

Jan. 5, 1 Roll: George Washington Carver
Jan. 5, 2 Rolls: *Bozo the Clown*
Jan. 5, 3 Rolls: The Taj Mahal. He ordered it to be created in memory of his wife Mumtaz Mahal.

Jan. 6, 1 Roll: Nancy Kerrigan
Jan. 6, 2 Rolls: Joan of Arc
Jan. 6, 3 Rolls: Martha Dandridge Custis

January 10

One Roll

Flip to pg. 17 for answers

Born on this date in 1949, this former Heavyweight Champion became better known for his grilling than his punching.

Two Rolls

In 1982, what San Francisco 49er made "the catch" in the NFC Championship game against the Dallas Cowboys?

Three Rolls

What socialist became President of Nicaragua today in 1985?

January 11

One Roll

On this date in 1973 baseball lineups in the American League got stronger? Why?

Two Rolls

In 1908, President Theodore Roosevelt made this a National Monument.

Three Rolls

What heroine of the Holocaust died at the age of 100 in 2010? She was one of the few who helped Anne Frank's family hide in the secret annex of Amsterdam.

January 12

One Roll

Whose 1969 "guarantee" lifted the New York Jets to victory in Super Bowl III?

Two Rolls

The "King of All Media" was born today in 1954. Who is he?

Three Rolls

In 1971, *All in the Family* debuted. Throughout the decade, audiences watched as Edith and Archie sang what song at the top of the show?

Answer Sheet | Answer Sheet | Answer Sheet

Name_____ | Name_____ | Name_____

January 10 | January 10 | January 10

1 Roll	1 Roll	1 Roll
2 Rolls	2 Rolls	2 Rolls
3 Rolls	3 Rolls	3 Rolls

January 11 | January 11 | January 11

1 Roll	1 Roll	1 Roll
2 Rolls	2 Rolls	2 Rolls
3 Rolls	3 Rolls	3 Rolls

January 12 | January 12 | January 12

1 Roll	1 Roll	1 Roll
2 Rolls	2 Rolls	2 Rolls
3 Rolls	3 Rolls	3 Rolls

After you have filled out the sheet, fold your column underneath along the dashed line so the next restroom user won't see your answers. *The first player uses the far right column.*

Answers - January 7-9
Jan. 7, 1 Roll: *Tarzan of the Apes*
Jan. 7, 2 Rolls: Japan's Emperor Hirohito died in 1989
Jan. 7, 3 Rolls: Pol Pot of Cambodia

Jan. 8, 1 Roll: Gabrielle Giffords
Jan. 8, 2 Rolls: Tupelo, Mississippi
Jan. 8, 3 Rolls: Treaty of Ghent

Jan. 9, 1 Roll: The iPhone
Jan. 9, 2 Rolls: *Common Sense*. The pamphlet convinced many that independence from the British Crown was justified.
Jan. 9, 3 Rolls: Bloody Sunday

January 13

One Roll

In 1962, what Chubby Checker hit reclaimed the #1 spot on the *Billboard* Hot 100 chart?

Two Rolls

For the first time in 1942, an aviation invention worked. It's a good thing in case of a crash.

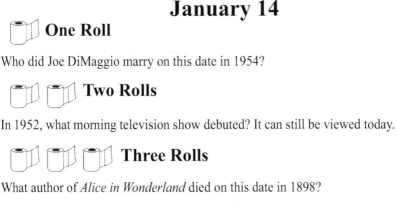

Flip to pg. 19 for answers

Three Rolls

Signed today, the Flag Act of 1794 changed the United States flag. How?

January 14

One Roll

Who did Joe DiMaggio marry on this date in 1954?

Two Rolls

In 1952, what morning television show debuted? It can still be viewed today.

Three Rolls

What author of *Alice in Wonderland* died on this date in 1898?

January 15

One Roll

What civil rights leader was born in Atlanta, Georgia today in 1929?

Two Rolls

What two teams battled in the first Super Bowl in 1967?

Three Rolls

James Heatherington of England is given credit for inventing and wearing something on his head for the first time. What?

Answer Sheet | Answer Sheet | Answer Sheet

Name_____ | Name_____ | Name_____

January 13	January 13	January 13
1 Roll	1 Roll	1 Roll
2 Rolls	2 Rolls	2 Rolls
3 Rolls	3 Rolls	3 Rolls

January 14	January 14	January 14
1 Roll	1 Roll	1 Roll
2 Rolls	2 Rolls	2 Rolls
3 Rolls	3 Rolls	3 Rolls

January 15	January 15	January 15
1 Roll	1 Roll	1 Roll
2 Rolls	2 Rolls	2 Rolls
3 Rolls	3 Rolls	3 Rolls

After you have filled out the sheet, fold your column underneath along the dashed line so the next restroom user won't see your answers. *The first player uses the far right column.*

Answers - January 10-12
Jan. 10, 1 Roll: George Foreman
Jan. 10, 2 Rolls: Dwight Clark caught a Joe Montana pass for the winning touchdown
Jan. 10, 3 Rolls: Daniel Ortega

Jan. 11, 1 Roll: The designated hitter (DH) was instituted
Jan. 11, 2 Rolls: The Grand Canyon
Jan. 11, 3 Rolls: Miep Gies

Jan. 12, 1 Roll: Quarterback Joe Namath shocked the football world, as he led the Jets to a 16-7 victory over the Baltimore Colts.
Jan. 12, 2 Rolls: Howard Stern
Jan. 12, 3 Rolls: *Those were the Days*

January 16

One Roll

Flip to pg. 21 for answers

In 1547 Ivan IV crowned himself "Czar of all Russia." What was this czar better known as?

Two Rolls

On this date in 1919, prohibition was ratified. What Amendment was prohibition?

Three Rolls

In 2001, President Bill Clinton posthumously awarded former President Theodore Roosevelt a Medal of Honor for serving in what war?

January 17

One Roll

Before he became a pet detective, this star born today in 1962 was seen on *In Living Color*.

Two Rolls

Who did George Burns marry in 1926? The first name will suffice.

Three Rolls

What Queen was dethroned in 1893, thereby making Hawaii a republic?

January 18

One Roll

In 1993, what national holiday was observed by Arizona for the first time?

Two Rolls

Willie O'Ree became the first African American to play which sport?

Three Rolls

Which President, who passed away on this date in 1862, was the first Vice President to take over for a President who died in office?

Answer Sheet | Answer Sheet | Answer Sheet

Name_____ | Name_____ | Name_____

January 16 | January 16 | January 16

1 Roll	1 Roll	1 Roll
2 Rolls	2 Rolls	2 Rolls
3 Rolls	3 Rolls	3 Rolls

January 17 | January 17 | January 17

1 Roll	1 Roll	1 Roll
2 Rolls	2 Rolls	2 Rolls
3 Rolls	3 Rolls	3 Rolls

January 18 | January 18 | January 18

1 Roll	1 Roll	1 Roll
2 Rolls	2 Rolls	2 Rolls
3 Rolls	3 Rolls	3 Rolls

After you have filled out the sheet, fold your column underneath along the dashed line so the next restroom user won't see your answers. *The first player uses the far right column.*

Answers - January 13-15
Jan. 13, 1 Roll: *The Twist*
Jan. 13, 2 Rolls: The ejection seat. It was done in a test flight.
Jan. 13, 3 Rolls: It added two stars and two stripes for Vermont and Kentucky

Jan. 14, 1 Roll: Marilyn Monroe
Jan. 14, 2 Rolls: *The Today Show*
Jan. 14, 3 Rolls: Charles Lutwidge Dodgson...better known as Lewis Carroll

Jan. 15, 1 Roll: Dr. Martin Luther King, Jr.
Jan. 15, 2 Rolls: The Packers defeated the Chiefs 35-10
Jan. 15, 3 Rolls: A top hat. He donned it today in 1797.

January 19

One Roll

Born today in 1946, what is Dolly Parton's Tennessee theme park called?

Flip to pg. 23 for answers

Two Rolls

Who became the first female leader of India in 1966?

Three Rolls

What famous European race was described to the public for the first time on this date in 1903?

January 20

One Roll

What happens in the United States every four years today?

Two Rolls

After over one year, what crisis ended in 1980?

Three Rolls

In 1892, James Naismith organized the first official basketball game at a YMCA in Springfield, Massachusetts. What was used for hoops?

January 21

One Roll

What American tennis star was kicked out of the men's Australian Open in 1990?

Two Rolls

Which Louis was executed today in 1793 during the French Revolution?

Three Rolls

In 1924 someone died...yet he is still visible on Earth. Who?

Answer Sheet | Answer Sheet | Answer Sheet

Name_____ | Name_____ | Name_____

January 19 | January 19 | January 19

January 19	January 19	January 19
1 Roll	1 Roll	1 Roll
2 Rolls	2 Rolls	2 Rolls
3 Rolls	3 Rolls	3 Rolls

January 20 | January 20 | January 20

January 20	January 20	January 20
1 Roll	1 Roll	1 Roll
2 Rolls	2 Rolls	2 Rolls
3 Rolls	3 Rolls	3 Rolls

January 21 | January 21 | January 21

January 21	January 21	January 21
1 Roll	1 Roll	1 Roll
2 Rolls	2 Rolls	2 Rolls
3 Rolls	3 Rolls	3 Rolls

After you have filled out the sheet, fold your column underneath along the dashed line so the next restroom user won't see your answers. *The first player uses the far right column.*

Answers - January 16-18
Jan. 16, 1 Roll: Ivan the Terrible
Jan. 16, 2 Rolls: Eighteenth Amendment
Jan. 16, 3 Rolls: Spanish-American War

Jan. 17, 1 Roll: Jim Carrey
Jan. 17, 2 Rolls: Gracie Allen
Jan. 17, 3 Rolls: Queen Liliuokalani

Jan. 18, 1 Roll: Martin Luther King, Jr. Day
Jan. 18, 2 Rolls: Hockey. He debuted on this date in 1958 for the Boston Bruins.
Jan. 18, 3 Rolls: John Tyler took over for William Henry Harrison who died one month into his term

January 22

One Roll

What Supreme Court decision, defining the legalities of abortion, was issued on this date in 1973?

Flip to pg. 25 for answers

Two Rolls

The Unabomber pleaded guilty to nearly two decades of terrorism. What is the Unabomber's real name?

Three Rolls

What former US President died on this date in 1973?

January 23

One Roll

What late-night talk show host died at the age of 79 in 2005?

Two Rolls

Take pity on the fools who don't know that this show debuted today in 1983.

Three Rolls

What company came out with the Frisbee (or Pluto Platter as it was called) on this date in 1957?

January 24

One Roll

In 1984, what juicy computer was introduced by Steve Jobs of Apple?

Two Rolls

What World War II leader, known for his Finest Hour Speech, died on this date in 1965?

Three Rolls

In 1964, which Amendment took effect which prevented poll taxes, or taxes to vote?

Answer Sheet | Answer Sheet | Answer Sheet

Name_____ Name_____ Name_____

January 22	**January 22**	**January 22**
1 Roll	1 Roll	1 Roll
2 Rolls	2 Rolls	2 Rolls
3 Rolls	3 Rolls	3 Rolls

January 23	**January 23**	**January 23**
1 Roll	1 Roll	1 Roll
2 Rolls	2 Rolls	2 Rolls
3 Rolls	3 Rolls	3 Rolls

January 24	**January 24**	**January 24**
1 Roll	1 Roll	1 Roll
2 Rolls	2 Rolls	2 Rolls
3 Rolls	3 Rolls	3 Rolls

After you have filled out the sheet, fold your column underneath along the dashed line so the next restroom user won't see your answers. ***The first player uses the far right column.***

Answers - January 19-21
Jan. 19, 1 Roll: Dollywood
Jan. 19, 2 Rolls: Indira Gandhi
Jan. 19, 3 Rolls: Tour de France

Jan. 20, 1 Roll: A presidential term begins on Inauguration Day
Jan. 20, 2 Rolls: The Iran-Hostage Crisis
Jan. 20, 3 Rolls: Peach baskets. The ball used was a soccer ball.

Jan. 21, 1 Roll: John McEnroe. He was ousted for bad conduct.
Jan. 21, 2 Rolls: Louis XVI
Jan. 21, 3 Rolls: Vladimir Lenin can still be viewed at a mausoleum in Moscow

January 25

One Roll

In 1939, John Lewis was knocked out by a rookie boxer with a similar name. Who?

Two Rolls

What international peacekeeping organization was founded on this date in 1919?

Three Rolls

After divorcing his first wife Catherine, Henry VIII married wife number 2 in 1533. Name her.

Flip to pg. 27 for answers

January 26

One Roll

What did Bill Clinton deny on this date in 1998?

Two Rolls

What star of the movie *Slap-Shot* was born on this date in 1925?

Three Rolls

What state became the first to prohibit alcohol in 1838?

January 27

One Roll

In 1984, what pop-star's hair caught fire while filming a commercial for Pepsi-Cola?

Two Rolls

Today in 1973, which President announced a cease-fire in the Vietnam War?

Three Rolls

What famed Russian dancer was born on this date in 1948?

Answer Sheet

Name_____

January 25

1 Roll	
2 Rolls	
3 Rolls	

January 26

1 Roll	
2 Rolls	
3 Rolls	

January 27

1 Roll	
2 Rolls	
3 Rolls	

Answer Sheet

Name_____

January 25

1 Roll	
2 Rolls	
3 Rolls	

January 26

1 Roll	
2 Rolls	
3 Rolls	

January 27

1 Roll	
2 Rolls	
3 Rolls	

Answer Sheet

Name_____

January 25

1 Roll	
2 Rolls	
3 Rolls	

January 26

1 Roll	
2 Rolls	
3 Rolls	

January 27

1 Roll	
2 Rolls	
3 Rolls	

After you have filled out the sheet, fold your column underneath along the dashed line so the next restroom user won't see your answers. ***The first player uses the far right column.***

Answers - January 22-24
Jan. 22, 1 Roll: *Roe v. Wade*
Jan. 22, 2 Rolls: Ted Kaczynski pleaded guilty in 1998
Jan. 22, 3 Rolls: Lyndon B. Johnson

Jan. 23, 1 Roll: Johnny Carson
Jan. 23, 2 Rolls: *A-Team*
Jan. 23, 3 Rolls: Wham-O

Jan. 24, 1 Roll: Macintosh
Jan. 24, 2 Rolls: Winston Churchill
Jan. 24, 3 Rolls: 24th Amendment

January 28

One Roll

The failure of an O-Ring seal was the likely cause behind what 1986 space-exploration tragedy?

Two Rolls

In 1935, Iceland became the first country to legalize a highly-debated procedure. Which one?

Three Rolls

What soon-to-be household name made his first national TV appearance in 1956?

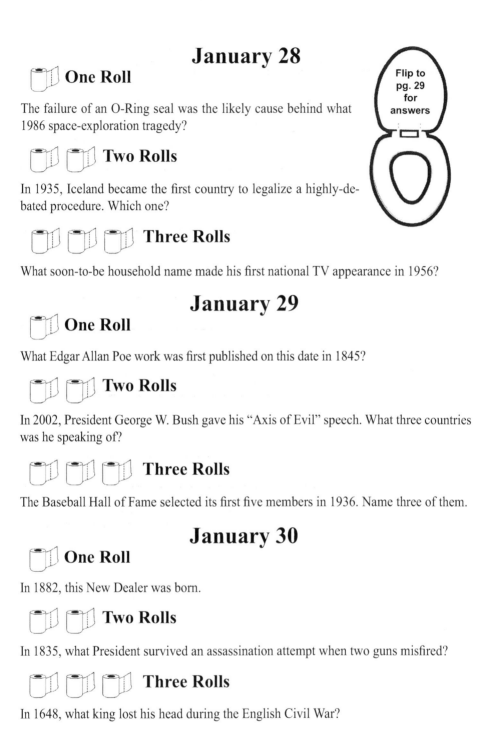

Flip to pg. 29 for answers

January 29

One Roll

What Edgar Allan Poe work was first published on this date in 1845?

Two Rolls

In 2002, President George W. Bush gave his "Axis of Evil" speech. What three countries was he speaking of?

Three Rolls

The Baseball Hall of Fame selected its first five members in 1936. Name three of them.

January 30

One Roll

In 1882, this New Dealer was born.

Two Rolls

In 1835, what President survived an assassination attempt when two guns misfired?

Three Rolls

In 1648, what king lost his head during the English Civil War?

Answer Sheet | Answer Sheet | Answer Sheet

Name_____ | Name_____ | Name_____

January 28 | January 28 | January 28

1 Roll	1 Roll	1 Roll
2 Rolls	2 Rolls	2 Rolls
3 Rolls	3 Rolls	3 Rolls

January 29 | January 29 | January 29

1 Roll	1 Roll	1 Roll
2 Rolls	2 Rolls	2 Rolls
3 Rolls	3 Rolls	3 Rolls

January 30 | January 30 | January 30

1 Roll	1 Roll	1 Roll
2 Rolls	2 Rolls	2 Rolls
3 Rolls	3 Rolls	3 Rolls

After you have filled out the sheet, fold your column underneath along the dashed line so the next restroom user won't see your answers. *The first player uses the far right column.*

Answers - January 25-27
Jan. 25, 1 Roll: Joe Louis
Jan. 25, 2 Rolls: League of Nations
Jan. 25, 3 Rolls: Anne Boleyn…who was later beheaded. Henry married six women.

Jan. 26, 1 Roll: Having sexual relations with his intern, Monica Lewinsky
Jan. 26, 2 Rolls: Paul Newman
Jan. 26, 3 Rolls: Tennessee

Jan. 27, 1 Roll: Michael Jackson
Jan. 27, 2 Rolls: Richard Nixon
Jan. 27, 3 Rolls: Mikhail Baryshnikov

January 31

🧻 **One Roll**

The first African American to play Major League Baseball was born on this date in 1919. Name him.

🧻🧻 **Two Rolls**

The first Prime Minister of Israel announced his resignation today in 1963. Name him.

🧻🧻🧻 **Three Rolls**

What Major League Baseball team did McDonalds head Ray Kroc purchase in 1974?

Flip to pg. 31 for answers

February 1

🧻 **One Roll**

This actor "might have given a damn" if you forgot his birthday. He was born in 1901.

 **Two Rolls**

Bill Murray was the first guest on this person's late night talk show which began today in 1982.

 **Three Rolls**

On this date in 1790, the Supreme Court was scheduled to meet for the first time. Who was the first Chief Justice?

February 2

🧻 **One Roll**

America's Movable Fighting Man debuted as an action figure today in 1964. What is he more commonly known as?

 **Two Rolls**

In 1943, where did the German army surrender today in a key battle of World War II?

 **Three Rolls**

Today in 1990, what leader of South Africa promised to free Nelson Mandela?

Answer Sheet | # Answer Sheet | # Answer Sheet

Name_____ | Name_____ | Name_____

January 31 | ### January 31 | ### January 31

1 Roll	1 Roll	1 Roll
2 Rolls	2 Rolls	2 Rolls
3 Rolls	3 Rolls	3 Rolls

February 1 | ### February 1 | ### February 1

1 Roll	1 Roll	1 Roll
2 Rolls	2 Rolls	2 Rolls
3 Rolls	3 Rolls	3 Rolls

February 2 | ### February 2 | ### February 2

1 Roll	1 Roll	1 Roll
2 Rolls	2 Rolls	2 Rolls
3 Rolls	3 Rolls	3 Rolls

After you have filled out the sheet, fold your column underneath along the dashed line so the next restroom user won't see your answers. *The first player uses the far right column.*

Answers - January 28-30
Jan. 28, 1 Roll: The *Challenger* disaster
Jan. 28, 2 Rolls: Abortion
Jan. 28, 3 Rolls: Elvis Presley appeared on the Dorsey Brothers Stage Show in New York

Jan. 29, 1 Roll: *The Raven*
Jan. 29, 2 Rolls: Iraq, Iran, and North Korea
Jan. 29, 3 Rolls: Ty Cobb, Walter Johnson, Christy Mathewson, Babe Ruth, and Honus Wagner

Jan. 30, 1 Roll: Franklin Delano Roosevelt
Jan. 30, 2 Rolls: Andrew Jackson. On January 30, 1835, Richard Lawrence pulled out two pistols and fired at the President. Both misfired. Later tests revealed that they should have worked.
Jan. 30, 3 Rolls: King Charles I

February 3

One Roll

What famous American artist, born today in 1894, drew for *The Saturday Evening Post*?

Two Rolls

Singer Don McLean believed today in 1959 was the day that music died. Why?

Flip to pg. 33 for answers

Three Rolls

In 1930, this former President, who later became Chief Justice, retired from the Court.

February 4

One Roll

Probably the most famous celebrity of his time, he was born today in 1902. Twenty-five years later, he flew across the Atlantic.

Two Rolls

After being unanimously elected as the first President of the US today in 1789, what city would George Washington be inaugurated in?

Three Rolls

The USO was founded today in 1941 to aid servicemen. What does USO stand for?

February 5

One Roll

With 715 home runs, he passed Babe Ruth in 1974. He was born today in 1934. Name him.

Two Rolls

What sweet boxer won his first pro fight today in 1977?

Three Rolls

What was the first Charlie Chaplin "talkie," which debuted today in 1936?

Answer Sheet | Answer Sheet | Answer Sheet

Name_____ Name_____ Name_____

February 3	**February 3**	**February 3**
1 Roll	1 Roll	1 Roll
2 Rolls	2 Rolls	2 Rolls
3 Rolls	3 Rolls	3 Rolls

February 4	**February 4**	**February 4**
1 Roll	1 Roll	1 Roll
2 Rolls	2 Rolls	2 Rolls
3 Rolls	3 Rolls	3 Rolls

February 5	**February 5**	**February 5**
1 Roll	1 Roll	1 Roll
2 Rolls	2 Rolls	2 Rolls
3 Rolls	3 Rolls	3 Rolls

After you have filled out the sheet, fold your column underneath along the dashed line so the next restroom user won't see your answers. *The first player uses the far right column.*

Answers - January 31-February 2
Jan. 31, 1 Roll: Jackie Robinson
Jan. 31, 2 Rolls: David Ben-Gurion
Jan. 31, 3 Rolls: San Diego Padres

Feb. 1, 1 Roll: Clark Gable
Feb. 1, 2 Rolls: David Letterman
Feb. 1, 3 Rolls: John Jay. Because only three justices showed up, they wound up meeting the next day.

Feb. 2, 1 Roll: G.I. Joe
Feb. 2, 2 Rolls: Battle of Stalingrad
Feb. 2, 3 Rolls: F.W. De Klerk

February 6

One Roll

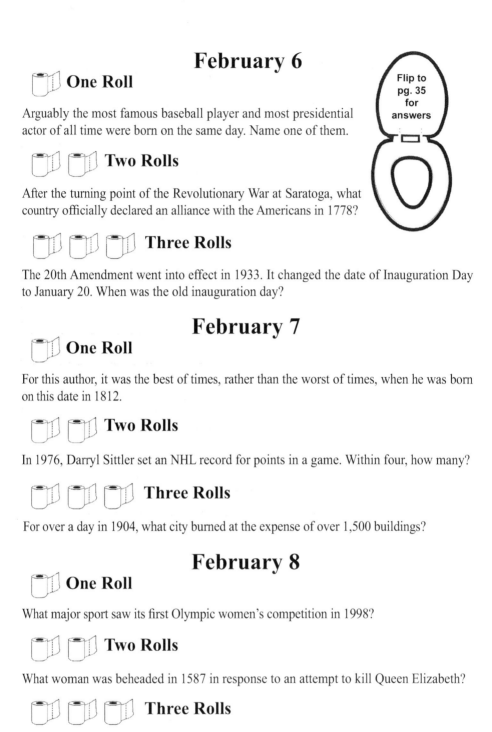

Flip to pg. 35 for answers

Arguably the most famous baseball player and most presidential actor of all time were born on the same day. Name one of them.

Two Rolls

After the turning point of the Revolutionary War at Saratoga, what country officially declared an alliance with the Americans in 1778?

Three Rolls

The 20th Amendment went into effect in 1933. It changed the date of Inauguration Day to January 20. When was the old inauguration day?

February 7

One Roll

For this author, it was the best of times, rather than the worst of times, when he was born on this date in 1812.

Two Rolls

In 1976, Darryl Sittler set an NHL record for points in a game. Within four, how many?

Three Rolls

For over a day in 1904, what city burned at the expense of over 1,500 buildings?

February 8

One Roll

What major sport saw its first Olympic women's competition in 1998?

Two Rolls

What woman was beheaded in 1587 in response to an attempt to kill Queen Elizabeth?

Three Rolls

What rather racist movie, shown in the White House by President Wilson, glorified the Ku Klux Klan as heroes? It opened today in 1915.

Answer Sheet | Answer Sheet | Answer Sheet

Name_____ Name_____ Name_____

February 6 | February 6 | February 6

1 Roll	1 Roll	1 Roll
2 Rolls	2 Rolls	2 Rolls
3 Rolls	3 Rolls	3 Rolls

February 7 | February 7 | February 7

1 Roll	1 Roll	1 Roll
2 Rolls	2 Rolls	2 Rolls
3 Rolls	3 Rolls	3 Rolls

February 8 | February 8 | February 8

1 Roll	1 Roll	1 Roll
2 Rolls	2 Rolls	2 Rolls
3 Rolls	3 Rolls	3 Rolls

After you have filled out the sheet, fold your column underneath along the dashed line so the next restroom user won't see your answers. *The first player uses the far right column.*

Answers - February 3-5

Feb. 3, 1 Roll: Norman Rockwell
Feb. 3, 2 Rolls: A plane carrying Buddy Holly, Ritchie Valens, and J.P. "The Big Bopper" Richardson, Jr. crashed in Iowa
Feb. 3, 3 Rolls: William Howard Taft

Feb. 4, 1 Roll: Charles Lindbergh. Though born in Detroit, he's buried on the Road to Hana in Hawaii.
Feb. 4, 2 Rolls: New York, the first capital
Feb. 4, 3 Rolls: United Service Organizations

Feb. 5, 1 Roll: Hank Aaron. He retired with 755 home runs.
Feb. 5, 2 Rolls: Sugar Ray Leonard defeated Luis "The Bull" Vega in six rounds
Feb. 5, 3 Rolls: *Modern Times*

February 9

One Roll

In 1997, what animated series took over *The Flintstones* as the longest running cartoon in television history?

Two Rolls

What Madonna album went to Number 1 on the *Billboard* 200 chart in 1985?

Three Rolls

The House of Representatives decided the Presidential Election today in 1825. Who became the first candidate to lose the electoral vote, despite winning the popular vote?

Flip to pg. 37 for answers

February 10

One Roll

Born today in 1940, he won 7 swimming Gold Medals at the 1972 Summer Games.

Two Rolls

Name the pair of animators who created *Tom and Jerry*, which debuted today in 1940.

Three Rolls

What war did the Treaty of Paris end today in 1763? It wasn't the American Revolution.

February 11

One Roll

What English King received the title of "Supreme Head of the Church of England" today in 1531? This probably helped him get a divorce.

Two Rolls

What did Robert Fulton patent on this date in 1809?

Three Rolls

Jennifer Aniston was born today in 1969. But did you know that her father, John, is also an actor? In what show is he Victor Kiriakis?

Answer Sheet | Answer Sheet | Answer Sheet

Name_____ Name_____ Name_____

February 9	February 9	February 9
1 Roll	1 Roll	1 Roll
2 Rolls	2 Rolls	2 Rolls
3 Rolls	3 Rolls	3 Rolls

February 10	February 10	February 10
1 Roll	1 Roll	1 Roll
2 Rolls	2 Rolls	2 Rolls
3 Rolls	3 Rolls	3 Rolls

February 11	February 11	February 11
1 Roll	1 Roll	1 Roll
2 Rolls	2 Rolls	2 Rolls
3 Rolls	3 Rolls	3 Rolls

After you have filled out the sheet, fold your column underneath along the dashed line so the next restroom user won't see your answers. *The first player uses the far right column.*

Answers - February 6-8
Feb. 6, 1 Roll: Babe Ruth, 1895; Ronald Reagan, 1911
Feb. 6, 2 Rolls: France
Feb. 6, 3 Rolls: March 4

Feb. 7, 1 Roll: Charles Dickens
Feb. 7, 2 Rolls: Ten. Six goals and four assists.
Feb. 7, 3 Rolls: Baltimore

Feb. 8, 1 Roll: Ice hockey
Feb. 8, 2 Rolls: Mary, Queen of Scots
Feb. 8, 3 Rolls: *Birth of a Nation*

February 12

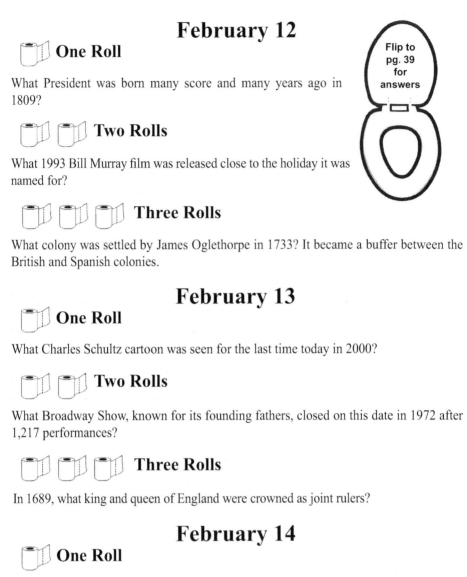

Flip to pg. 39 for answers

One Roll

What President was born many score and many years ago in 1809?

Two Rolls

What 1993 Bill Murray film was released close to the holiday it was named for?

Three Rolls

What colony was settled by James Oglethorpe in 1733? It became a buffer between the British and Spanish colonies.

February 13

One Roll

What Charles Schultz cartoon was seen for the last time today in 2000?

Two Rolls

What Broadway Show, known for its founding fathers, closed on this date in 1972 after 1,217 performances?

Three Rolls

In 1689, what king and queen of England were crowned as joint rulers?

February 14

One Roll

On this date in 1929, seven of George "Bugs" Moran's Chicago mobsters were gunned down by Al Capone's gang. What has history remembered this event as?

Two Rolls

Tragically, what future president's wife and mother died on Valentine's Day in 1884?

Three Rolls

Why is Valentine's Day celebrated on February 14?

Answer Sheet

Name_____

February 12

1 Roll	
2 Rolls	
3 Rolls	

February 13

1 Roll	
2 Rolls	
3 Rolls	

February 14

1 Roll	
2 Rolls	
3 Rolls	

Answer Sheet

Name_____

February 12

1 Roll	
2 Rolls	
3 Rolls	

February 13

1 Roll	
2 Rolls	
3 Rolls	

February 14

1 Roll	
2 Rolls	
3 Rolls	

Answer Sheet

Name_____

February 12

1 Roll	
2 Rolls	
3 Rolls	

February 13

1 Roll	
2 Rolls	
3 Rolls	

February 14

1 Roll	
2 Rolls	
3 Rolls	

After you have filled out the sheet, fold your column underneath along the dashed line so the next restroom user won't see your answers. *The first player uses the far right column.*

Answers - February 9-11
Feb. 9, 1 Roll: *The Simpsons*. It would also become the longest running television sitcom of all time.
Feb. 9, 2 Rolls: *Like a Virgin*
Feb. 9, 3 Rolls: Andrew Jackson

Feb. 10, 1 Roll: Mark Spitz
Feb. 10, 2 Rolls: Hanna-Barbera (William Hanna and Joseph Barbera). *Tom and Jerry* first appeared in *Puss Gets the Boot*.
Feb. 10, 3 Rolls: The Seven Years' War or French and Indian War (as it was called in the colonies)

Feb. 11, 1 Roll: King Henry VIII
Feb. 11, 2 Rolls: Steamboat. Fulton is buried next to Alexander Hamilton at Trinity Church in New York City.
Feb. 11, 3 Rolls: *Days of our Lives*

February 15

One Roll

What "Brat Pack" film about detention was released today in 1985?

Two Rolls

What philosopher was sentenced to death in 399 BC?

Three Rolls

On this date in 1898, what US ship sank off the coast of Cuba? The sinking greatly contributed to the Spanish-American War.

Flip to pg. 41 for answers

February 16

One Roll

Whose Egyptian tomb was opened in 1923, thousands of years after he was mummified?

Two Rolls

Born in 1958, musician and actor Tracy Marrow is better known as what *cool* nickname?

Three Rolls

Today in 1959, Fidel Castro was sworn in as leader of Cuba. Who did he overthrow?

February 17

One Roll

Michael Jordan was born today in 1963. Name one of the two numbers he wore in the NBA.

Two Rolls

Thomas Jefferson won the Election of 1800, but it wasn't easy. The House of Representatives chose him over what man who tried to steal the election?

Three Rolls

In 1969, two male music legends met and recorded some duets. One duet made it onto the album *Nashville Skyline*. The others were not released. Name one of these two legends.

Answer Sheet | # Answer Sheet | # Answer Sheet

Name_____ | Name_____ | Name_____

February 15 | ### February 15 | ### February 15

1 Roll	1 Roll	1 Roll
2 Rolls	2 Rolls	2 Rolls
3 Rolls	3 Rolls	3 Rolls

February 16 | ### February 16 | ### February 16

1 Roll	1 Roll	1 Roll
2 Rolls	2 Rolls	2 Rolls
3 Rolls	3 Rolls	3 Rolls

February 17 | ### February 17 | ### February 17

1 Roll	1 Roll	1 Roll
2 Rolls	2 Rolls	2 Rolls
3 Rolls	3 Rolls	3 Rolls

After you have filled out the sheet, fold your column underneath along the dashed line so the next restroom user won't see your answers. *The first player uses the far right column.*

Answers - February 12-14
Feb. 12, 1 Roll: Abraham Lincoln
Feb. 12, 2 Rolls: *Groundhog Day*
Feb. 12, 3 Rolls: Georgia

Feb. 13, 1 Roll: *Peanuts*
Feb. 13, 2 Rolls: *1776*
Feb. 13, 3 Rolls: William and Mary

Feb. 14, 1 Roll: St. Valentine's Day Massacre. Capone claimed his innocence, as he was vacationing in Florida at the time.
Feb. 14, 2 Rolls: Theodore Roosevelt
Feb. 14, 3 Rolls: That was the day that St. Valentine was executed. He defied Roman Emperor Claudius' decree that no marriages shall be performed.

February 18

🧻 One Roll

What did Mark Twain publish today in 1885?

🧻🧻 Two Rolls

What weather event happened in the Sahara Desert in 1979?

🧻🧻🧻 Three Rolls

In 1978, the first Iron Man Triathlon was held. It involved a 2.4 mile swim, followed by a 112 mile bike ride, and a running distance of how long?

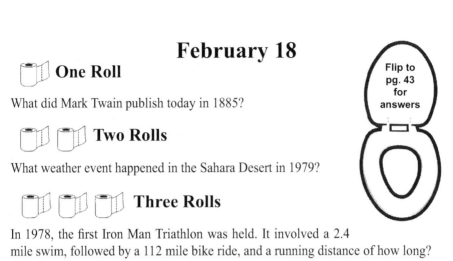

Flip to pg. 43 for answers

February 19

🧻 One Roll

In 2010, what professional golfer admitted to being unfaithful to his wife?

🧻🧻 Two Rolls

Bad enough that he killed Alexander Hamilton, but what former Vice President was arrested on treason charges today in 1807?

🧻🧻🧻 Three Rolls

Today in 1473, Nicolas Copernicus was born. What model did he propose whereby the Earth revolved around the sun?

February 20

🧻 One Roll

What did George Washington create when he signed a law today in 1792? The weather shouldn't hamper the answering of this question.

🧻🧻 Two Rolls

In 1992, who announced his third-party candidacy for President on *Larry King Live*?

🧻🧻🧻 Three Rolls

Today in 1963, who became the first Major League Baseball player to make 6 figures?

Answer Sheet | Answer Sheet | Answer Sheet

Name_____ | Name_____ | Name_____

February 18 | February 18 | February 18

1 Roll	1 Roll	1 Roll
2 Rolls	2 Rolls	2 Rolls
3 Rolls	3 Rolls	3 Rolls

February 19 | February 19 | February 19

1 Roll	1 Roll	1 Roll
2 Rolls	2 Rolls	2 Rolls
3 Rolls	3 Rolls	3 Rolls

February 20 | February 20 | February 20

1 Roll	1 Roll	1 Roll
2 Rolls	2 Rolls	2 Rolls
3 Rolls	3 Rolls	3 Rolls

After you have filled out the sheet, fold your column underneath along the dashed line so the next restroom user won't see your answers. *The first player uses the far right column.*

Answers - February 15-17
Feb. 15, 1 Roll: *The Breakfast Club*
Feb. 15, 2 Rolls: Socrates. He was found guilty of corrupting the youth of Athens, and drank poisonous hemlock.
Feb. 15, 3 Rolls: USS *Maine*. It was later proven that the ship caught fire and sunk on its own, rather than being detonated by a Spanish mine.

Feb. 16, 1 Roll: King Tutankhamun, or King Tut
Feb. 16, 2 Rolls: Ice-T
Feb. 16, 3 Rolls: Fulgencio Batista

Feb. 17, 1 Roll: 23 and 45. He also once wore number 12 when his uniform was stolen in Orlando.
Feb. 17, 2 Rolls: Aaron Burr. He wound up being Jefferson's Vice President for one term.
Feb. 17, 3 Rolls: Johnny Cash and Bob Dylan

February 21

One Roll

What African American religious leader, portrayed by Denzel Washington in the movies, was assassinated today in 1965?

Flip to pg. 45 for answers

Two Rolls

What obelisk, dedicated today in 1885, took more than forty years to complete?

Three Rolls

In 1848, the *Communist Manifesto* was published. Along with Karl Marx, who wrote it?

February 22

One Roll

What film out of Bollywood won 8 Oscars today in 2009?

Two Rolls

What pop-artist, known for his soup cans, died today in 1987?

Three Rolls

A decade before Franklin Roosevelt gave his Fireside Chats, what President provided the first public radio address today in 1924?

February 23

One Roll

Who printed the first Bible on a printing press today in 1455?

Two Rolls

On this date in 1945, US soldiers raised the American flag for a famous snapshot. On what Japanese island was the picture taken?

Three Rolls

Today in 1836, the siege on the Alamo began. Who led the Mexican army?

Answer Sheet | # Answer Sheet | # Answer Sheet

Name_____ | Name_____ | Name_____

February 21	February 21	February 21
1 Roll	1 Roll	1 Roll
2 Rolls	2 Rolls	2 Rolls
3 Rolls	3 Rolls	3 Rolls

February 22	February 22	February 22
1 Roll	1 Roll	1 Roll
2 Rolls	2 Rolls	2 Rolls
3 Rolls	3 Rolls	3 Rolls

February 23	February 23	February 23
1 Roll	1 Roll	1 Roll
2 Rolls	2 Rolls	2 Rolls
3 Rolls	3 Rolls	3 Rolls

After you have filled out the sheet, fold your column underneath along the dashed line so the next restroom user won't see your answers. *The first player uses the far right column.*

Answers - February 18-20
Feb. 18, 1 Roll: *The Adventures of Huckleberry Finn*
Feb. 18, 2 Rolls: Snow. It lasted for about 30 minutes, and evaporated rather quickly.
Feb. 18, 3 Rolls: 26.2 miles, or a marathon

Feb. 19, 1 Roll: Tiger Woods
Feb. 19, 2 Rolls: Aaron Burr. He was acquitted of treason charges concerning a secessionist plot.
Feb. 19, 3 Rolls: Heliocentric Model

Feb. 20, 1 Roll: The US Postal Service
Feb. 20, 2 Rolls: H. Ross Perot
Feb. 20, 3 Rolls: Willie Mays. He signed a contract worth $100,000 per year.

February 24

 **One Roll**

Flip to pg. 47 for answers

Who was the first President to be impeached? It happened on this date in 1868.

 **Two Rolls**

What Supreme Court decision of John Marshall set a precedent for judicial review in 1803?

 **Three Rolls**

What actor, known for his role as Mr. Furley on *Three's Company*, died today in 2006 at the age of 81?

February 25

 **One Roll**

Today in 1932, what infamous Austrian officially became a German citizen?

 **Two Rolls**

What president fled his native Philippines in 1986, amid an election scandal?

 **Three Rolls**

What amendment, that instituted a graduated income tax, was ratified today in 1913?

February 26

 **One Roll**

The best-selling album of all time went to Number 1 today in 1983? Who was the artist?

 **Two Rolls**

What actor, who played opposite Jack Klugman in the television version of *The Odd Couple*, was born today in 1920?

 **Three Rolls**

What island did Napoleon Bonaparte leave on this date in 1815 to begin his Hundred Days of resurgence?

Answer Sheet | Answer Sheet | Answer Sheet

Name_____ | Name_____ | Name_____

| February 24 | February 24 | February 24 |

1 Roll	1 Roll	1 Roll
2 Rolls	2 Rolls	2 Rolls
3 Rolls	3 Rolls	3 Rolls

| February 25 | February 25 | February 25 |

1 Roll	1 Roll	1 Roll
2 Rolls	2 Rolls	2 Rolls
3 Rolls	3 Rolls	3 Rolls

| February 26 | February 26 | February 26 |

1 Roll	1 Roll	1 Roll
2 Rolls	2 Rolls	2 Rolls
3 Rolls	3 Rolls	3 Rolls

After you have filled out the sheet, fold your column underneath along the dashed line so the next restroom user won't see your answers. *The first player uses the far right column.*

Answers - February 21-23
Feb. 21, 1 Roll: Malcolm X
Feb. 21, 2 Rolls: Washington Monument. Construction began in 1848, but a lack of funding, political disagreements, and the Civil War, left it unfinished for decades.
Feb. 21, 3 Rolls: Friedrich Engels

Feb. 22, 1 Roll: *Slumdog Millionaire*
Feb. 22, 2 Rolls: Andy Warhol
Feb. 22, 3 Rolls: Calvin Coolidge

Feb. 23, 1 Roll: Johannes Gutenberg
Feb. 23, 2 Rolls: Iwo Jima, atop Mount Suribachi
Feb. 23, 3 Rolls: Santa Anna

February 27

One Roll

What New Orleans celebration was held for the first time today in 1827?

Flip to pg. 49 for answers

Two Rolls

Author John Steinbeck was born today in 1902. What famous book did he pen that detailed harsh life during the Dust Bowl?

Three Rolls

In 1992, Tiger Woods became the youngest man to play in a PGA event. How old was he?

February 28

One Roll

What London religious landmark was open for prayer on this date in 1066?

Two Rolls

What changed about the purchase of cigarettes today in 1997?

Three Rolls

What President was nearly killed when a naval gun exploded on this date in 1844?

February 29

One Roll

Happy Leap Year! How long does it take the Earth to revolve around the sun in a given year? (To the second decimal)

Two Rolls

The star of *Dinah's Place*, and *Dinah and Friends*, this entertainment legend was born today in 1916. She died at age 77...or 19, depending on how you look at it.

Three Rolls

2096 will be a leap year. When is the next leap year after that?

Answer Sheet

Name_____

February 27

1 Roll
2 Rolls
3 Rolls

February 28

1 Roll
2 Rolls
3 Rolls

February 29

1 Roll
2 Rolls
3 Rolls

Answer Sheet

Name_____

February 27

1 Roll
2 Rolls
3 Rolls

February 28

1 Roll
2 Rolls
3 Rolls

February 29

1 Roll
2 Rolls
3 Rolls

Answer Sheet

Name_____

February 27

1 Roll
2 Rolls
3 Rolls

February 28

1 Roll
2 Rolls
3 Rolls

February 29

1 Roll
2 Rolls
3 Rolls

After you have filled out the sheet, fold your column underneath along the dashed line so the next restroom user won't see your answers. *The first player uses the far right column.*

Answers - February 24-26
Feb. 24, 1 Roll: Andrew Johnson. He was never thrown out of office. Bill Clinton was the only other President to be impeached (1998).
Feb. 24, 2 Rolls: *Marbury v. Madison*
Feb. 24, 3 Rolls: Don Knotts. He was also famous as Barney Fife on *The Andy Griffith Show*.

Feb. 25, 1 Roll: Adolf Hitler. He was born in Austria, and naturalized a German.
Feb. 25, 2 Rolls: Ferdinand Marcos
Feb. 25, 3 Rolls: 16th Amendment

Feb. 26, 1 Roll: Michael Jackson's Thriller has recorded millions of worldwide sales
Feb. 26, 2 Rolls: Tony Randall
Feb. 26, 3 Rolls: Elba

March 1

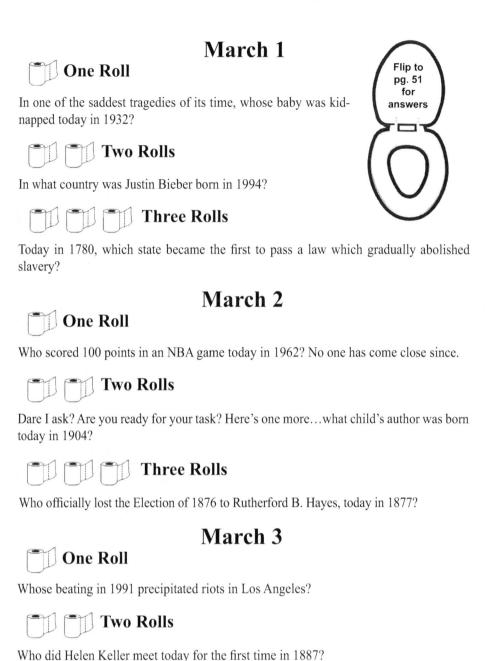

One Roll

In one of the saddest tragedies of its time, whose baby was kidnapped today in 1932?

Two Rolls

In what country was Justin Bieber born in 1994?

Flip to pg. 51 for answers

Three Rolls

Today in 1780, which state became the first to pass a law which gradually abolished slavery?

March 2

One Roll

Who scored 100 points in an NBA game today in 1962? No one has come close since.

Two Rolls

Dare I ask? Are you ready for your task? Here's one more…what child's author was born today in 1904?

Three Rolls

Who officially lost the Election of 1876 to Rutherford B. Hayes, today in 1877?

March 3

One Roll

Whose beating in 1991 precipitated riots in Los Angeles?

Two Rolls

Who did Helen Keller meet today for the first time in 1887?

Three Rolls

Today in 1820, the Missouri Compromise was brokered by Henry Clay. Missouri came into the Union as a slave state, but what state entered without slavery?

Answer Sheet

Name_____

March 1

1 Roll
2 Rolls
3 Rolls

March 2

1 Roll
2 Rolls
3 Rolls

March 3

1 Roll
2 Rolls
3 Rolls

Answer Sheet

Name_____

March 1

1 Roll
2 Rolls
3 Rolls

March 2

1 Roll
2 Rolls
3 Rolls

March 3

1 Roll
2 Rolls
3 Rolls

Answer Sheet

Name_____

March 1

1 Roll
2 Rolls
3 Rolls

March 2

1 Roll
2 Rolls
3 Rolls

March 3

1 Roll
2 Rolls
3 Rolls

After you have filled out the sheet, fold your column underneath along the dashed line so the next restroom user won't see your answers. *The first player uses the far right column.*

Answers - February 27-29
Feb. 27, 1 Roll: Mardi Gras
Feb. 27, 2 Rolls: *The Grapes of Wrath*
Feb. 27, 3 Rolls: 16 years-old

Feb. 28, 1 Roll: Westminster Abbey
Feb. 28, 2 Rolls: One had to prove they were over 18 years old to purchase cigarettes
Feb. 28, 3 Rolls: President John Tyler. The explosion on board the USS *Princeton* killed seven, including his fiancé's father. The gun—the world's largest naval gun—was ironically named the Peacemaker. However it caused the deadliest US disaster during a time of peace.

Feb. 29, 1 Roll: 365.2425 days…hence the need to add a day to the calendar every four years
Feb. 29, 2 Rolls: Dinah Shore
Feb. 29, 3 Rolls: 2104. There will be no leap year in 2100, because under the rules of the Gregorian calendar, years ending in 00 are not leap years unless they are evenly divisible by 400.

March 4

One Roll

Flip to pg. 53 for answers

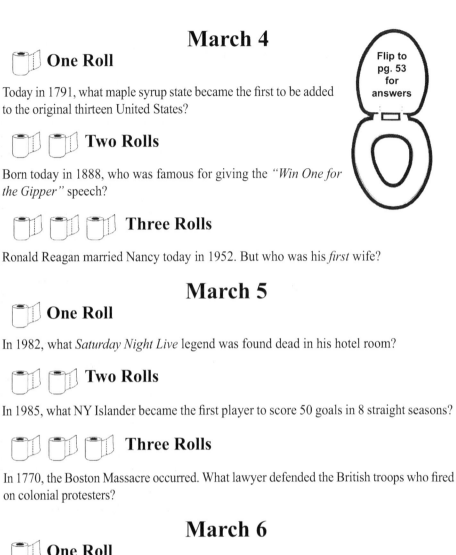

Today in 1791, what maple syrup state became the first to be added to the original thirteen United States?

Two Rolls

Born today in 1888, who was famous for giving the *"Win One for the Gipper"* speech?

Three Rolls

Ronald Reagan married Nancy today in 1952. But who was his *first* wife?

March 5

One Roll

In 1982, what *Saturday Night Live* legend was found dead in his hotel room?

Two Rolls

In 1985, what NY Islander became the first player to score 50 goals in 8 straight seasons?

Three Rolls

In 1770, the Boston Massacre occurred. What lawyer defended the British troops who fired on colonial protesters?

March 6

One Roll

What 7 foot 1 inch basketball star, actor, and rapper was born today in 1972?

Two Rolls

What Supreme Court decision, that struck down a slave's ability to sue for freedom, was handed down by Roger B. Taney today in 1857?

Three Rolls

What Russian scientist presented his periodic chart of elements today in 1869?

Answer Sheet | Answer Sheet | Answer Sheet

Name_____ Name_____ Name_____

| March 4 | March 4 | March 4 |

1 Roll	1 Roll	1 Roll
2 Rolls	2 Rolls	2 Rolls
3 Rolls	3 Rolls	3 Rolls

| March 5 | March 5 | March 5 |

1 Roll	1 Roll	1 Roll
2 Rolls	2 Rolls	2 Rolls
3 Rolls	3 Rolls	3 Rolls

| March 6 | March 6 | March 6 |

1 Roll	1 Roll	1 Roll
2 Rolls	2 Rolls	2 Rolls
3 Rolls	3 Rolls	3 Rolls

After you have filled out the sheet, fold your column underneath along the dashed line so the next restroom user won't see your answers. *The first player uses the far right column.*

Answers - March 1-3

Mar. 1, 1 Roll: Charles Lindbergh's son. After the child's body was found, the investigation pointed to Bruno Hauptmann as the perpetrator. He was electrocuted in 1935.
Mar. 1, 2 Rolls: Canada
Mar. 1, 3 Rolls: Pennsylvania

Mar. 2, 1 Roll: Wilt Chamberlain
Mar. 2, 2 Rolls: Dr. Seuss
Mar. 2, 3 Rolls: Samuel J. Tilden. A compromise was garnered ending Reconstruction, and gave the Republicans the White House. Tilden is among four candidates who have won the popular vote, but lost the electoral vote (Andrew Jackson in 1824, Grover Cleveland in 1888, and Al Gore in 2000).

Mar. 3, 1 Roll: Rodney King
Mar. 3, 2 Rolls: Anne Sullivan…also known as, the "miracle worker"
Mar. 3, 3 Rolls: Maine. There would also be no slavery north of the 36°30′ latitude line in the Louisiana Territory.

March 7

One Roll

What did Alexander Graham Bell patent today in 1876?

Two Rolls

What country's famine did *We are the World* look to raise money for? The song was released today in 1985.

Three Rolls

Today in 1857, it was decided that a baseball game would go 9 innings. Before there were innings, how would the winner of a game be determined?

Flip to pg. 55 for answers

March 8

One Roll

Who beat Muhammad Ali in a legendary fight today in 1971? It was dubbed the "Fight of the Century."

Two Rolls

Like, I bet you can't guess what show debuted on MTV today in 1993. You should like, use your head and stuff.

Three Rolls

What busy European airport, named for a World War II leader, opened today in 1974?

March 9

One Roll

How old was George Burns when he died today in 1996?

Two Rolls

Who did Napoleon Bonaparte marry today in 1796?

Three Rolls

Today in 1562, what action between two people of Naples was banned from taking place in public?

Answer Sheet   Answer Sheet   Answer Sheet

Name_____   Name_____   Name_____

March 7	**March 7**	**March 7**
1 Roll	1 Roll	1 Roll
2 Rolls	2 Rolls	2 Rolls
3 Rolls	3 Rolls	3 Rolls

March 8	**March 8**	**March 8**
1 Roll	1 Roll	1 Roll
2 Rolls	2 Rolls	2 Rolls
3 Rolls	3 Rolls	3 Rolls

March 9	**March 9**	**March 9**
1 Roll	1 Roll	1 Roll
2 Rolls	2 Rolls	2 Rolls
3 Rolls	3 Rolls	3 Rolls

After you have filled out the sheet, fold your column underneath along the dashed line so the next restroom user won't see your answers. *The first player uses the far right column.*

Answers - March 4-6
Mar. 4, 1 Roll: Vermont
Mar. 4, 2 Rolls: Knute Rockne
Mar. 4, 3 Rolls: Jane Wyman. Reagan remains the only President to ever get a divorce.

Mar. 5, 1 Roll: John Belushi
Mar. 5, 2 Rolls: Mike Bossy
Mar. 5, 3 Rolls: John Adams

Mar. 6, 1 Roll: Shaquille O'Neal
Mar. 6, 2 Rolls: *Dred Scott v. Sandford*
Mar. 6, 3 Rolls: Dmitri Mendeleev

March 10

 **One Roll**

What hero of the underground railroad died today in 1913?

  **Two Rolls**

What martial arts actor, who has his own line of jokes, was born today in 1940?

   **Three Rolls**

The only President to patent an invention did so on this date. It was for lifting boats over river obstacles. Who patented it?

Flip to
pg. 57
for
answers

March 11

 **One Roll**

Here's a toss-up: On what side of Mikhail Gorbachev's head would one find his birthmark leaning? He became the leader of the USSR today in 1985.

  **Two Rolls**

What Yugoslavian war criminal died in his cell on this date in 2006?

   **Three Rolls**

In the infamous game show scandal of 1956, what contestant on *Twenty-One* was handed victory over Herb Stempel? He finally lost today in 1957.

March 12

 **One Roll**

What Broadway show, based on a Victor Hugo novel, opened today in 1987?

  **Two Rolls**

What Beat Generation writer was "on the road" to life, as he was born today in 1922?

   **Three Rolls**

In 1903, the team that would become the New York Yankees joined the American League. What was their name?

54

Answer Sheet

Name_____

March 10

1 Roll
2 Rolls
3 Rolls

March 11

1 Roll
2 Rolls
3 Rolls

March 12

1 Roll
2 Rolls
3 Rolls

Answer Sheet

Name_____

March 10

1 Roll
2 Rolls
3 Rolls

March 11

1 Roll
2 Rolls
3 Rolls

March 12

1 Roll
2 Rolls
3 Rolls

Answer Sheet

Name_____

March 10

1 Roll
2 Rolls
3 Rolls

March 11

1 Roll
2 Rolls
3 Rolls

March 12

1 Roll
2 Rolls
3 Rolls

After you have filled out the sheet, fold your column underneath along the dashed line so the next restroom user won't see your answers. *The first player uses the far right column.*

Answers - March 7-9
Mar. 7, 1 Roll: The telephone
Mar. 7, 2 Rolls: USA for Africa looked to raise money for all of Africa, with specific emphasis on the famine-stricken country of Ethiopia
Mar. 7, 3 Rolls: Whoever scored 21 runs first. The original rules, written by Alexander Cartwright, didn't use the word "runs." Instead they were "counts" or "aces."

Mar. 8, 1 Roll: Joe Frazier. He knocked Ali to the canvas in the 15th round.
Mar. 8, 2 Rolls: *Beavis and Butt-Head*
Mar. 8, 3 Rolls: Charles de Gaulle Airport

Mar. 9, 1 Roll: 100 years-old
Mar. 9, 2 Rolls: Josephine de Beauharnais
Mar. 9, 3 Rolls: Kissing. Doing so in public could result in a death sentence.

March 13

One Roll

Today in 1933, who became the head of Nazi propaganda for the Third Reich?

 ### Two Rolls

In 1781, Sir William Herschel thought he saw a comet. But truly, he discovered what planet a little further out than Saturn?

Flip to pg. 59 for answers

Three Rolls

The defense attorney in the Scopes Trial died today in 1938. Who was this man who battled William Jennings Bryan in the 1925 trial that rocked the country?

March 14

 ### One Roll

Invented in 1793, what did Eli Whitney patent the following year on this date?

Two Rolls

What did Albert Einstein, born today in 1879, think World War IV would be fought with?

Three Rolls

What did Bill Clinton injure on this date in 1997? He required surgery.

March 15

 ### One Roll

Who was stabbed to death today, the Ides of March, in 44 BC?

Two Rolls

Russia no longer had a czar when in 1917, this man abdicated the throne.

Three Rolls

What former US President, born today in 1767, was scarred as a youth when a British soldier slashed him in the face with a sword?

Answer Sheet | Answer Sheet | Answer Sheet

Name_____   Name_____   Name_____

March 13	March 13	March 13
1 Roll	1 Roll	1 Roll
2 Rolls	2 Rolls	2 Rolls
3 Rolls	3 Rolls	3 Rolls

March 14	March 14	March 14
1 Roll	1 Roll	1 Roll
2 Rolls	2 Rolls	2 Rolls
3 Rolls	3 Rolls	3 Rolls

March 15	March 15	March 15
1 Roll	1 Roll	1 Roll
2 Rolls	2 Rolls	2 Rolls
3 Rolls	3 Rolls	3 Rolls

After you have filled out the sheet, fold your column underneath along the dashed line so the next restroom user won't see your answers. *The first player uses the far right column.*

Answers - March 10-12

Mar. 10, 1 Roll: Harriet Tubman. The "railroad" was a network of safe-houses that brought slaves to freedom up north.
Mar. 10, 2 Rolls: Chuck Norris
Mar. 10, 3 Rolls: Abraham Lincoln in 1849

Mar. 11, 1 Roll: The "port-wine stain" flows just right of center. Going bald can be tough. But for the leader of the Soviet Union, this must have been especially devastating.
Mar. 11, 2 Rolls: Slobodan Milosevic
Mar. 11, 3 Rolls: Charles Van Doren. Stempel answered a question wrong on purpose. He needed to identify the Best Picture of 1955 (*Marty*), but instead responded with 1954's Best Picture (*On the Waterfront*).

Mar. 12, 1 Roll: *Les Misérables*
Mar. 12, 2 Rolls: Jack Kerouac, author of *On the Road*
Mar. 12, 3 Rolls: New York Highlanders

March 16

 **One Roll**

Flip to pg. 61 for answers

In 1850, Nathaniel Hawthorne's *The Scarlet Letter* was published. What letter did Hester Prynne wear on her clothing?

 **Two Rolls**

Standing at 5 feet, four inches, the shortest President was born today in 1751. Name him.

 **Three Rolls**

$3,470.25 could have bought you all of the shares traded today in 1830...the weakest trading day in the history of Wall Street. Within 10, how many shares were traded?

March 17

 **One Roll**

Who fled Tibet today in 1959 to escape the Chinese government?

 **Two Rolls**

Born in 1972, she retired with more international soccer goals than any other player.

 **Three Rolls**

Within 30 years, when was the first official St. Patrick's Day Parade in NY City?

March 18

 **One Roll**

Today in 1959, there were finally 50 United States. What state became Number 50?

 **Two Rolls**

What notorious British taxing law was repealed today in 1766? Benjamin Franklin traveled across the Atlantic to argue against it.

 **Three Rolls**

Where did the Boston Braves move to on this date in 1953?

Answer Sheet | Answer Sheet | Answer Sheet

Name_____ Name_____ Name_____

| **March 16** | **March 16** | **March 16** |

1 Roll	1 Roll	1 Roll
2 Rolls	2 Rolls	2 Rolls
3 Rolls	3 Rolls	3 Rolls

| **March 17** | **March 17** | **March 17** |

1 Roll	1 Roll	1 Roll
2 Rolls	2 Rolls	2 Rolls
3 Rolls	3 Rolls	3 Rolls

| **March 18** | **March 18** | **March 18** |

1 Roll	1 Roll	1 Roll
2 Rolls	2 Rolls	2 Rolls
3 Rolls	3 Rolls	3 Rolls

After you have filled out the sheet, fold your column underneath along the dashed line so the next restroom user won't see your answers. *The first player uses the far right column.*

Answers - March 13-15

Mar. 13, 1 Roll: Joseph Goebbels
Mar. 13, 2 Rolls: Uranus
Mar. 13, 3 Rolls: Clarence Darrow. The case involved the teaching of evolution in schools.

Mar. 14, 1 Roll: The cotton gin
Mar. 14, 2 Rolls: Sticks and stones. For everyone would have been killed by atomic weapons in World War III.
Mar. 14, 3 Rolls: His leg, or knee. He tore a tendon in his right knee when he tripped going down a flight of stairs.

Mar. 15, 1 Roll: Julius Caesar
Mar. 15, 2 Rolls: Czar Nicholas II
Mar. 15, 3 Rolls: Andrew Jackson. The officer was upset that Jackson refused to shine his shoes. The event took place during the American Revolution.

March 19

One Roll

Flip to pg. 63 for answers

After a short stint in the minor leagues with the White Sox, who returned to the Chicago hardwood today in 1995?

Two Rolls

What minority-based show debuted on the radio today in 1928? Though incredibly popular for its day, it would never fly these days.

Three Rolls

The War in Iraq began today in 2003. What was the official name of the mission?

March 20

One Roll

What political party was founded today in 1854? It was against the expansion of slavery.

Two Rolls

On the subject of slavery, *Uncle Tom's Cabin* was published today in 1852. Who wrote it?

Three Rolls

Today in 1942, General Douglas MacArthur uttered a three-word promise. What was it?

March 21

One Roll

On this date in 1980, the United States announced that it was boycotting the Summer Olympics. Where were they held?

Two Rolls

Who did Kristin Shepard shoot on this date in 1980?

Three Rolls

Born today in 1685, what composer and musician of the Baroque period was known for the Brandenburg Concertos?

Answer Sheet   Answer Sheet   Answer Sheet

Name_____   Name_____   Name_____

March 19   March 19   March 19

1 Roll	1 Roll	1 Roll
2 Rolls	2 Rolls	2 Rolls
3 Rolls	3 Rolls	3 Rolls

March 20   March 20   March 20

1 Roll	1 Roll	1 Roll
2 Rolls	2 Rolls	2 Rolls
3 Rolls	3 Rolls	3 Rolls

March 21   March 21   March 21

1 Roll	1 Roll	1 Roll
2 Rolls	2 Rolls	2 Rolls
3 Rolls	3 Rolls	3 Rolls

After you have filled out the sheet, fold your column underneath along the dashed line so the next restroom user won't see your answers. *The first player uses the far right column.*

Answers - March 16-18
Mar. 16, 1 Roll: A…for adultery
Mar. 16, 2 Rolls: James Madison
Mar. 16, 3 Rolls: 31 shares

Mar. 17, 1 Roll: The Dalai Lama
Mar. 17, 2 Rolls: Mia Hamm…158 goals, more than any other player, male or female. Her record was surpassed by Abby Wambach in 2013.
Mar. 17, 3 Rolls: Today in 1762, well before independence. It was held by Irish soldiers in the British army.

Mar. 18, 1 Roll: Hawaii
Mar. 18, 2 Rolls: Stamp Act
Mar. 18, 3 Rolls: Milwaukee. They later moved to Atlanta after the 1965 season.

March 22

 **One Roll**

It's no coincidence that William Shatner shares a birthday with a science fiction icon. Which one?

 **Two Rolls**

What ended 15 years after it began today in 1933?

 **Three Rolls**

Along with George Whitefield, what preacher was associated with the eighteenth century religious movement known as the Great Awakening? He died today in 1758.

Flip to pg. 65 for answers

March 23

 **One Roll**

What girl from uptown did Billy Joel marry today in 1985?

 **Two Rolls**

Who famously uttered today in 1775, "Give me liberty, or give me death"?

Three Rolls

Barney Clark, the world's first artificial heart recipient, died today in 1983. How long did he live for with the artificial heart? (Within 50 days)

March 24

One Roll

What ship spilled an estimated 11 million gallons of oil in Alaska on this date in 1989?

 **Two Rolls**

In 1664, what man was granted a charter to create a colony in Rhode Island? The colony ultimately promoted religious freedom.

 **Three Rolls**

Who was crowned King of England today in 1603 after the death of Elizabeth I?

Answer Sheet   Answer Sheet   Answer Sheet

Name_____   Name_____   Name_____

March 22   March 22   March 22

1 Roll	1 Roll	1 Roll
2 Rolls	2 Rolls	2 Rolls
3 Rolls	3 Rolls	3 Rolls

March 23   March 23   March 23

1 Roll	1 Roll	1 Roll
2 Rolls	2 Rolls	2 Rolls
3 Rolls	3 Rolls	3 Rolls

March 24   March 24   March 24

1 Roll	1 Roll	1 Roll
2 Rolls	2 Rolls	2 Rolls
3 Rolls	3 Rolls	3 Rolls

After you have filled out the sheet, fold your column underneath along the dashed line so the next restroom user won't see your answers. *The first player uses the far right column.*

Answers - March 19-21
Mar. 19, 1 Roll: Michael Jordan
Mar. 19, 2 Rolls: *Amos 'n' Andy*. The radio and television show stereotyped African American culture from the 1920s through the 1950s.
Mar. 19, 3 Rolls: Operation Iraqi Freedom

Mar. 20, 1 Roll: Republican Party
Mar. 20, 2 Rolls: Harriet Beecher Stowe
Mar. 20, 3 Rolls: "I shall return." He proclaimed this as he left Bataan.

Mar. 21, 1 Roll: Soviet Union. The US was protesting Soviet occupation of Afghanistan.
Mar. 21, 2 Rolls: She shot J.R. Ewing on Dallas. Fans had to wait an extra two months to find out she pulled the trigger because of a Screen Actors Guild strike in 1980. The reveal was watched by over 3/4 of the viewing audience.
Mar. 21, 3 Rolls: Johann Sebastian Bach

March 25

Flip to pg. 67 for answers

 **One Roll**

What broadcaster, known for his antics with Muhammad Ali, was born today in 1918?

 **Two Rolls**

What tragedy occurred in New York City today in 1911? 146 died.

 **Three Rolls**

What breakfast staple was made in a demonstration for the first time at a New York department store today in 1882?

March 26

 **One Roll**

Born today in 1930, she was the first woman to ever be appointed to the Supreme Court.

 **Two Rolls**

Today in 1999, a jury deliberated and found what doctor guilty of second-degree murder?

Three Rolls

Ludwig van Beethoven died on this date in 1827. What city is he buried in?

March 27

One Roll

Much to the delight of sexually active senior citizens everywhere, what drug was approved by the FDA today in 1998?

Two Rolls

What Japanese flowers were planted in Washington, DC on this date in 1912?

Three Rolls

Marlon Brando won the Oscar for Best Actor for *The Godfather* in 1973. But who gave his non-acceptance speech?

Answer Sheet | Answer Sheet | Answer Sheet

Name_____   Name_____   Name_____

| March 25 | March 25 | March 25 |

| 1 Roll |
| 2 Rolls |
| 3 Rolls |

| March 26 | March 26 | March 26 |

| 1 Roll |
| 2 Rolls |
| 3 Rolls |

| March 27 | March 27 | March 27 |

| 1 Roll |
| 2 Rolls |
| 3 Rolls |

After you have filled out the sheet, fold your column underneath along the dashed line so the next restroom user won't see your answers. *The first player uses the far right column.*

Answers - March 22-24

Mar. 22, 1 Roll: Captain James T. Kirk will be born today in 2233…in Riverside, Iowa of Earth
Mar. 22, 2 Rolls: Prohibition. First, Franklin Delano Roosevelt signed the Beer and Wine Act today in 1933. Later that year, the 21st Amendment repealed the 18th Amendment which established prohibition.
Mar. 22, 3 Rolls: Jonathan Edwards

Mar. 23, 1 Roll: Christie Brinkley
Mar. 23, 2 Rolls: Patrick Henry
Mar. 23, 3 Rolls: Clark lived for 112 days. Five others patients received one during the 1980s, including William Schroeder, who lived for nearly two years.

Mar. 24, 1 Roll: *Exxon Valdez.* The supertanker ran aground in Prince William Sound, Alaska. Did you know that this disaster wasn't even close to being the worst oil spill of all time? Over thirty spills are ranked worse as of 2012. Still, it was catastrophic to the marine life of Alaska.
Mar. 24, 2 Rolls: Roger Williams
Mar. 24, 3 Rolls: James I, her cousin. The Virgin Queen had no kids. So began a century-long reign of the Stuarts.

March 28

 **One Roll**

Today, the biggest nuclear disaster in US history occurred at Three Mile Island. What state was home to this event?

 **Two Rolls**

Who did P.T. Barnum team up with in 1881 to create "The Greatest Show on Earth"?

 **Three Rolls**

"America's Sweetheart" married Douglas Fairbanks in 1920. Name her.

Flip to pg. 69 for answers

March 29

 **One Roll**

What song did Stevie Wonder and Paul McCartney release today in 1982?

 **Two Rolls**

In 1987, who did nearly 100,000 people watch Hulk Hogan pin at WrestleMania III?

 **Three Rolls**

How did the 23rd Amendment, ratified today in 1961, change the total of Electoral Votes?

March 30

 **One Roll**

Which famed impressionist painter, born today in 1853, handed over his left ear to a prostitute? Whether or not he cut if off himself is still open to debate.

 **Two Rolls**

Who was Ronald Reagan's press secretary that, along with the President, was shot by John Hinckley, Jr. today in 1981? His name today is associated with gun control.

 **Three Rolls**

Which Amendment, ratified today in 1870, guaranteed universal male suffrage?

Answer Sheet

Name_____

March 28

1 Roll	
2 Rolls	
3 Rolls	

March 29

1 Roll	
2 Rolls	
3 Rolls	

March 30

1 Roll	
2 Rolls	
3 Rolls	

Answer Sheet

Name_____

March 28

1 Roll	
2 Rolls	
3 Rolls	

March 29

1 Roll	
2 Rolls	
3 Rolls	

March 30

1 Roll	
2 Rolls	
3 Rolls	

Answer Sheet

Name_____

March 28

1 Roll	
2 Rolls	
3 Rolls	

March 29

1 Roll	
2 Rolls	
3 Rolls	

March 30

1 Roll	
2 Rolls	
3 Rolls	

After you have filled out the sheet, fold your column underneath along the dashed line so the next restroom user won't see your answers. *The first player uses the far right column.*

Answers - March 25-27
Mar. 25, 1 Roll: Howard Cosell
Mar. 25, 2 Rolls: Triangle Shirtwaist Fire
Mar. 25, 3 Rolls: Pancake

Mar. 26, 1 Roll: Sandra Day O'Connor
Mar. 26, 2 Rolls: Dr. Jack Kevorkian, who administered lethal injection to induce euthanasia. He was sentenced to 10-25 years. He was paroled in 2007.
Mar. 26, 3 Rolls: Vienna. Though he was exhumed twice (1863 and 1888). His body was eventually moved to Zentralfriedhof (Central Cemetery). He's been there ever since.

Mar. 27, 1 Roll: Viagra
Mar. 27, 2 Rolls: Cherry Blossoms
Mar. 27, 3 Rolls: A Native American woman named Sacheen Littlefeather. Brando wanted to bring attention to Native American society, so he didn't accept the award.

March 31

 **One Roll**

Opening today in 1889, what structure was once thought to be an eye-sore to the beautiful city of Paris?

Flip to pg. 71 for answers

 **Two Rolls**

What household name of the chicken industry died today in 2005?

 **Three Rolls**

Born today in 1878, who became the first African American to win the heavyweight boxing title?

April 1

 **One Roll**

Born April 1, 1961, she was no fool when she sang *I Dreamed a Dream* on *Britain's Got Talent* in 2009. Her performance immediately drew millions of hits on YouTube.

 **Two Rolls**

What Motown legend was tragically shot and killed by his own father today in 1984?

 **Three Rolls**

Today in 1748, the ancient city of Pompeii was first excavated. What volcano buried it under ash in 79 AD?

April 2

 **One Roll**

Today in 1513, Ponce de Leon found Florida. What was he supposedly looking for?

 **Two Rolls**

What two Yankee stars were K'd by a teenage girl during an exhibition game in 1931?

 **Three Rolls**

What vampire soap opera had its series finale today in 1971?

Answer Sheet | Answer Sheet | Answer Sheet

Name_____ | Name_____ | Name_____

March 31 | March 31 | March 31

1 Roll	1 Roll	1 Roll
2 Rolls	2 Rolls	2 Rolls
3 Rolls	3 Rolls	3 Rolls

April 1 | April 1 | April 1

1 Roll	1 Roll	1 Roll
2 Rolls	2 Rolls	2 Rolls
3 Rolls	3 Rolls	3 Rolls

April 2 | April 2 | April 2

1 Roll	1 Roll	1 Roll
2 Rolls	2 Rolls	2 Rolls
3 Rolls	3 Rolls	3 Rolls

After you have filled out the sheet, fold your column underneath along the dashed line so the next restroom user won't see your answers. *The first player uses the far right column.*

Answers - March 28-30
Mar. 28, 1 Roll: Pennsylvania
Mar. 28, 2 Rolls: James Bailey (Hence: Barnum & Bailey Circus)
Mar. 28, 3 Rolls: Mary Pickford

Mar. 29, 1 Roll: *Ebony and Ivory*
Mar. 29, 2 Rolls: Andre the Giant. Hogan pinned him in front of a packed Pontiac Silverdome.
Mar. 29, 3 Rolls: It gave Washington, DC its own Electoral Votes. They have 3.

Mar. 30, 1 Roll: Vincent van Gogh. It probably wasn't his entire ear, but his ear lobe. There's even a case that van Gogh didn't do this himself, and it was either accidentally or purposely cut off by his friend in a fight. That friend was artist, and fencer, Paul Gauguin.
Mar. 30, 2 Rolls: James Brady…as in "the Brady Bill" which requires stricter background checks for firearm licenses
Mar. 30, 3 Rolls: 15th Amendment

April 3

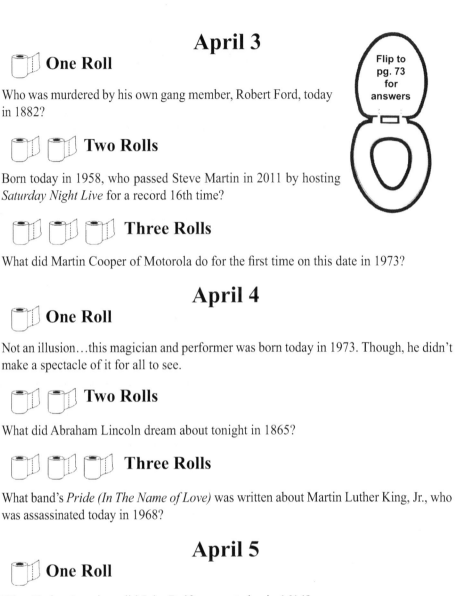

Flip to pg. 73 for answers

One Roll

Who was murdered by his own gang member, Robert Ford, today in 1882?

Two Rolls

Born today in 1958, who passed Steve Martin in 2011 by hosting *Saturday Night Live* for a record 16th time?

Three Rolls

What did Martin Cooper of Motorola do for the first time on this date in 1973?

April 4

One Roll

Not an illusion…this magician and performer was born today in 1973. Though, he didn't make a spectacle of it for all to see.

Two Rolls

What did Abraham Lincoln dream about tonight in 1865?

Three Rolls

What band's *Pride (In The Name of Love)* was written about Martin Luther King, Jr., who was assassinated today in 1968?

April 5

One Roll

What Native American did John Rolfe marry today in 1614?

Two Rolls

What famous boat's wood is claimed to be a barn on a farm 25 miles northwest of London? The ship set sail back to England today in 1621.

Three Rolls

On whose late night show in 1961 did Barbra Streisand make her television debut?

Answer Sheet   Answer Sheet   Answer Sheet

Name_____   Name_____   Name_____

April 3   April 3   April 3

1 Roll	1 Roll	1 Roll
2 Rolls	2 Rolls	2 Rolls
3 Rolls	3 Rolls	3 Rolls

April 4   April 4   April 4

1 Roll	1 Roll	1 Roll
2 Rolls	2 Rolls	2 Rolls
3 Rolls	3 Rolls	3 Rolls

April 5   April 5   April 5

1 Roll	1 Roll	1 Roll
2 Rolls	2 Rolls	2 Rolls
3 Rolls	3 Rolls	3 Rolls

After you have filled out the sheet, fold your column underneath along the dashed line so the next restroom user won't see your answers. *The first player uses the far right column.*

Answers - March 31-April 2
Mar. 31, 1 Roll: Eiffel Tower
Mar. 31, 2 Rolls: Frank Perdue
Mar. 31, 3 Rolls: Jack Johnson

Apr. 1, 1 Roll: Susan Boyle
Apr. 1, 2 Rolls: Marvin Gaye
Apr. 1, 3 Rolls: Mt. Vesuvius

Apr. 2, 1 Roll: The fountain of youth
Apr. 2, 2 Rolls: Jackie Mitchell struck out Babe Ruth and Lou Gehrig. She was never given a crack at the Major Leagues.
Apr. 2, 3 Rolls: *Dark Shadows*

April 6

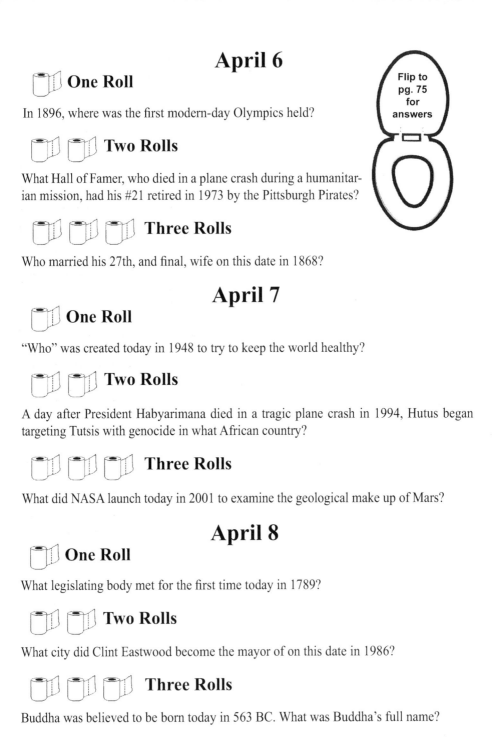

One Roll

In 1896, where was the first modern-day Olympics held?

Two Rolls

What Hall of Famer, who died in a plane crash during a humanitarian mission, had his #21 retired in 1973 by the Pittsburgh Pirates?

Three Rolls

Who married his 27th, and final, wife on this date in 1868?

Flip to pg. 75 for answers

April 7

One Roll

"Who" was created today in 1948 to try to keep the world healthy?

Two Rolls

A day after President Habyarimana died in a tragic plane crash in 1994, Hutus began targeting Tutsis with genocide in what African country?

Three Rolls

What did NASA launch today in 2001 to examine the geological make up of Mars?

April 8

One Roll

What legislating body met for the first time today in 1789?

Two Rolls

What city did Clint Eastwood become the mayor of on this date in 1986?

Three Rolls

Buddha was believed to be born today in 563 BC. What was Buddha's full name?

Answer Sheet | Answer Sheet | Answer Sheet

Name_____   Name_____   Name_____

April 6	April 6	April 6
1 Roll	1 Roll	1 Roll
2 Rolls	2 Rolls	2 Rolls
3 Rolls	3 Rolls	3 Rolls

April 7	April 7	April 7
1 Roll	1 Roll	1 Roll
2 Rolls	2 Rolls	2 Rolls
3 Rolls	3 Rolls	3 Rolls

April 8	April 8	April 8
1 Roll	1 Roll	1 Roll
2 Rolls	2 Rolls	2 Rolls
3 Rolls	3 Rolls	3 Rolls

After you have filled out the sheet, fold your column underneath along the dashed line so the next restroom user won't see your answers. *The first player uses the far right column.*

Answers - April 3-5

Apr. 3, 1 Roll: Jesse James

Apr. 3, 2 Rolls: Alec Baldwin

Apr. 3, 3 Rolls: He made the first cellphone call. He called his rival at AT&T to rub it in. The call was made on 6th Avenue in Manhattan.

Apr. 4, 1 Roll: David Blaine

Apr. 4, 2 Rolls: His impending assassination and funeral. Lincoln envisioned a casket surrounded by mourners. He was assassinated ten days later.

Apr. 4, 3 Rolls: U2

Apr. 5, 1 Roll: Pocahantas

Apr. 5, 2 Rolls: The *Mayflower*. According to oral history, rather than save their boat for a future Smithsonian, the Pilgrims sold the lumber it was made of. At least that is the claim in rural Jordans in England. The Mayflower Barn is open for banquets if you wish to get married beneath the timbers that landed at Plymouth.

Apr. 5, 3 Rolls: *The Jack Paar Tonight Show*

April 9

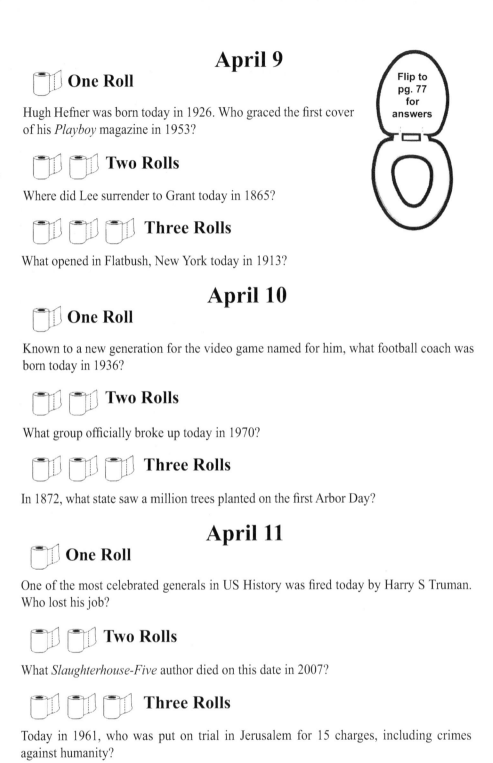

🧻 One Roll

Hugh Hefner was born today in 1926. Who graced the first cover of his *Playboy* magazine in 1953?

Flip to pg. 77 for answers

🧻🧻 Two Rolls

Where did Lee surrender to Grant today in 1865?

🧻🧻🧻 Three Rolls

What opened in Flatbush, New York today in 1913?

April 10

🧻 One Roll

Known to a new generation for the video game named for him, what football coach was born today in 1936?

🧻🧻 Two Rolls

What group officially broke up today in 1970?

🧻🧻🧻 Three Rolls

In 1872, what state saw a million trees planted on the first Arbor Day?

April 11

🧻 One Roll

One of the most celebrated generals in US History was fired today by Harry S Truman. Who lost his job?

🧻🧻 Two Rolls

What *Slaughterhouse-Five* author died on this date in 2007?

🧻🧻🧻 Three Rolls

Today in 1961, who was put on trial in Jerusalem for 15 charges, including crimes against humanity?

Answer Sheet   Answer Sheet   Answer Sheet

Name_____   Name_____   Name_____

April 9 | April 9 | April 9

1 Roll	1 Roll	1 Roll
2 Rolls	2 Rolls	2 Rolls
3 Rolls	3 Rolls	3 Rolls

April 10 | April 10 | April 10

1 Roll	1 Roll	1 Roll
2 Rolls	2 Rolls	2 Rolls
3 Rolls	3 Rolls	3 Rolls

April 11 | April 11 | April 11

1 Roll	1 Roll	1 Roll
2 Rolls	2 Rolls	2 Rolls
3 Rolls	3 Rolls	3 Rolls

After you have filled out the sheet, fold your column underneath along the dashed line so the next restroom user won't see your answers. *The first player uses the far right column.*

Answers - April 6-8
Apr. 6, 1 Roll: In Athens, Greece of course
Apr. 6, 2 Rolls: Roberto Clemente
Apr. 6, 3 Rolls: Brigham Young

Apr. 7, 1 Roll: World Health Organization (WHO)
Apr. 7, 2 Rolls: Rwanda
Apr. 7, 3 Rolls: Mars Odyssey

Apr. 8, 1 Roll: House of Representatives
Apr. 8, 2 Rolls: Carmel, California
Apr. 8, 3 Rolls: Siddhartha Gautama

April 12

One Roll

Flip to pg. 79 for answers

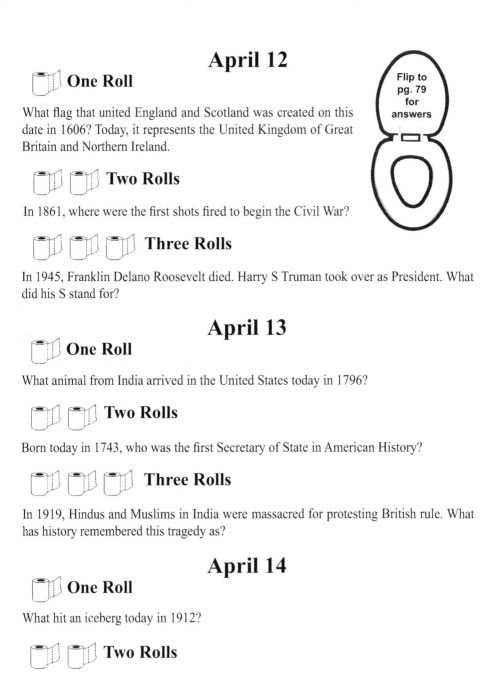

What flag that united England and Scotland was created on this date in 1606? Today, it represents the United Kingdom of Great Britain and Northern Ireland.

Two Rolls

In 1861, where were the first shots fired to begin the Civil War?

Three Rolls

In 1945, Franklin Delano Roosevelt died. Harry S Truman took over as President. What did his S stand for?

April 13

One Roll

What animal from India arrived in the United States today in 1796?

Two Rolls

Born today in 1743, who was the first Secretary of State in American History?

Three Rolls

In 1919, Hindus and Muslims in India were massacred for protesting British rule. What has history remembered this tragedy as?

April 14

One Roll

What hit an iceberg today in 1912?

Two Rolls

Lincoln was shot tonight in 1865. What Secretary of State was almost killed as well.

Three Rolls

Who published his roughly 70,000-word book today in 1828?

Answer Sheet | Answer Sheet | Answer Sheet

Name_____ | Name_____ | Name_____

April 12 | April 12 | April 12

1 Roll	1 Roll	1 Roll
2 Rolls	2 Rolls	2 Rolls
3 Rolls	3 Rolls	3 Rolls

April 13 | April 13 | April 13

1 Roll	1 Roll	1 Roll
2 Rolls	2 Rolls	2 Rolls
3 Rolls	3 Rolls	3 Rolls

April 14 | April 14 | April 14

1 Roll	1 Roll	1 Roll
2 Rolls	2 Rolls	2 Rolls
3 Rolls	3 Rolls	3 Rolls

After you have filled out the sheet, fold your column underneath along the dashed line so the next restroom user won't see your answers. *The first player uses the far right column.*

Answers - April 9-11

Apr. 9, 1 Roll: Marilyn Monroe
Apr. 9, 2 Rolls: Appomattox Court House
Apr. 9, 3 Rolls: Ebbets Field, home of the Brooklyn Dodgers

Apr. 10, 1 Roll: John Madden
Apr. 10, 2 Rolls: The Beatles. Paul McCartney announced the release of his solo album.
Apr. 10, 3 Rolls: Nebraska

Apr. 11, 1 Roll: Douglas MacArthur. As Commander-in-Chief, Truman had the final say as to how the military would be run.
Apr. 11, 2 Rolls: Kurt Vonnegut
Apr. 11, 3 Rolls: Adolf Eichmann

April 15

One Roll

Much to the joy of beer drinkers everywhere, what common key chain item was invented today in 1738?

Two Rolls

Born in 1452, whose Vitruvian Man drawing depicted symmetry and proportion of the human body?

Three Rolls

What baseball executive signed Jackie Robinson to break the color barrier today in 1947?

Flip to pg. 81 for answers

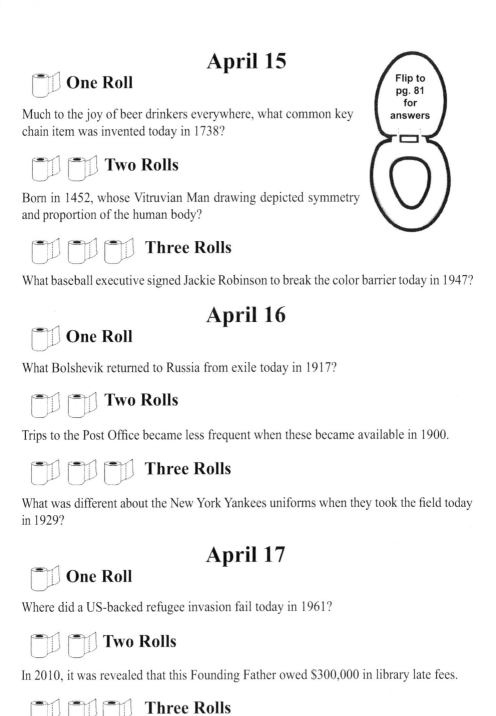

April 16

One Roll

What Bolshevik returned to Russia from exile today in 1917?

Two Rolls

Trips to the Post Office became less frequent when these became available in 1900.

Three Rolls

What was different about the New York Yankees uniforms when they took the field today in 1929?

April 17

One Roll

Where did a US-backed refugee invasion fail today in 1961?

Two Rolls

In 2010, it was revealed that this Founding Father owed $300,000 in library late fees.

Three Rolls

Today in 1790, Benjamin Franklin died. What war was his famous "Join, or Die" cartoon created during?

Answer Sheet | Answer Sheet | Answer Sheet

Name_____ | Name_____ | Name_____

April 15	**April 15**	**April 15**
1 Roll	1 Roll	1 Roll
2 Rolls	2 Rolls	2 Rolls
3 Rolls	3 Rolls	3 Rolls

April 16	**April 16**	**April 16**
1 Roll	1 Roll	1 Roll
2 Rolls	2 Rolls	2 Rolls
3 Rolls	3 Rolls	3 Rolls

April 17	**April 17**	**April 17**
1 Roll	1 Roll	1 Roll
2 Rolls	2 Rolls	2 Rolls
3 Rolls	3 Rolls	3 Rolls

After you have filled out the sheet, fold your column underneath along the dashed line so the next restroom user won't see your answers. *The first player uses the far right column.*

Answers - April 12-14

Apr. 12, 1 Roll: Union Jack, or Union Flag
Apr. 12, 2 Rolls: Fort Sumter, South Carolina
Apr. 12, 3 Rolls: Nothing. Just plain S. It seems that his mother's relatives were battling his father's relatives over what his middle name should be. Since both family names began with S, they compromised and essentially made his middle name S.

Apr. 13, 1 Roll: Elephant
Apr. 13, 2 Rolls: Thomas Jefferson. He wrote the Declaration of Independence, by the way.
Apr. 13, 3 Rolls: The Amritsar Massacre

Apr. 14, 1 Roll: The *Titanic*. It sank the next day.
Apr. 14, 2 Rolls: William Seward. As part of a larger conspiracy, Seward was attacked. The assailant tried to cut his throat, but he sliced a metal neck-brace that the Secretary had been wearing in the wake of a carriage accident.
Apr. 14, 3 Rolls: Noah Webster published *An American Dictionary of the English Language*

April 18

One Roll

What fault shook today in 1906 during the Great San Francisco Earthquake?

Two Rolls

Who did Prince Ranier marry today in Monaco in 1956?

Three Rolls

Paul Revere wasn't the only Bostonian to warn colonists that the British were coming. Who departed Boston on a separate route tonight in 1775?

Flip to pg. 83 for answers

April 19

One Roll

On this date in 1982, who did NASA name as the first female astronaut to go into space?

Two Rolls

In 1943, what city saw Jews rise up against Nazi aggression during the Holocaust?

Three Rolls

The Bill of Rights went into effect in 1791. But what state became the last to ratify it today in 1939?

April 20

One Roll

Who became the first woman to win an Indy-car race today in 2008?

Two Rolls

What environmental catastrophe in the Gulf of Mexico began today in 2010?

Three Rolls

What landmark invention of the twentieth century were people introduced to at the World's Fair today in 1939?

Answer Sheet

Name_____

April 18

1 Roll
2 Rolls
3 Rolls

April 19

1 Roll
2 Rolls
3 Rolls

April 20

1 Roll
2 Rolls
3 Rolls

Answer Sheet

Name_____

April 18

1 Roll
2 Rolls
3 Rolls

April 19

1 Roll
2 Rolls
3 Rolls

April 20

1 Roll
2 Rolls
3 Rolls

Answer Sheet

Name_____

April 18

1 Roll
2 Rolls
3 Rolls

April 19

1 Roll
2 Rolls
3 Rolls

April 20

1 Roll
2 Rolls
3 Rolls

After you have filled out the sheet, fold your column underneath along the dashed line so the next restroom user won't see your answers. ***The first player uses the far right column.***

Answers - April 15-17
Apr. 15, 1 Roll: Bottle opener
Apr. 15, 2 Rolls: Leonardo da Vinci
Apr. 15, 3 Rolls: Branch Rickey

Apr. 16, 1 Roll: Vladimir Lenin
Apr. 16, 2 Rolls: Books of stamps
Apr. 16, 3 Rolls: They had numbers on them. The game was rained out. Miles away, the Cleveland Indians took to a dry field to become the first team to wear numbers.

Apr. 17, 1 Roll: Bay of Pigs, in Cuba
Apr. 17, 2 Rolls: George Washington
Apr. 17, 3 Rolls: French and Indian War, or Seven Years' War. It was intended for the Albany Plan of Union. The cartoon was later used in the Revolution, and throughout American history.

April 21

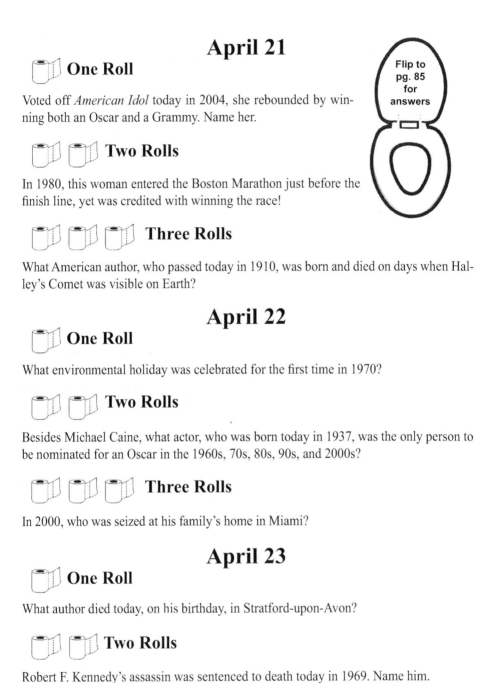

One Roll

Flip to pg. 85 for answers

Voted off *American Idol* today in 2004, she rebounded by winning both an Oscar and a Grammy. Name her.

Two Rolls

In 1980, this woman entered the Boston Marathon just before the finish line, yet was credited with winning the race!

Three Rolls

What American author, who passed today in 1910, was born and died on days when Halley's Comet was visible on Earth?

April 22

One Roll

What environmental holiday was celebrated for the first time in 1970?

Two Rolls

Besides Michael Caine, what actor, who was born today in 1937, was the only person to be nominated for an Oscar in the 1960s, 70s, 80s, 90s, and 2000s?

Three Rolls

In 2000, who was seized at his family's home in Miami?

April 23

One Roll

What author died today, on his birthday, in Stratford-upon-Avon?

Two Rolls

Robert F. Kennedy's assassin was sentenced to death today in 1969. Name him.

Three Rolls

What English King was *restored* to the throne in 1661? Habeas Corpus soon became law.

Answer Sheet   Answer Sheet   Answer Sheet

Name_____   Name_____   Name_____

April 21   April 21   April 21

1 Roll	1 Roll	1 Roll
2 Rolls	2 Rolls	2 Rolls
3 Rolls	3 Rolls	3 Rolls

April 22   April 22   April 22

1 Roll	1 Roll	1 Roll
2 Rolls	2 Rolls	2 Rolls
3 Rolls	3 Rolls	3 Rolls

April 23   April 23   April 23

1 Roll	1 Roll	1 Roll
2 Rolls	2 Rolls	2 Rolls
3 Rolls	3 Rolls	3 Rolls

After you have filled out the sheet, fold your column underneath along the dashed line so the next restroom user won't see your answers. *The first player uses the far right column.*

Answers - April 18-20
Apr. 18, 1 Roll: San Andreas Fault. The earthquake registered over an eight on the Richter scale.
Apr. 18, 2 Rolls: Grace Kelly
Apr. 18, 3 Rolls: William Dawes. Dr. Samuel Prescott also warned the colonists, and made it from Lexington to Concord after Revere and Dawes were caught. It is believed that poet Henry Wadsworth Longfellow's 1860 poem, *Paul Revere's Ride*, propelled Revere to historic immortality.

Apr. 19, 1 Roll: Sally Ride
Apr. 19, 2 Rolls: Warsaw
Apr. 19, 3 Rolls: Connecticut. Massachusetts and Georgia also ratified it that year. It was to mark the 150th anniversary of both its writing, and the ratification of the Constitution.

Apr. 20, 1 Roll: Danica Patrick
Apr. 20, 2 Rolls: BP Oil Spill, or *Deepwater Horizon* Oil Spill
Apr. 20, 3 Rolls: Television

April 24

 **One Roll**

Umpire Frank Umont was the first to wear something today in 1956. He probably just took everyone's advice.

 **Two Rolls**

Pope Benedict XVI took his name today in 2005 as the 265th pope. What was his name the day before?

 **Three Rolls**

What cosmetics giant died today in 2004?

Flip to pg. 87 for answers

April 25

 **One Roll**

Today in 1792, Frenchman Nicolas-Jacques Pelletier became the first person to be executed by what new device?

 **Two Rolls**

Which Golden Girl died today in 2009?

 **Three Rolls**

In 1886, who opened up his private practice in Vienna?

April 26

One Roll

Dubbed the most famous nightclub of all time, what New York City hotspot with digits in its name opened its doors on this date in 1977?

Two Rolls

In 1865, who was tracked down to a barn and killed...so we think?

Three Rolls

They didn't want his body. What pop star's Porsche was carjacked in LA today in 1982?

Answer Sheet | Answer Sheet | Answer Sheet

Name_____ | Name_____ | Name_____

April 24 | April 24 | April 24

1 Roll	1 Roll	1 Roll
2 Rolls	2 Rolls	2 Rolls
3 Rolls	3 Rolls	3 Rolls

April 25 | April 25 | April 25

1 Roll	1 Roll	1 Roll
2 Rolls	2 Rolls	2 Rolls
3 Rolls	3 Rolls	3 Rolls

April 26 | April 26 | April 26

1 Roll	1 Roll	1 Roll
2 Rolls	2 Rolls	2 Rolls
3 Rolls	3 Rolls	3 Rolls

After you have filled out the sheet, fold your column underneath along the dashed line so the next restroom user won't see your answers. *The first player uses the far right column.*

Answers - April 21-23

Apr. 21, 1 Roll: Jennifer Hudson
Apr. 21, 2 Rolls: Rosie Ruiz. About a week later, she was exposed.
Apr. 21, 3 Rolls: Mark Twain

Apr. 22, 1 Roll: Earth Day
Apr. 22, 2 Rolls: Jack Nicholson
Apr. 22, 3 Rolls: Elian Gonzalez. The boy was taken to Andrews Air Force Base and reunited with his father.

Apr. 23, 1 Roll: William Shakespeare, in 1616
Apr. 23, 2 Rolls: Sirhan Sirhan. However, after California did away with capital punishment, his sentence was changed to life in prison.
Apr. 23, 3 Rolls: Charles II. The event was known as the Restoration, as a monarch once again ruled England.

April 27

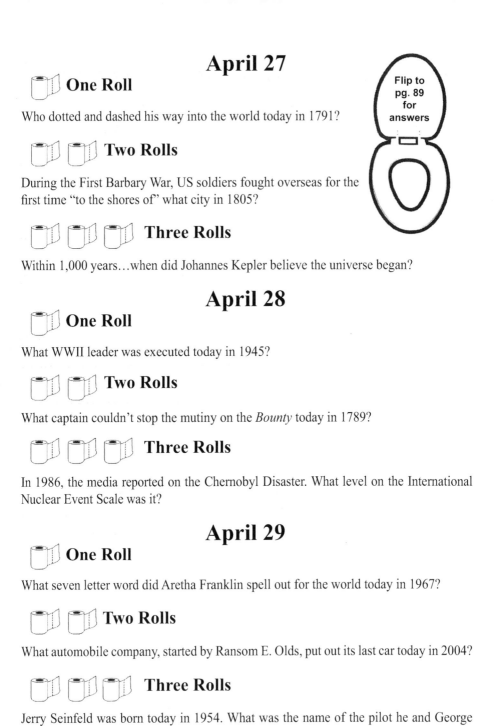

One Roll

Who dotted and dashed his way into the world today in 1791?

Flip to pg. 89 for answers

Two Rolls

During the First Barbary War, US soldiers fought overseas for the first time "to the shores of" what city in 1805?

Three Rolls

Within 1,000 years…when did Johannes Kepler believe the universe began?

April 28

One Roll

What WWII leader was executed today in 1945?

Two Rolls

What captain couldn't stop the mutiny on the *Bounty* today in 1789?

Three Rolls

In 1986, the media reported on the Chernobyl Disaster. What level on the International Nuclear Event Scale was it?

April 29

One Roll

What seven letter word did Aretha Franklin spell out for the world today in 1967?

Two Rolls

What automobile company, started by Ransom E. Olds, put out its last car today in 2004?

Three Rolls

Jerry Seinfeld was born today in 1954. What was the name of the pilot he and George wrote on *Seinfeld?*

Answer Sheet | Answer Sheet | Answer Sheet

Name_____ Name_____ Name_____

April 27 | **April 27** | **April 27**

1 Roll	1 Roll	1 Roll
2 Rolls	2 Rolls	2 Rolls
3 Rolls	3 Rolls	3 Rolls

April 28 | **April 28** | **April 28**

1 Roll	1 Roll	1 Roll
2 Rolls	2 Rolls	2 Rolls
3 Rolls	3 Rolls	3 Rolls

April 29 | **April 29** | **April 29**

1 Roll	1 Roll	1 Roll
2 Rolls	2 Rolls	2 Rolls
3 Rolls	3 Rolls	3 Rolls

After you have filled out the sheet, fold your column underneath along the dashed line so the next restroom user won't see your answers. *The first player uses the far right column.*

Answers - April 24-26
Apr. 24, 1 Roll: Glasses
Apr. 24, 2 Rolls: Cardinal Joseph Ratzinger
Apr. 24, 3 Rolls: Estée Lauder

Apr. 25, 1 Roll: Guillotine
Apr. 25, 2 Rolls: Bea Arthur
Apr. 25, 3 Rolls: Sigmund Freud

Apr. 26, 1 Roll: Studio 54
Apr. 26, 2 Rolls: John Wilkes Booth. There have been conspiracy theories indicating that he survived and lived in Tennessee.
Apr. 26, 3 Rolls: Rod Stewart

April 30

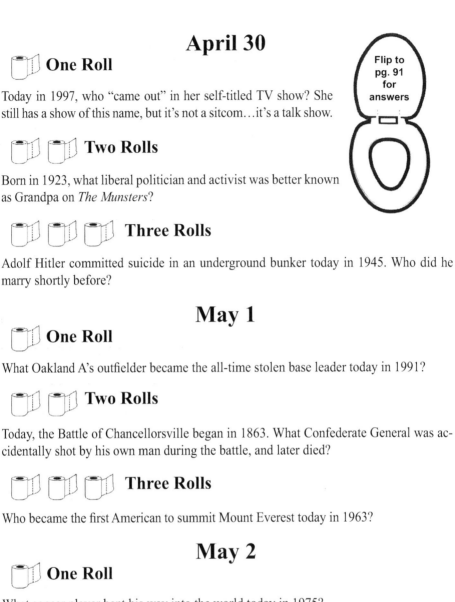

🧻 One Roll

Today in 1997, who "came out" in her self-titled TV show? She still has a show of this name, but it's not a sitcom…it's a talk show.

🧻🧻 Two Rolls

Born in 1923, what liberal politician and activist was better known as Grandpa on *The Munsters*?

🧻🧻🧻 Three Rolls

Adolf Hitler committed suicide in an underground bunker today in 1945. Who did he marry shortly before?

Flip to pg. 91 for answers

May 1

🧻 One Roll

What Oakland A's outfielder became the all-time stolen base leader today in 1991?

🧻🧻 Two Rolls

Today, the Battle of Chancellorsville began in 1863. What Confederate General was accidentally shot by his own man during the battle, and later died?

🧻🧻🧻 Three Rolls

Who became the first American to summit Mount Everest today in 1963?

May 2

🧻 One Roll

What soccer player bent his way into the world today in 1975?

🧻🧻 Two Rolls

What controversial Senator from Wisconsin died today in 1957?

🧻🧻🧻 Three Rolls

What play by Tennessee Williams won the Pulitzer Prize for Drama today in 1955?

Answer Sheet | Answer Sheet | Answer Sheet

Name_____ | Name_____ | Name_____

April 30 | April 30 | April 30

1 Roll	1 Roll	1 Roll
2 Rolls	2 Rolls	2 Rolls
3 Rolls	3 Rolls	3 Rolls

May 1 | May 1 | May 1

1 Roll	1 Roll	1 Roll
2 Rolls	2 Rolls	2 Rolls
3 Rolls	3 Rolls	3 Rolls

May 2 | May 2 | May 2

1 Roll	1 Roll	1 Roll
2 Rolls	2 Rolls	2 Rolls
3 Rolls	3 Rolls	3 Rolls

After you have filled out the sheet, fold your column underneath along the dashed line so the next restroom user won't see your answers. *The first player uses the far right column.*

Answers - April 27-29
Apr. 27, 1 Roll: Samuel Morse
Apr. 27, 2 Rolls: Tripoli
Apr. 27, 3 Rolls: 4977 BC

Apr. 28, 1 Roll: Benito Mussolini
Apr. 28, 2 Rolls: Captain William Bligh
Apr. 28, 3 Rolls: A seven, or major accident. The meltdown took place on the 26th, but was kept a secret.

Apr. 29, 1 Roll: R-E-S-P-E-C-T
Apr. 29, 2 Rolls: Oldsmobile
Apr. 29, 3 Rolls: *Jerry*

May 3

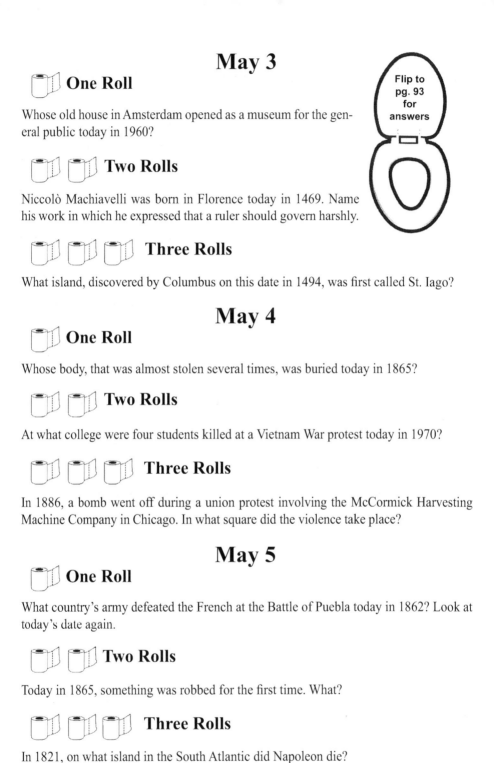

One Roll

Whose old house in Amsterdam opened as a museum for the general public today in 1960?

Two Rolls

Niccolò Machiavelli was born in Florence today in 1469. Name his work in which he expressed that a ruler should govern harshly.

Flip to pg. 93 for answers

Three Rolls

What island, discovered by Columbus on this date in 1494, was first called St. Iago?

May 4

One Roll

Whose body, that was almost stolen several times, was buried today in 1865?

Two Rolls

At what college were four students killed at a Vietnam War protest today in 1970?

Three Rolls

In 1886, a bomb went off during a union protest involving the McCormick Harvesting Machine Company in Chicago. In what square did the violence take place?

May 5

One Roll

What country's army defeated the French at the Battle of Puebla today in 1862? Look at today's date again.

Two Rolls

Today in 1865, something was robbed for the first time. What?

Three Rolls

In 1821, on what island in the South Atlantic did Napoleon die?

Answer Sheet | Answer Sheet | Answer Sheet

Name_____ | Name_____ | Name_____

May 3	**May 3**	**May 3**
1 Roll	1 Roll	1 Roll
2 Rolls	2 Rolls	2 Rolls
3 Rolls	3 Rolls	3 Rolls

May 4	**May 4**	**May 4**
1 Roll	1 Roll	1 Roll
2 Rolls	2 Rolls	2 Rolls
3 Rolls	3 Rolls	3 Rolls

May 5	**May 5**	**May 5**
1 Roll	1 Roll	1 Roll
2 Rolls	2 Rolls	2 Rolls
3 Rolls	3 Rolls	3 Rolls

After you have filled out the sheet, fold your column underneath along the dashed line so the next restroom user won't see your answers. *The first player uses the far right column.*

Answers - April 30-May 2
Apr. 30, 1 Roll: Ellen DeGeneres, of *Ellen*
Apr. 30, 2 Rolls: Al Lewis
Apr. 30, 3 Rolls: Eva Braun

May 1, 1 Roll: Rickey Henderson. Henderson once framed a million dollar check instead of cashing it. He finally got to a bank a few months later. He just wanted to remind himself that he was a millionaire. The A's asked him to cash it for record-keeping purposes.
May 1, 2 Rolls: Stonewall Jackson
May 1, 3 Rolls: James Whittaker

May 2, 1 Roll: David Beckham
May 2, 2 Rolls: Joseph McCarthy. McCarthyism supporters targeted communist traitors in the government. This often became a witch hunt.
May 2, 3 Rolls: *Cat on a Hot Tin Roof*

May 6

One Roll

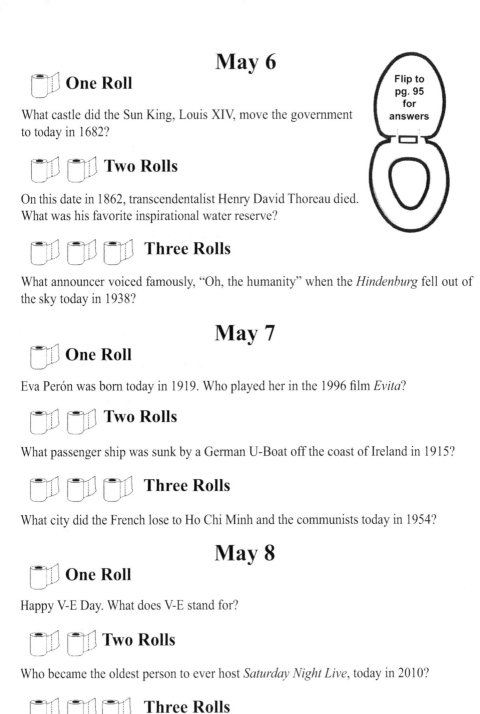

Flip to pg. 95 for answers

What castle did the Sun King, Louis XIV, move the government to today in 1682?

Two Rolls

On this date in 1862, transcendentalist Henry David Thoreau died. What was his favorite inspirational water reserve?

Three Rolls

What announcer voiced famously, "Oh, the humanity" when the *Hindenburg* fell out of the sky today in 1938?

May 7

One Roll

Eva Perón was born today in 1919. Who played her in the 1996 film *Evita*?

Two Rolls

What passenger ship was sunk by a German U-Boat off the coast of Ireland in 1915?

Three Rolls

What city did the French lose to Ho Chi Minh and the communists today in 1954?

May 8

One Roll

Happy V-E Day. What does V-E stand for?

Two Rolls

Who became the oldest person to ever host *Saturday Night Live*, today in 2010?

Three Rolls

In 1909, Neal Ball pulled off the rarest play in baseball for the first time in the modern era…what is it?

Answer Sheet

Name_____

May 6

1 Roll
2 Rolls
3 Rolls

May 7

1 Roll
2 Rolls
3 Rolls

May 8

1 Roll
2 Rolls
3 Rolls

Answer Sheet

Name_____

May 6

1 Roll
2 Rolls
3 Rolls

May 7

1 Roll
2 Rolls
3 Rolls

May 8

1 Roll
2 Rolls
3 Rolls

Answer Sheet

Name_____

May 6

1 Roll
2 Rolls
3 Rolls

May 7

1 Roll
2 Rolls
3 Rolls

May 8

1 Roll
2 Rolls
3 Rolls

After you have filled out the sheet, fold your column underneath along the dashed line so the next restroom user won't see your answers. *The first player uses the far right column.*

Answers - May 3-5
May 3, 1 Roll: Anne Frank's House
May 3, 2 Rolls: *The Prince*
May 3, 3 Rolls: Jamaica

May 4, 1 Roll: Abraham Lincoln. Lincoln's body was almost stolen in 1876, and the sound of gunfire rattled the cemetery. After authorities chased away the bandits, Lincoln's body was hidden for decades. In 1901, he was placed in his renovated tomb in Springfield, Illinois.
May 4, 2 Rolls: Kent State
May 4, 3 Rolls: Haymarket Square. The event was blamed on immigrant union members, and led to both a rise in nativism and a decrease in unionization.

May 5, 1 Roll: Mexico. Hence, why Cinco de Mayo is celebrated today.
May 5, 2 Rolls: A train—it was traveling between St. Louis and Cincinnati.
May 5, 3 Rolls: St. Helena

May 9

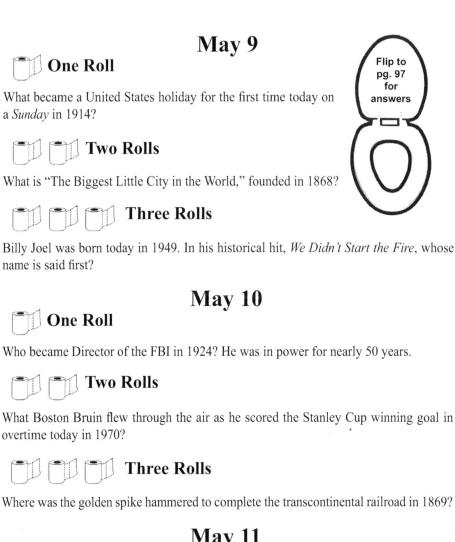

Flip to pg. 97 for answers

One Roll

What became a United States holiday for the first time today on a *Sunday* in 1914?

Two Rolls

What is "The Biggest Little City in the World," founded in 1868?

Three Rolls

Billy Joel was born today in 1949. In his historical hit, *We Didn't Start the Fire*, whose name is said first?

May 10

One Roll

Who became Director of the FBI in 1924? He was in power for nearly 50 years.

Two Rolls

What Boston Bruin flew through the air as he scored the Stanley Cup winning goal in overtime today in 1970?

Three Rolls

Where was the golden spike hammered to complete the transcontinental railroad in 1869?

May 11

One Roll

What Andrew Lloyd Weber musical both opened and closed on this date in 1981 and 2002? It finally ran out of lives.

Two Rolls

What contraceptive method was approved for sale today in 1961?

Three Rolls

Constantinople was founded today in 330AD. What two names has it also been known as?

94

Answer Sheet

Name_____

Answer Sheet

Name_____

Answer Sheet

Name_____

May 9   May 9   May 9

1 Roll	1 Roll	1 Roll
2 Rolls	2 Rolls	2 Rolls
3 Rolls	3 Rolls	3 Rolls

May 10   May 10   May 10

1 Roll	1 Roll	1 Roll
2 Rolls	2 Rolls	2 Rolls
3 Rolls	3 Rolls	3 Rolls

May 11   May 11   May 11

1 Roll	1 Roll	1 Roll
2 Rolls	2 Rolls	2 Rolls
3 Rolls	3 Rolls	3 Rolls

After you have filled out the sheet, fold your column underneath along the dashed line so the next restroom user won't see your answers. *The first player uses the far right column.*

Answers - May 6-8
May 6, 1 Roll: The Palace of Versailles
May 6, 2 Rolls: Walden Pond. It was the inspiration behind his famous book *Walden*.
May 6, 3 Rolls: Herbert Morrison. Urban legend has it that he was fired after the broadcast because he editorialized with emotion. However, this is unproven.

May 7, 1 Roll: Madonna
May 7, 2 Rolls: The *Lusitania*
May 7, 3 Rolls: Dien Bien Phu. The event can be considered to be the beginning of the Vietnam War.

May 8, 1 Roll: Victory in Europe Day for the Allies of World War II (1945)
May 8, 2 Rolls: Betty White at age 88
May 8, 3 Rolls: Unassisted Triple Play. It's only occurred fifteen times since the beginning of the twentieth century.

May 12

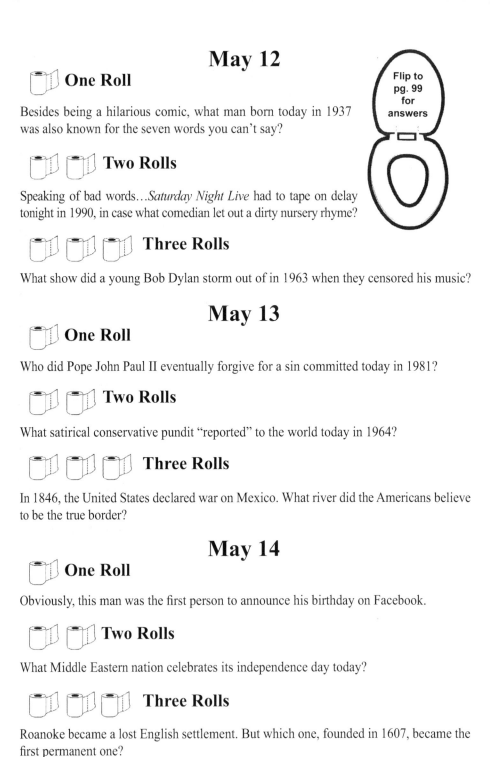

One Roll

Besides being a hilarious comic, what man born today in 1937 was also known for the seven words you can't say?

Flip to pg. 99 for answers

Two Rolls

Speaking of bad words...*Saturday Night Live* had to tape on delay tonight in 1990, in case what comedian let out a dirty nursery rhyme?

Three Rolls

What show did a young Bob Dylan storm out of in 1963 when they censored his music?

May 13

One Roll

Who did Pope John Paul II eventually forgive for a sin committed today in 1981?

Two Rolls

What satirical conservative pundit "reported" to the world today in 1964?

Three Rolls

In 1846, the United States declared war on Mexico. What river did the Americans believe to be the true border?

May 14

One Roll

Obviously, this man was the first person to announce his birthday on Facebook.

Two Rolls

What Middle Eastern nation celebrates its independence day today?

Three Rolls

Roanoke became a lost English settlement. But which one, founded in 1607, became the first permanent one?

Answer Sheet | Answer Sheet | Answer Sheet

Name_____ | Name_____ | Name_____

| May 12 | May 12 | May 12 |

May 12	May 12	May 12
1 Roll	1 Roll	1 Roll
2 Rolls	2 Rolls	2 Rolls
3 Rolls	3 Rolls	3 Rolls

May 13	May 13	May 13
1 Roll	1 Roll	1 Roll
2 Rolls	2 Rolls	2 Rolls
3 Rolls	3 Rolls	3 Rolls

May 14	May 14	May 14
1 Roll	1 Roll	1 Roll
2 Rolls	2 Rolls	2 Rolls
3 Rolls	3 Rolls	3 Rolls

After you have filled out the sheet, fold your column underneath along the dashed line so the next restroom user won't see your answers. *The first player uses the far right column.*

Answers - May 9-11
May 9, 1 Roll: Mother's Day
May 9, 2 Rolls: Reno, Nevada
May 9, 3 Rolls: Harry Truman

May 10, 1 Roll: J. Edgar Hoover
May 10, 2 Rolls: Bobby Orr
May 10, 3 Rolls: Promontory Summit, Utah. Leland Stanford swung and missed in his first attempt to hammer it in.

May 11, 1 Roll: *Cats*
May 11, 2 Rolls: Birth control pills
May 11, 3 Rolls: Earlier it was Byzantium and in 1930 it became Istanbul

May 15

Flip to pg. 101 for answers

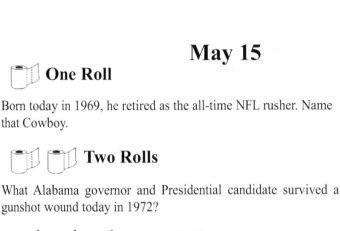 **One Roll**

Born today in 1969, he retired as the all-time NFL rusher. Name that Cowboy.

 **Two Rolls**

What Alabama governor and Presidential candidate survived a gunshot wound today in 1972?

Three Rolls

What Scandinavian country's civil war ended today in 1918?

May 16

One Roll

Born today in 1966, who suffered a wardrobe malfunction at the 2004 Super Bowl?

 **Two Rolls**

What circular pasta in tomato sauce was made available by the Franco-American Food Company today in 1965?

Three Rolls

At the Oscars, "Best Picture" used to be referred to as "Outstanding Picture." What film won the first Oscar for this category in 1929?

May 17

One Roll

What Supreme Court decision in 1954 ended segregation in schools?

 **Two Rolls**

In what Nebraskan city did Buffalo Bill Cody's Wild West Show debut today in 1883?

 **Three Rolls**

What agricultural inventor died today in 1886?

Answer Sheet

Name_____

May 15

1 Roll
2 Rolls
3 Rolls

May 16

1 Roll
2 Rolls
3 Rolls

May 17

1 Roll
2 Rolls
3 Rolls

Answer Sheet

Name_____

May 15

1 Roll
2 Rolls
3 Rolls

May 16

1 Roll
2 Rolls
3 Rolls

May 17

1 Roll
2 Rolls
3 Rolls

Answer Sheet

Name_____

May 15

1 Roll
2 Rolls
3 Rolls

May 16

1 Roll
2 Rolls
3 Rolls

May 17

1 Roll
2 Rolls
3 Rolls

After you have filled out the sheet, fold your column underneath along the dashed line so the next restroom user won't see your answers. *The first player uses the far right column.*

Answers - May 12-14
May 12, 1 Roll: George Carlin. Use your imagination for the words, we'll keep it clean.
May 12, 2 Rolls: Andrew Dice Clay
May 12, 3 Rolls: *The Ed Sullivan Show*. He wanted to play a song criticizing the John Birch Society, an organization which finger-pointed communist activity.

May 13, 1 Roll: His attempted assassin. The Pope survived the gunshot wounds inflicted by Mehmet Ali Ağca. Despite the forgiveness, the Vatican equipped the Popemobile with bullet-proof glass.
May 13, 2 Rolls: Stephen Colbert of *The Colbert Report*
May 13, 3 Rolls: The Rio Grande. The Mexican government contested that the Nueces River, further north, was the border.

May 14, 1 Roll: Mark Zuckerberg. He was born today in 1984.
May 14, 2 Rolls: Israel (1948)
May 14, 3 Rolls: Jamestown

May 18

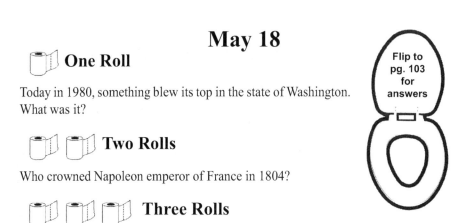

Flip to pg. 103 for answers

One Roll

Today in 1980, something blew its top in the state of Washington. What was it?

Two Rolls

Who crowned Napoleon emperor of France in 1804?

Three Rolls

Who was elected governor of the Massachusetts Bay colony today in 1631?

May 19

One Roll

In 1962, Marilyn Monroe sang *Happy Birthday* to President John F. Kennedy. Within three years, what birthday was it?

 **Two Rolls**

What drama series, whose five letter title could fit on a license plate, had its finale tonight in 1994?

 **Three Rolls**

What was the nickname given to the infamous tariff passed today in 1828?

May 20

One Roll

Who patented blue jeans today in 1873?

 **Two Rolls**

What first lady, born today in 1768, was known to serve ice cream in the White House?

 **Three Rolls**

During the US Civil War, "free land" became abundant for settlement out west. What landmark act encouraged people to move? It became law today in 1862.

Answer Sheet | Answer Sheet | Answer Sheet

Name_____ | Name_____ | Name_____

May 18		May 18		May 18
1 Roll		1 Roll		1 Roll
2 Rolls		2 Rolls		2 Rolls
3 Rolls		3 Rolls		3 Rolls

May 19		May 19		May 19
1 Roll		1 Roll		1 Roll
2 Rolls		2 Rolls		2 Rolls
3 Rolls		3 Rolls		3 Rolls

May 20		May 20		May 20
1 Roll		1 Roll		1 Roll
2 Rolls		2 Rolls		2 Rolls
3 Rolls		3 Rolls		3 Rolls

After you have filled out the sheet, fold your column underneath along the dashed line so the next restroom user won't see your answers. *The first player uses the far right column.*

Answers - May 15-17
May 15, 1 Roll: Emmitt Smith rushed for 18,355 yards
May 15, 2 Rolls: George Wallace
May 15, 3 Rolls: Finland

May 16, 1 Roll: Janet Jackson
May 16, 2 Rolls: SpaghettiOs
May 16, 3 Rolls: *Wings* won for 1927-28. It was a silent film about a World War I fighter pilot.

May 17, 1 Roll: *Brown v. Board of Education of Topeka, Kansas*
May 17, 2 Rolls: Omaha
May 17, 3 Rolls: John Deere. Yes, he was a real person.

May 21

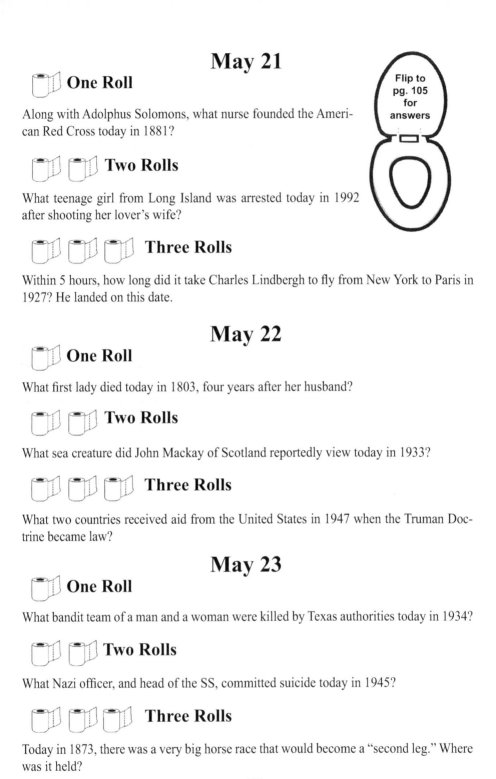

One Roll

Flip to pg. 105 for answers

Along with Adolphus Solomons, what nurse founded the American Red Cross today in 1881?

Two Rolls

What teenage girl from Long Island was arrested today in 1992 after shooting her lover's wife?

Three Rolls

Within 5 hours, how long did it take Charles Lindbergh to fly from New York to Paris in 1927? He landed on this date.

May 22

One Roll

What first lady died today in 1803, four years after her husband?

Two Rolls

What sea creature did John Mackay of Scotland reportedly view today in 1933?

Three Rolls

What two countries received aid from the United States in 1947 when the Truman Doctrine became law?

May 23

One Roll

What bandit team of a man and a woman were killed by Texas authorities today in 1934?

Two Rolls

What Nazi officer, and head of the SS, committed suicide today in 1945?

Three Rolls

Today in 1873, there was a very big horse race that would become a "second leg." Where was it held?

102

Answer Sheet | Answer Sheet | Answer Sheet

Name _____

Name _____

Name _____

May 21	May 21	May 21
1 Roll	1 Roll	1 Roll
2 Rolls	2 Rolls	2 Rolls
3 Rolls	3 Rolls	3 Rolls

May 22	May 22	May 22
1 Roll	1 Roll	1 Roll
2 Rolls	2 Rolls	2 Rolls
3 Rolls	3 Rolls	3 Rolls

May 23	May 23	May 23
1 Roll	1 Roll	1 Roll
2 Rolls	2 Rolls	2 Rolls
3 Rolls	3 Rolls	3 Rolls

After you have filled out the sheet, fold your column underneath along the dashed line so the next restroom user won't see your answers. ***The first player uses the far right column.***

Answers - May 18-20

May 18, 1 Roll: Mount St. Helens
May 18, 2 Rolls: Napoleon crowned himself. He took the crown from the pope, and placed it on his own head.
May 18, 3 Rolls: John Winthrop. He advocated for a religious "city upon a hill."

May 19, 1 Roll: He turned 45. Actually, the President's birthday wasn't until May 29. She sang it at Madison Square Garden. The dress has since been auctioned off for over a million dollars.
May 19, 2 Rolls: *L.A. Law*
May 19, 3 Rolls: Tariff of Abominations

May 20, 1 Roll: Levi Strauss. He applied for the patent with Jacob Davis. Some people made money by finding nuggets during the gold rush. Strauss made his fortune giving miners stronger pants.
May 20, 2 Rolls: Dolley Madison
May 20, 3 Rolls: Homestead Act

May 24

One Roll

Flip to pg. 107 for answers

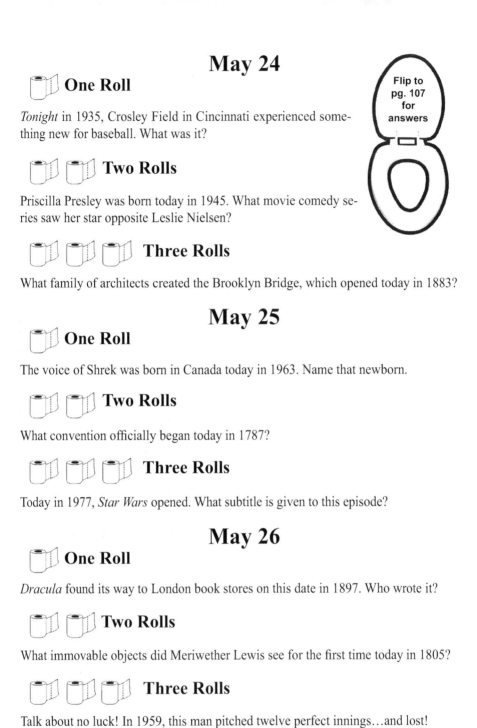

Tonight in 1935, Crosley Field in Cincinnati experienced something new for baseball. What was it?

Two Rolls

Priscilla Presley was born today in 1945. What movie comedy series saw her star opposite Leslie Nielsen?

Three Rolls

What family of architects created the Brooklyn Bridge, which opened today in 1883?

May 25

One Roll

The voice of Shrek was born in Canada today in 1963. Name that newborn.

Two Rolls

What convention officially began today in 1787?

Three Rolls

Today in 1977, *Star Wars* opened. What subtitle is given to this episode?

May 26

One Roll

Dracula found its way to London book stores on this date in 1897. Who wrote it?

Two Rolls

What immovable objects did Meriwether Lewis see for the first time today in 1805?

Three Rolls

Talk about no luck! In 1959, this man pitched twelve perfect innings…and lost!

Answer Sheet | Answer Sheet | Answer Sheet

Name_____ Name_____ Name_____

May 24	**May 24**	**May 24**
1 Roll	1 Roll	1 Roll
2 Rolls	2 Rolls	2 Rolls
3 Rolls	3 Rolls	3 Rolls

May 25	**May 25**	**May 25**
1 Roll	1 Roll	1 Roll
2 Rolls	2 Rolls	2 Rolls
3 Rolls	3 Rolls	3 Rolls

May 26	**May 26**	**May 26**
1 Roll	1 Roll	1 Roll
2 Rolls	2 Rolls	2 Rolls
3 Rolls	3 Rolls	3 Rolls

After you have filled out the sheet, fold your column underneath along the dashed line so the next restroom user won't see your answers. *The first player uses the far right column.*

Answers - May 21-23
May 21, 1 Roll: Clara Barton
May 21, 2 Rolls: Amy Fisher
May 21, 3 Rolls: 33.5 hours

May 22, 1 Roll: Martha Washington. George Washington died in December of 1799…a man truly of the eighteenth century.
May 22, 2 Rolls: Nessie, or the Loch Ness Monster
May 22, 3 Rolls: Greece and Turkey

May 23, 1 Roll: Bonnie and Clyde
May 23, 2 Rolls: Heinrich Himmler. He committed suicide after being captured by the British.
May 23, 3 Rolls: The first Preakness Stakes was held at Pimlico Race Course in Baltimore, with a purse just over $2,000.

May 27

Flip to pg. 109 for answers

One Roll

What Bay Area landmark officially opened for business on this date in 1937?

Two Rolls

What German battleship was sunk by the British today in 1941?

Three Rolls

Born today in 1837, this quick gunslinger of the west was holding Aces and Eights when he was killed. Name him.

May 28

One Roll

Today in 1972, there was a break-in at a hotel complex in Washington, DC. Which hotel?

Two Rolls

In 1754, what British soldier triggered an international incident when he attacked a French garrison in the Ohio River Valley?

Three Rolls

What British Prime Minister, who took office today in 1937, thought he found "peace in our time" with Hitler at the Munich Conference?

May 29

One Roll

What comedian turned 100 today in 2003? We hope you know the answer.

Two Rolls

Who beat out Magic Johnson to become the NBA Rookie-of-the-Year today in 1980?

Three Rolls

What African American delivered her famous "Ain't I a Woman?" speech today in 1851 at the Women's Rights Convention in Akron, Ohio?

Answer Sheet | Answer Sheet | Answer Sheet

Name_____ | Name_____ | Name_____

May 27	**May 27**	**May 27**
1 Roll	1 Roll	1 Roll
2 Rolls	2 Rolls	2 Rolls
3 Rolls	3 Rolls	3 Rolls

May 28	**May 28**	**May 28**
1 Roll	1 Roll	1 Roll
2 Rolls	2 Rolls	2 Rolls
3 Rolls	3 Rolls	3 Rolls

May 29	**May 29**	**May 29**
1 Roll	1 Roll	1 Roll
2 Rolls	2 Rolls	2 Rolls
3 Rolls	3 Rolls	3 Rolls

After you have filled out the sheet, fold your column underneath along the dashed line so the next restroom user won't see your answers. ***The first player uses the far right column.***

Answers - May 24-26
May 24, 1 Roll: The first night game in baseball history. The Reds beat the Phillies 2-1.
May 24, 2 Rolls: *The Naked Gun*
May 24, 3 Rolls: The Roeblings (John and Washington)

May 25, 1 Roll: Mike Myers
May 25, 2 Rolls: The Constitutional Convention
May 25, 3 Rolls: *Episode IV: A New Hope*

May 26, 1 Roll: Bram Stoker
May 26, 2 Rolls: The Rocky Mountains
May 26, 3 Rolls: Harvey Haddix of the Pittsburgh Pirates

May 30

One Roll

Born today in 1972, it's a good thing he was named Manny. Otherwise, it would have been very hard for him to be Manny.

Two Rolls

What future President was shot in a duel today in 1806?

Three Rolls

What act regarding slavery became law today in 1854? Shortly thereafter, one of the states it was named for would bleed.

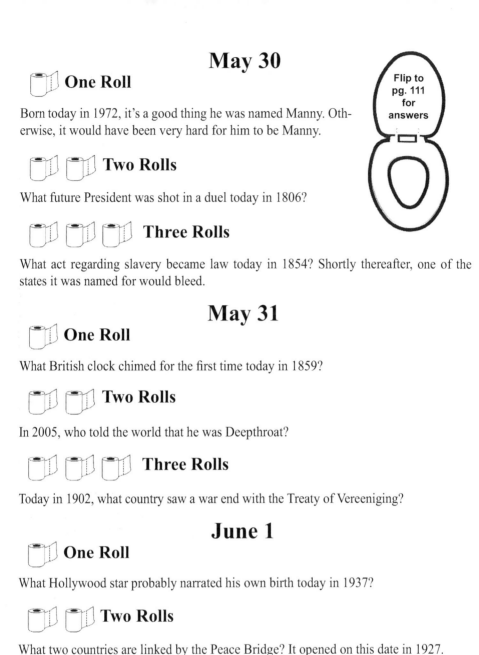

Flip to pg. 111 for answers

May 31

One Roll

What British clock chimed for the first time today in 1859?

Two Rolls

In 2005, who told the world that he was Deepthroat?

Three Rolls

Today in 1902, what country saw a war end with the Treaty of Vereeniging?

June 1

One Roll

What Hollywood star probably narrated his own birth today in 1937?

Two Rolls

What two countries are linked by the Peace Bridge? It opened on this date in 1927.

Three Rolls

Thomas Edison gained his first patent today in 1869. It was designed to be used five months from now. What was it?

Answer Sheet

Name_____

May 30

1 Roll	
2 Rolls	
3 Rolls	

May 31

1 Roll	
2 Rolls	
3 Rolls	

June 1

1 Roll	
2 Rolls	
3 Rolls	

Answer Sheet

Name_____

May 30

1 Roll	
2 Rolls	
3 Rolls	

May 31

1 Roll	
2 Rolls	
3 Rolls	

June 1

1 Roll	
2 Rolls	
3 Rolls	

Answer Sheet

Name_____

May 30

1 Roll	
2 Rolls	
3 Rolls	

May 31

1 Roll	
2 Rolls	
3 Rolls	

June 1

1 Roll	
2 Rolls	
3 Rolls	

After you have filled out the sheet, fold your column underneath along the dashed line so the next restroom user won't see your answers. *The first player uses the far right column.*

Answers - May 27-29
May 27, 1 Roll: Golden Gate Bridge
May 27, 2 Rolls: The *Bismarck*
May 27, 3 Rolls: Wild Bill Hickok. Aces and Eights became known as the "Dead Man's Hand."

May 28, 1 Roll: The office complex of the Watergate Hotel. Files were tampered with, and phones were bugged. So began the great scandal.
May 28, 2 Rolls: George Washington, then a red coat. The incident would escalate into the French and Indian War.
May 28, 3 Rolls: Neville Chamberlain. By giving Hitler the Sudetenland in Czechoslovakia, he hoped there would be peace. This appeasement attempt only made Hitler want more.

May 29, 1 Roll: Bob Hope
May 29, 2 Rolls: Larry Bird
May 29, 3 Rolls: Sojourner Truth

June 2

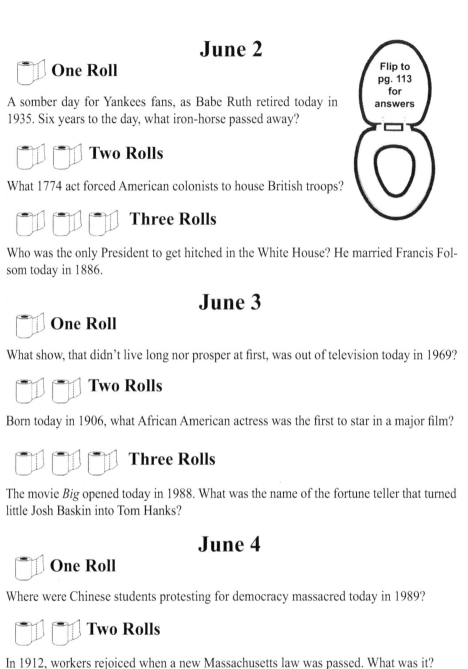

One Roll

Flip to pg. 113 for answers

A somber day for Yankees fans, as Babe Ruth retired today in 1935. Six years to the day, what iron-horse passed away?

Two Rolls

What 1774 act forced American colonists to house British troops?

Three Rolls

Who was the only President to get hitched in the White House? He married Francis Folsom today in 1886.

June 3

One Roll

What show, that didn't live long nor prosper at first, was out of television today in 1969?

Two Rolls

Born today in 1906, what African American actress was the first to star in a major film?

Three Rolls

The movie *Big* opened today in 1988. What was the name of the fortune teller that turned little Josh Baskin into Tom Hanks?

June 4

One Roll

Where were Chinese students protesting for democracy massacred today in 1989?

Two Rolls

In 1912, workers rejoiced when a new Massachusetts law was passed. What was it?

Three Rolls

In 1892, what non-profit organization that seeks to protect nature was established in San Francisco? John Muir was the first president.

Answer Sheet

Name_____

June 2

1 Roll
2 Rolls
3 Rolls

June 3

1 Roll
2 Rolls
3 Rolls

June 4

1 Roll
2 Rolls
3 Rolls

Answer Sheet

Name_____

June 2

1 Roll
2 Rolls
3 Rolls

June 3

1 Roll
2 Rolls
3 Rolls

June 4

1 Roll
2 Rolls
3 Rolls

Answer Sheet

Name_____

June 2

1 Roll
2 Rolls
3 Rolls

June 3

1 Roll
2 Rolls
3 Rolls

June 4

1 Roll
2 Rolls
3 Rolls

After you have filled out the sheet, fold your column underneath along the dashed line so the next restroom user won't see your answers. *The first player uses the far right column.*

Answers - May 30-June 1
May 30, 1 Roll: Manny Ramirez
May 30, 2 Rolls: Andrew Jackson. He carried metal in his body for the rest of his life. He killed Charles Dickinson in the duel.
May 30, 3 Rolls: The Kansas-Nebraska Act instituted popular sovereignty, which gave each territory the right to choose if they wanted slavery or not. Bleeding Kansas resulted from this choice.

May 31, 1 Roll: Big Ben
May 31, 2 Rolls: Mark Felt, formerly of the FBI, admitted that he was the informant of the Watergate Scandal. Journalists Bob Woodward and Carl Bernstein verified the fact.
May 31, 3 Rolls: South Africa

June 1, 1 Roll: Morgan Freeman
June 1, 2 Rolls: United States and Canada. It connects New York to Ontario.
June 1, 3 Rolls: It was a vote counting machine. Edison had a total of 1,093 patents.

June 5

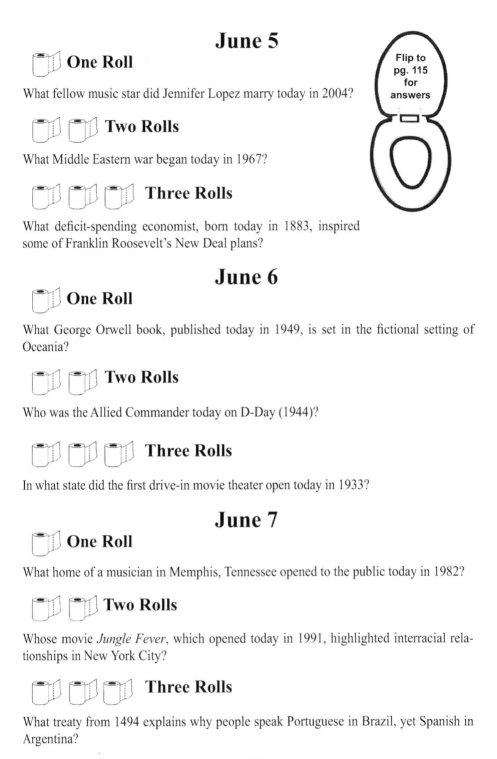

One Roll

What fellow music star did Jennifer Lopez marry today in 2004?

Flip to pg. 115 for answers

Two Rolls

What Middle Eastern war began today in 1967?

Three Rolls

What deficit-spending economist, born today in 1883, inspired some of Franklin Roosevelt's New Deal plans?

June 6

One Roll

What George Orwell book, published today in 1949, is set in the fictional setting of Oceania?

Two Rolls

Who was the Allied Commander today on D-Day (1944)?

Three Rolls

In what state did the first drive-in movie theater open today in 1933?

June 7

One Roll

What home of a musician in Memphis, Tennessee opened to the public today in 1982?

Two Rolls

Whose movie *Jungle Fever*, which opened today in 1991, highlighted interracial relationships in New York City?

Three Rolls

What treaty from 1494 explains why people speak Portuguese in Brazil, yet Spanish in Argentina?

Answer Sheet | Answer Sheet | Answer Sheet

Name_____ | Name_____ | Name_____

June 5 | June 5 | June 5

June 5	June 5	June 5
1 Roll	1 Roll	1 Roll
2 Rolls	2 Rolls	2 Rolls
3 Rolls	3 Rolls	3 Rolls

June 6 | June 6 | June 6

June 6	June 6	June 6
1 Roll	1 Roll	1 Roll
2 Rolls	2 Rolls	2 Rolls
3 Rolls	3 Rolls	3 Rolls

June 7 | June 7 | June 7

June 7	June 7	June 7
1 Roll	1 Roll	1 Roll
2 Rolls	2 Rolls	2 Rolls
3 Rolls	3 Rolls	3 Rolls

After you have filled out the sheet, fold your column underneath along the dashed line so the next restroom user won't see your answers. *The first player uses the far right column.*

Answers - June 2-4

June 2, 1 Roll: Lou Gehrig. Note that Babe Ruth retired from the Boston Braves.
June 2, 2 Rolls: Quartering Act. It was passed along with the other Intolerable Acts in the wake of the Boston Tea Party.
June 2, 3 Rolls: Grover Cleveland. John Tyler and Woodrow Wilson also married while in office, just not in the White House. Cleveland was also the only President to win office twice, yet serve two non-successive terms.

June 3, 1 Roll: *Star Trek*. In its original television format, it only lasted three seasons.
June 3, 2 Rolls: Josephine Baker
June 3, 3 Rolls: Zoltar Speaks

June 4, 1 Roll: Tiananmen Square
June 4, 2 Rolls: The nation's first minimum wage law. It was meant to protect women and children from sweatshops.
June 4, 3 Rolls: Sierra Club

June 8

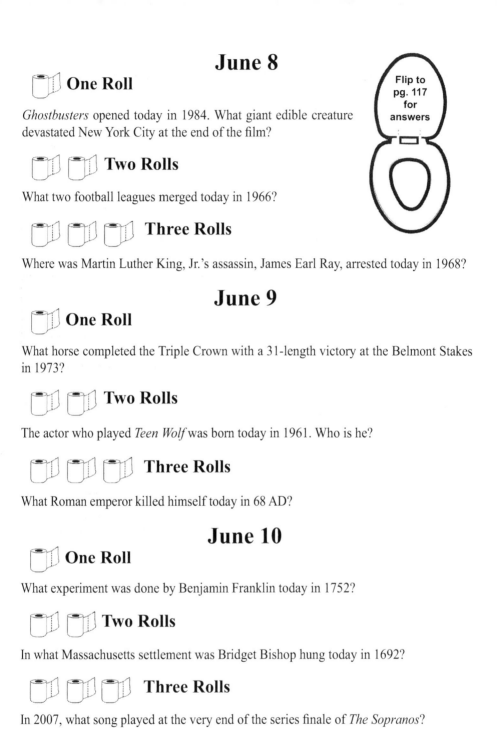

🧻 One Roll

Ghostbusters opened today in 1984. What giant edible creature devastated New York City at the end of the film?

Flip to pg. 117 for answers

🧻 🧻 Two Rolls

What two football leagues merged today in 1966?

🧻 🧻 🧻 Three Rolls

Where was Martin Luther King, Jr.'s assassin, James Earl Ray, arrested today in 1968?

June 9

🧻 One Roll

What horse completed the Triple Crown with a 31-length victory at the Belmont Stakes in 1973?

🧻 🧻 Two Rolls

The actor who played *Teen Wolf* was born today in 1961. Who is he?

🧻 🧻 🧻 Three Rolls

What Roman emperor killed himself today in 68 AD?

June 10

🧻 One Roll

What experiment was done by Benjamin Franklin today in 1752?

🧻 🧻 Two Rolls

In what Massachusetts settlement was Bridget Bishop hung today in 1692?

🧻 🧻 🧻 Three Rolls

In 2007, what song played at the very end of the series finale of *The Sopranos*?

Answer Sheet | Answer Sheet | Answer Sheet

Name_____   Name_____   Name_____

June 8	June 8	June 8
1 Roll	1 Roll	1 Roll
2 Rolls	2 Rolls	2 Rolls
3 Rolls	3 Rolls	3 Rolls

June 9	June 9	June 9
1 Roll	1 Roll	1 Roll
2 Rolls	2 Rolls	2 Rolls
3 Rolls	3 Rolls	3 Rolls

June 10	June 10	June 10
1 Roll	1 Roll	1 Roll
2 Rolls	2 Rolls	2 Rolls
3 Rolls	3 Rolls	3 Rolls

After you have filled out the sheet, fold your column underneath along the dashed line so the next restroom user won't see your answers. *The first player uses the far right column.*

Answers - June 5-7
June 5, 1 Roll: Marc Anthony
June 5, 2 Rolls: Six-Day War
June 5, 3 Rolls: John Maynard Keynes, father of Keynesian Economics

June 6, 1 Roll: *Nineteen Eighty-Four*
June 6, 2 Rolls: Dwight Eisenhower
June 6, 3 Rolls: New Jersey. Camden to be exact.

June 7, 1 Roll: Graceland, home of Elvis Presley
June 7, 2 Rolls: Spike Lee
June 7, 3 Rolls: In 1494, the Treaty of Tordesillas determined the line of demarcation which would separate Spanish and Portuguese land. Today, this is why most people in South America speak Spanish, yet Brazil to the east of the line speaks Portuguese.

June 11

One Roll

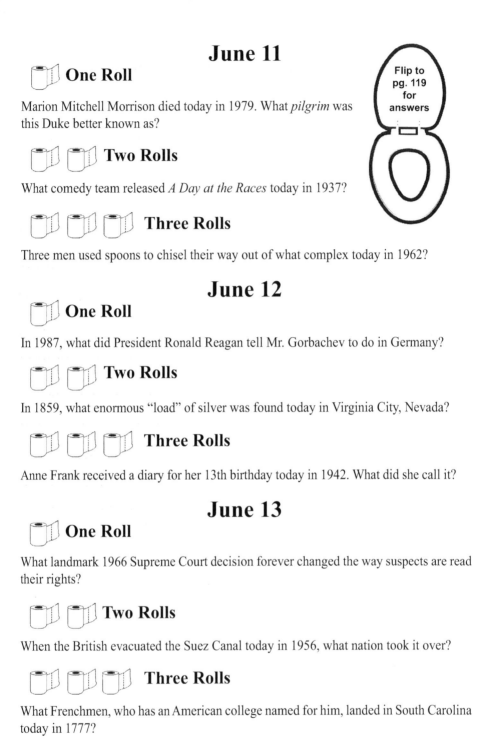

Marion Mitchell Morrison died today in 1979. What *pilgrim* was this Duke better known as?

Flip to pg. 119 for answers

Two Rolls

What comedy team released *A Day at the Races* today in 1937?

Three Rolls

Three men used spoons to chisel their way out of what complex today in 1962?

June 12

One Roll

In 1987, what did President Ronald Reagan tell Mr. Gorbachev to do in Germany?

Two Rolls

In 1859, what enormous "load" of silver was found today in Virginia City, Nevada?

Three Rolls

Anne Frank received a diary for her 13th birthday today in 1942. What did she call it?

June 13

One Roll

What landmark 1966 Supreme Court decision forever changed the way suspects are read their rights?

Two Rolls

When the British evacuated the Suez Canal today in 1956, what nation took it over?

Three Rolls

What Frenchmen, who has an American college named for him, landed in South Carolina today in 1777?

Answer Sheet | Answer Sheet | Answer Sheet

Name_____ | Name_____ | Name_____

June 11 | June 11 | June 11

1 Roll	1 Roll	1 Roll
2 Rolls	2 Rolls	2 Rolls
3 Rolls	3 Rolls	3 Rolls

June 12 | June 12 | June 12

1 Roll	1 Roll	1 Roll
2 Rolls	2 Rolls	2 Rolls
3 Rolls	3 Rolls	3 Rolls

June 13 | June 13 | June 13

1 Roll	1 Roll	1 Roll
2 Rolls	2 Rolls	2 Rolls
3 Rolls	3 Rolls	3 Rolls

After you have filled out the sheet, fold your column underneath along the dashed line so the next restroom user won't see your answers. *The first player uses the far right column.*

Answers - June 8-10
June 8, 1 Roll: The Stay Puft Marshmallow Man
June 8, 2 Rolls: NFL and AFL (National Football League and American Football League)
June 8, 3 Rolls: London, England

June 9, 1 Roll: Secretariat
June 9, 2 Rolls: Michael J. Fox
June 9, 3 Rolls: Nero

June 10, 1 Roll: The Kite Experiment to observe lightning and electricity. He took his son out to witness it. Contrary to myth, his son William wasn't a kid. He was in his 20s.
June 10, 2 Rolls: Salem. She was the first to be executed during the Salem Witch Trials.
June 10, 3 Rolls: *Don't Stop Believin'* by Journey

June 14

One Roll

If you didn't get this businessman a cake on his birthday, then you might get fired.

Two Rolls

What Hungarian actress was accused of slapping a cop in the face after a traffic stop today in 1989?

Three Rolls

What VP, whose grandson lost to Dwight Eisenhower in 1952 and 1956, died in 1914?

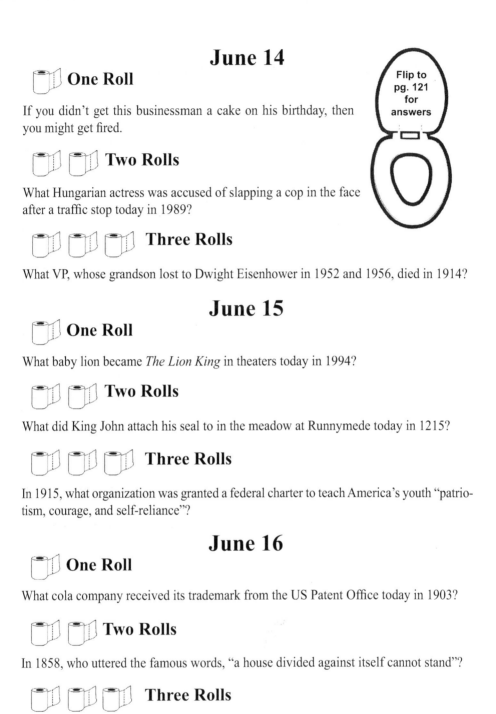

Flip to pg. 121 for answers

June 15

One Roll

What baby lion became *The Lion King* in theaters today in 1994?

Two Rolls

What did King John attach his seal to in the meadow at Runnymede today in 1215?

Three Rolls

In 1915, what organization was granted a federal charter to teach America's youth "patriotism, courage, and self-reliance"?

June 16

One Roll

What cola company received its trademark from the US Patent Office today in 1903?

Two Rolls

In 1858, who uttered the famous words, "a house divided against itself cannot stand"?

Three Rolls

Psycho opened today in 1960. What special effect was used to simulate blood in the shower scene?

Answer Sheet | Answer Sheet | Answer Sheet

Name_____   Name_____   Name_____

June 14	June 14	June 14
1 Roll	1 Roll	1 Roll
2 Rolls	2 Rolls	2 Rolls
3 Rolls	3 Rolls	3 Rolls

June 15	June 15	June 15
1 Roll	1 Roll	1 Roll
2 Rolls	2 Rolls	2 Rolls
3 Rolls	3 Rolls	3 Rolls

June 16	June 16	June 16
1 Roll	1 Roll	1 Roll
2 Rolls	2 Rolls	2 Rolls
3 Rolls	3 Rolls	3 Rolls

After you have filled out the sheet, fold your column underneath along the dashed line so the next restroom user won't see your answers. *The first player uses the far right column.*

Answers - June 11-13
June 11, 1 Roll: John Wayne
June 11, 2 Rolls: The Marx Brothers
June 11, 3 Rolls: Alcatraz. The men used papier-mâché dummies to fool guards into thinking they were asleep. They then escaped through vents, hopped onto a raft-like contraption made from raincoats, and were never heard from again. They either drowned leaving The Rock, or fled the country.

June 12, 1 Roll: "Tear down this wall." He was referring to the Berlin Wall.
June 12, 2 Rolls: The Comstock Lode
June 12, 3 Rolls: Kitty. She began her entries, "Dear Kitty."

June 13, 1 Roll: *Miranda* v. *Arizona*…hence, Miranda rights
June 13, 2 Rolls: Egypt
June 13, 3 Rolls: Marquis de Lafayette

June 17

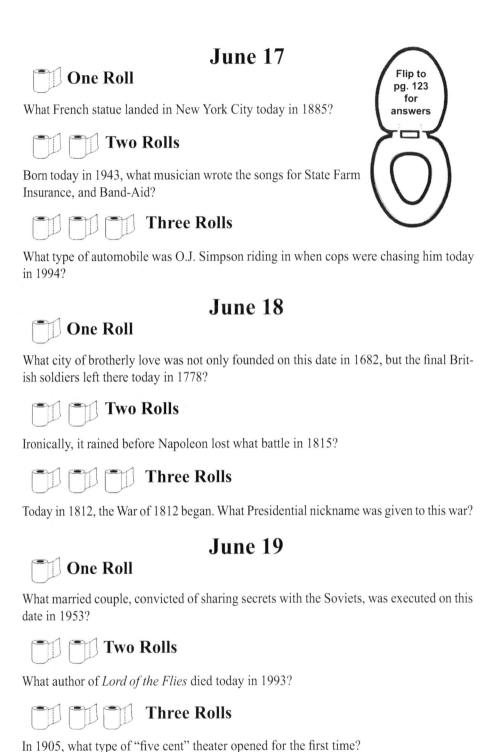

One Roll

What French statue landed in New York City today in 1885?

Flip to
pg. 123
for
answers

Two Rolls

Born today in 1943, what musician wrote the songs for State Farm Insurance, and Band-Aid?

Three Rolls

What type of automobile was O.J. Simpson riding in when cops were chasing him today in 1994?

June 18

One Roll

What city of brotherly love was not only founded on this date in 1682, but the final British soldiers left there today in 1778?

Two Rolls

Ironically, it rained before Napoleon lost what battle in 1815?

Three Rolls

Today in 1812, the War of 1812 began. What Presidential nickname was given to this war?

June 19

One Roll

What married couple, convicted of sharing secrets with the Soviets, was executed on this date in 1953?

Two Rolls

What author of *Lord of the Flies* died today in 1993?

Three Rolls

In 1905, what type of "five cent" theater opened for the first time?

Answer Sheet | Answer Sheet | Answer Sheet

Name_____ | Name_____ | Name_____

| June 17 | June 17 | June 17 |

1 Roll	1 Roll	1 Roll
2 Rolls	2 Rolls	2 Rolls
3 Rolls	3 Rolls	3 Rolls

| June 18 | June 18 | June 18 |

1 Roll	1 Roll	1 Roll
2 Rolls	2 Rolls	2 Rolls
3 Rolls	3 Rolls	3 Rolls

| June 19 | June 19 | June 19 |

1 Roll	1 Roll	1 Roll
2 Rolls	2 Rolls	2 Rolls
3 Rolls	3 Rolls	3 Rolls

After you have filled out the sheet, fold your column underneath along the dashed line so the next restroom user won't see your answers. *The first player uses the far right column.*

Answers - June 14-16
June 14, 1 Roll: Donald Trump
June 14, 2 Rolls: Zsa Zsa Gabor
June 14, 3 Rolls: Adlai Stevenson. He was Grover Cleveland's Vice President, and grandfather of the Democratic candidate with the same name.

June 15, 1 Roll: Simba
June 15, 2 Rolls: The Magna Carta
June 15, 3 Rolls: The Boy Scouts of America

June 16, 1 Roll: Pepsi-Cola
June 16, 2 Rolls: Abraham Lincoln, then a candidate for Senator
June 16, 3 Rolls: Chocolate syrup. The movie was in black and white.

June 20

🧻 One Roll

In 1967, what boxer was convicted of violating the US Selective Service Act when he refused to be drafted?

🧻 🧻 Two Rolls

At what type of sporting venue did the French Third Estate pledge to make a new constitution in 1789?

🧻 🧻 🧻 Three Rolls

Today in 1975, *Jaws* was released. On what fictional venue did the story take place?

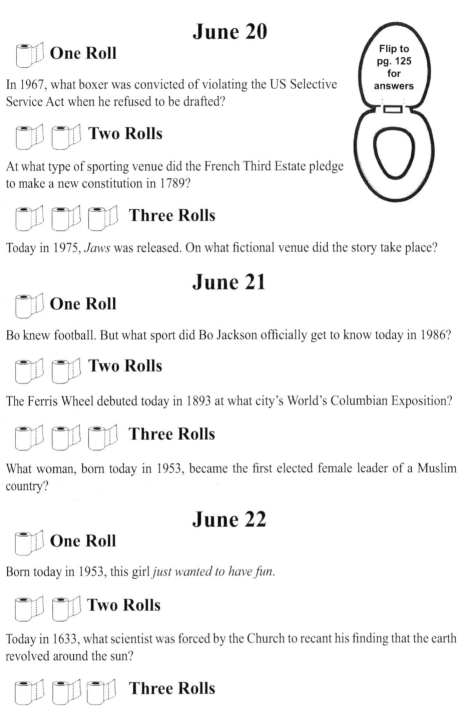

Flip to pg. 125 for answers

June 21

🧻 One Roll

Bo knew football. But what sport did Bo Jackson officially get to know today in 1986?

🧻 🧻 Two Rolls

The Ferris Wheel debuted today in 1893 at what city's World's Columbian Exposition?

🧻 🧻 🧻 Three Rolls

What woman, born today in 1953, became the first elected female leader of a Muslim country?

June 22

🧻 One Roll

Born today in 1953, this girl *just wanted to have fun.*

🧻 🧻 Two Rolls

Today in 1633, what scientist was forced by the Church to recant his finding that the earth revolved around the sun?

🧻 🧻 🧻 Three Rolls

What producer of *Gone with the Wind* died today in 1965?

122

Answer Sheet | Answer Sheet | Answer Sheet

Name_____ | Name_____ | Name_____

June 20	**June 20**	**June 20**
1 Roll	1 Roll	1 Roll
2 Rolls	2 Rolls	2 Rolls
3 Rolls	3 Rolls	3 Rolls

June 21	**June 21**	**June 21**
1 Roll	1 Roll	1 Roll
2 Rolls	2 Rolls	2 Rolls
3 Rolls	3 Rolls	3 Rolls

June 22	**June 22**	**June 22**
1 Roll	1 Roll	1 Roll
2 Rolls	2 Rolls	2 Rolls
3 Rolls	3 Rolls	3 Rolls

After you have filled out the sheet, fold your column underneath along the dashed line so the next restroom user won't see your answers. *The first player uses the far right column.*

Answers - June 17-19
June 17, 1 Roll: The Statue of Liberty
June 17, 2 Rolls: Barry Manilow. He wrote many other jingles for companies including soft drinks Tab and Dr. Pepper. He has been honored at the Clio Awards.
June 17, 3 Rolls: Ford Bronco

June 18, 1 Roll: Philadelphia
June 18, 2 Rolls: Waterloo
June 18, 3 Rolls: Mr. Madison's War

June 19, 1 Roll: Julius and Ethel Rosenberg
June 19, 2 Rolls: William Golding
June 19, 3 Rolls: A nickelodeon. It opened in Pittsburgh.

June 23

One Roll

Who played *Batman* for Tim Burton when it opened today in 1989?

Two Rolls

Going into effect today in 1972, what law gives women equal opportunities in collegiate sports?

Three Rolls

He died today in 79 AD. What emperor was in power when ground was broken for the Roman Colosseum?

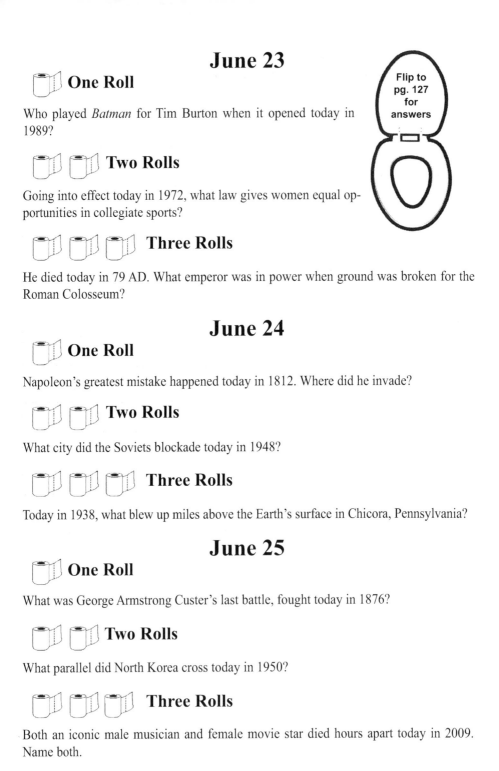

Flip to pg. 127 for answers

June 24

One Roll

Napoleon's greatest mistake happened today in 1812. Where did he invade?

Two Rolls

What city did the Soviets blockade today in 1948?

Three Rolls

Today in 1938, what blew up miles above the Earth's surface in Chicora, Pennsylvania?

June 25

One Roll

What was George Armstrong Custer's last battle, fought today in 1876?

Two Rolls

What parallel did North Korea cross today in 1950?

Three Rolls

Both an iconic male musician and female movie star died hours apart today in 2009. Name both.

Answer Sheet | Answer Sheet | Answer Sheet

Name_____ Name_____ Name_____

| June 23 | June 23 | June 23 |

1 Roll	1 Roll	1 Roll
2 Rolls	2 Rolls	2 Rolls
3 Rolls	3 Rolls	3 Rolls

| June 24 | June 24 | June 24 |

1 Roll	1 Roll	1 Roll
2 Rolls	2 Rolls	2 Rolls
3 Rolls	3 Rolls	3 Rolls

| June 25 | June 25 | June 25 |

1 Roll	1 Roll	1 Roll
2 Rolls	2 Rolls	2 Rolls
3 Rolls	3 Rolls	3 Rolls

After you have filled out the sheet, fold your column underneath along the dashed line so the next restroom user won't see your answers. *The first player uses the far right column.*

Answers - June 20-22
June 20, 1 Roll: Muhammad Ali
June 20, 2 Rolls: They made the Tennis Court Oath
June 20, 3 Rolls: Amity Island

June 21, 1 Roll: Baseball. He signed with the Kansas City Royals.
June 21, 2 Rolls: Chicago
June 21, 3 Rolls: Benazir Bhutto

June 22, 1 Roll: Cyndi Lauper
June 22, 2 Rolls: Galileo. His research confirmed the heliocentric model of Copernicus. The Church accused him of heresy. He abandoned his findings, and lived the rest of his life under house arrest.
June 22, 3 Rolls: David O. Selznick

June 26

🧻 One Roll

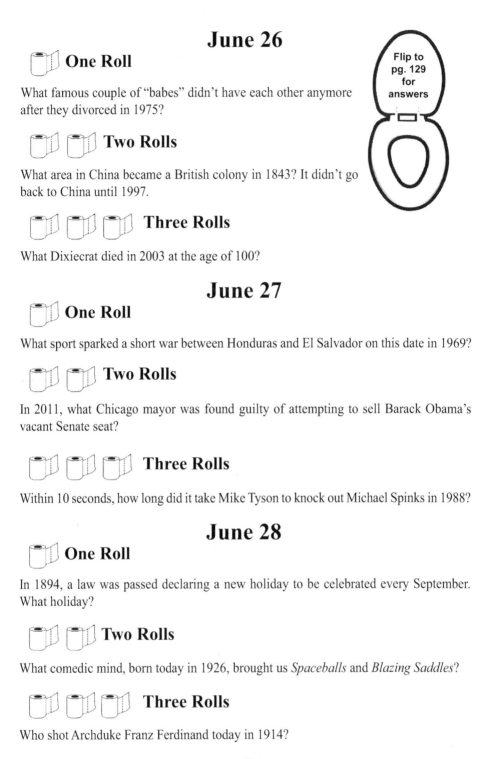

Flip to pg. 129 for answers

What famous couple of "babes" didn't have each other anymore after they divorced in 1975?

🧻🧻 Two Rolls

What area in China became a British colony in 1843? It didn't go back to China until 1997.

🧻🧻🧻 Three Rolls

What Dixiecrat died in 2003 at the age of 100?

June 27

🧻 One Roll

What sport sparked a short war between Honduras and El Salvador on this date in 1969?

🧻🧻 Two Rolls

In 2011, what Chicago mayor was found guilty of attempting to sell Barack Obama's vacant Senate seat?

🧻🧻🧻 Three Rolls

Within 10 seconds, how long did it take Mike Tyson to knock out Michael Spinks in 1988?

June 28

🧻 One Roll

In 1894, a law was passed declaring a new holiday to be celebrated every September. What holiday?

🧻🧻 Two Rolls

What comedic mind, born today in 1926, brought us *Spaceballs* and *Blazing Saddles*?

🧻🧻🧻 Three Rolls

Who shot Archduke Franz Ferdinand today in 1914?

126

Answer Sheet | Answer Sheet | Answer Sheet

Name_____ | Name_____ | Name_____

June 26 | June 26 | June 26

1 Roll	1 Roll	1 Roll
2 Rolls	2 Rolls	2 Rolls
3 Rolls	3 Rolls	3 Rolls

June 27 | June 27 | June 27

1 Roll	1 Roll	1 Roll
2 Rolls	2 Rolls	2 Rolls
3 Rolls	3 Rolls	3 Rolls

June 28 | June 28 | June 28

1 Roll	1 Roll	1 Roll
2 Rolls	2 Rolls	2 Rolls
3 Rolls	3 Rolls	3 Rolls

After you have filled out the sheet, fold your column underneath along the dashed line so the next restroom user won't see your answers. *The first player uses the far right column.*

Answers - June 23-25
June 23, 1 Roll: Michael Keaton
June 23, 2 Rolls: Title IX
June 23, 3 Rolls: Vespasian

June 24, 1 Roll: Russia. The miscalculation wiped out nearly his entire army.
June 24, 2 Rolls: West Berlin. The incident led to the Berlin Airlift, where American and British planes dropped supplies to the people of that city.
June 24, 3 Rolls: A meteor, estimated to be between 400-500 tons

June 25, 1 Roll: Little Big Horn
June 25, 2 Rolls: 38th Parallel. So began the Korean War.
June 25, 3 Rolls: Michael Jackson and Farrah Fawcett

June 29

One Roll

In 1613 what burned to the ground during a production of *Henry VIII*?

Flip to pg. 131 for answers

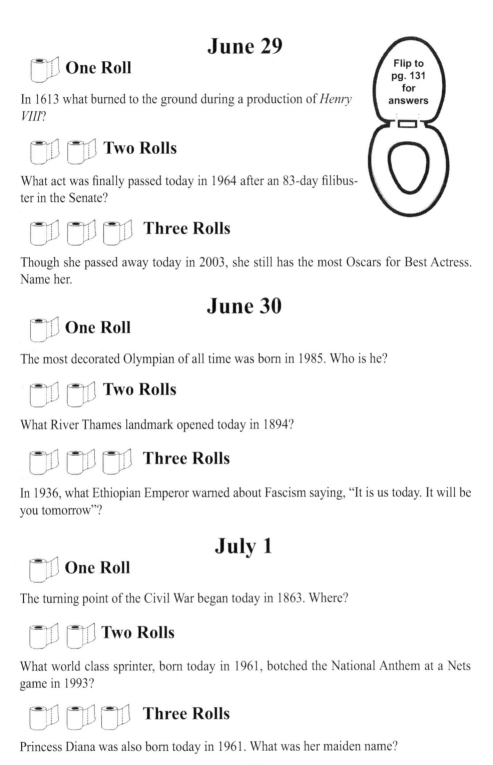

Two Rolls

What act was finally passed today in 1964 after an 83-day filibuster in the Senate?

Three Rolls

Though she passed away today in 2003, she still has the most Oscars for Best Actress. Name her.

June 30

One Roll

The most decorated Olympian of all time was born in 1985. Who is he?

Two Rolls

What River Thames landmark opened today in 1894?

Three Rolls

In 1936, what Ethiopian Emperor warned about Fascism saying, "It is us today. It will be you tomorrow"?

July 1

One Roll

The turning point of the Civil War began today in 1863. Where?

Two Rolls

What world class sprinter, born today in 1961, botched the National Anthem at a Nets game in 1993?

Three Rolls

Princess Diana was also born today in 1961. What was her maiden name?

Answer Sheet | Answer Sheet | Answer Sheet

Name_____ | Name_____ | Name_____

<table>
<tr><td align="center">June 29</td><td align="center">June 29</td><td align="center">June 29</td></tr>
<tr><td>1 Roll</td><td>1 Roll</td><td>1 Roll</td></tr>
<tr><td>2 Rolls</td><td>2 Rolls</td><td>2 Rolls</td></tr>
<tr><td>3 Rolls</td><td>3 Rolls</td><td>3 Rolls</td></tr>
</table>

<table>
<tr><td align="center">June 30</td><td align="center">June 30</td><td align="center">June 30</td></tr>
<tr><td>1 Roll</td><td>1 Roll</td><td>1 Roll</td></tr>
<tr><td>2 Rolls</td><td>2 Rolls</td><td>2 Rolls</td></tr>
<tr><td>3 Rolls</td><td>3 Rolls</td><td>3 Rolls</td></tr>
</table>

<table>
<tr><td align="center">July 1</td><td align="center">July 1</td><td align="center">July 1</td></tr>
<tr><td>1 Roll</td><td>1 Roll</td><td>1 Roll</td></tr>
<tr><td>2 Rolls</td><td>2 Rolls</td><td>2 Rolls</td></tr>
<tr><td>3 Rolls</td><td>3 Rolls</td><td>3 Rolls</td></tr>
</table>

After you have filled out the sheet, fold your column underneath along the dashed line so the next restroom user won't see your answers. *The first player uses the far right column.*

Answers - June 26-28
June 26, 1 Roll: Sonny Bono and Cher
June 26, 2 Rolls: Hong Kong
June 26, 3 Rolls: Strom Thurmond

June 27, 1 Roll: Soccer. On the 26th, after El Salvador won a playoff game to get into the FIFA World Cup, they cut ties to Honduras. Fighting began on July 14. The "Football War" lasted about 100 hours.
June 27, 2 Rolls: Rod Blagojevich
June 27, 3 Rolls: 91 seconds. For the fight, Tyson made about $220,000 per second!

June 28, 1 Roll: Labor Day
June 28, 2 Rolls: Mel Brooks
June 28, 3 Rolls: Gavrilo Princip. The assassination precipitated the chain reaction that would become World War I.

July 2

🧻 One Roll

What pilot disappeared over the Pacific while trying to fly around the world in 1937?

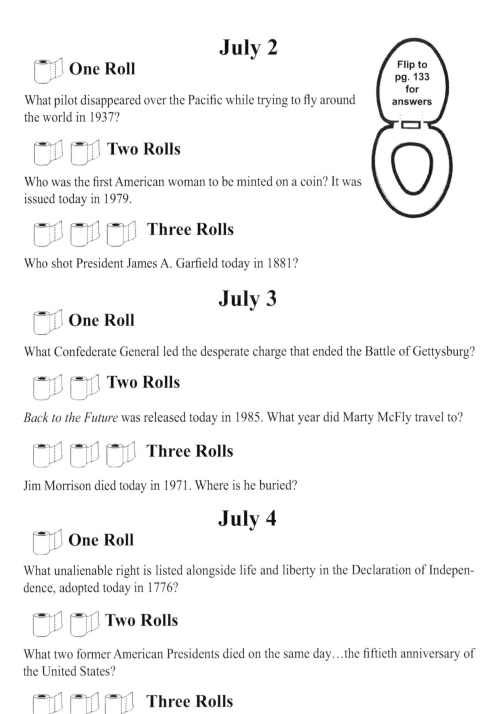

Flip to pg. 133 for answers

🧻 🧻 Two Rolls

Who was the first American woman to be minted on a coin? It was issued today in 1979.

🧻 🧻 🧻 Three Rolls

Who shot President James A. Garfield today in 1881?

July 3

🧻 One Roll

What Confederate General led the desperate charge that ended the Battle of Gettysburg?

🧻 🧻 Two Rolls

Back to the Future was released today in 1985. What year did Marty McFly travel to?

🧻 🧻 🧻 Three Rolls

Jim Morrison died today in 1971. Where is he buried?

July 4

🧻 One Roll

What unalienable right is listed alongside life and liberty in the Declaration of Independence, adopted today in 1776?

🧻 🧻 Two Rolls

What two former American Presidents died on the same day…the fiftieth anniversary of the United States?

🧻 🧻 🧻 Three Rolls

It didn't happen today. But on what day did most sign the Declaration of Independence?

Answer Sheet

Name_____

July 2

1 Roll
2 Rolls
3 Rolls

July 3

1 Roll
2 Rolls
3 Rolls

July 4

1 Roll
2 Rolls
3 Rolls

Answer Sheet

Name_____

July 2

1 Roll
2 Rolls
3 Rolls

July 3

1 Roll
2 Rolls
3 Rolls

July 4

1 Roll
2 Rolls
3 Rolls

Answer Sheet

Name_____

July 2

1 Roll
2 Rolls
3 Rolls

July 3

1 Roll
2 Rolls
3 Rolls

July 4

1 Roll
2 Rolls
3 Rolls

After you have filled out the sheet, fold your column underneath along the dashed line so the next restroom user won't see your answers. ***The first player uses the far right column.***

Answers - June 29-July 1
June 29, 1 Roll: Shakespeare's Globe Theatre. A cannon set the stage on fire.
June 29, 2 Rolls: Civil Rights Act
June 29, 3 Rolls: Katharine Hepburn. She won four almost fifty years apart. She won in 1934 for *Morning Glory* and in 1982 for *On Golden Pond*.

June 30, 1 Roll: Michael Phelps
June 30, 2 Rolls: Tower Bridge
June 30, 3 Rolls: Haile Selassie

July 1, 1 Roll: Gettysburg. The battle ended on July 3rd.
July 1, 2 Rolls: Carl Lewis. *TIME Magazine* ranked his performance as one of the Top 10 worst National Anthem renditions of all time. It is the only one on record that included an apology to a booing crowd, and a promise to improve as the song progressed.
July 1, 3 Rolls: Spencer

July 5

One Roll

Flip to pg. 135 for answers

What European capital was the first to display the bikini on this date in 1946?

Two Rolls

"The greatest hitter who ever lived" died today in 2005. Name him.

Three Rolls

In 1935, Franklin Roosevelt signed the National Labor Relations Act. What else was this act known as?

July 6

One Roll

In 1923, the USSR formed its first government. What did USSR stand for?

Two Rolls

Born today in 1946, he starred in the first sports movie to win the Oscar for Best Picture.

Three Rolls

What Beatles movie premiered in London today in 1964?

July 7

One Roll

Sir Arthur Conan Doyle died today in 1930. What detective did he create?

Two Rolls

In 1891, what did Marcellus Berry of the American Express Company patent for purchases abroad?

Three Rolls

Today in 1930, work on the Hoover Dam began. What other name did the Dam go by?

Answer Sheet | Answer Sheet | Answer Sheet

Name_____ Name_____ Name_____

July 5	July 5	July 5
1 Roll	1 Roll	1 Roll
2 Rolls	2 Rolls	2 Rolls
3 Rolls	3 Rolls	3 Rolls

July 6	July 6	July 6
1 Roll	1 Roll	1 Roll
2 Rolls	2 Rolls	2 Rolls
3 Rolls	3 Rolls	3 Rolls

July 7	July 7	July 7
1 Roll	1 Roll	1 Roll
2 Rolls	2 Rolls	2 Rolls
3 Rolls	3 Rolls	3 Rolls

After you have filled out the sheet, fold your column underneath along the dashed line so the next restroom user won't see your answers. *The first player uses the far right column.*

Answers - July 2-4
July 2, 1 Roll: Amelia Earhart
July 2, 2 Rolls: Susan B. Anthony. Lady Liberty had been on money too, but she was obviously fictional.
July 2, 3 Rolls: Charles Guiteau…a deranged office seeker

July 3, 1 Roll: George C. Pickett. The charge was a failure, and the Union turned the tide of the Civil War in 1863.
July 3, 2 Rolls: 1955…November 5th
July 3, 3 Rolls: In Paris, at Père Lachaise Cemetery

July 4, 1 Roll: The pursuit of happiness
July 4, 2 Rolls: John Adams and Thomas Jefferson, in 1826. According to eyewitnesses, Adams' last words were, "Thomas Jefferson survives." He was wrong, as Jefferson passed away a few hours earlier.
July 4, 3 Rolls: Though independence was declared today in 1776, most signed on August 2. The famous John Turnbull painting showing them all together never happened.

July 8

One Roll

What basketball star took his talents to South Beach today in 2010?

Flip to
pg. 137
for
answers

Two Rolls

You might be within six degrees of this man's birthday party. He was born in 1958.

Three Rolls

In 1776, the Liberty Bell rang in Philadelphia. What two names are on the bell?

July 9

One Roll

What tennis tournament began for the first time ever, today in 1877?

Two Rolls

What President, who died today in 1846, was exhumed in 1991 to see if he was poisoned?

Three Rolls

Today in 1979, Voyager 2 came within 350,000 miles of what planet?

July 10

One Roll

Amidst the fall of communism, who became President of Russia today in 1991?

Two Rolls

What voice of Bugs Bunny died today in 1989?

Three Rolls

In 1890, women could vote in what new state that entered the Union?

Answer Sheet

Name_____

July 8

1 Roll	
2 Rolls	
3 Rolls	

July 9

1 Roll	
2 Rolls	
3 Rolls	

July 10

1 Roll	
2 Rolls	
3 Rolls	

Answer Sheet

Name_____

July 8

1 Roll	
2 Rolls	
3 Rolls	

July 9

1 Roll	
2 Rolls	
3 Rolls	

July 10

1 Roll	
2 Rolls	
3 Rolls	

Answer Sheet

Name_____

July 8

1 Roll	
2 Rolls	
3 Rolls	

July 9

1 Roll	
2 Rolls	
3 Rolls	

July 10

1 Roll	
2 Rolls	
3 Rolls	

After you have filled out the sheet, fold your column underneath along the dashed line so the next restroom user won't see your answers. *The first player uses the far right column.*

Answers - July 5-7
July 5, 1 Roll: Paris
July 5, 2 Rolls: Ted Williams. He batted .406 in 1941. He missed several years of his career, as he was a fighter-pilot in both World War II and the Korean War.
July 5, 3 Rolls: The Wagner Act. It was named for Robert F. Wagner, the New York Senator who sponsored it. The act expanded the rights of workers.

July 6, 1 Roll: Union of Soviet Socialist Republics
July 6, 2 Rolls: Sylvester Stallone. *Rocky* was released in 1976.
July 6, 3 Rolls: *Hard Day's Night*

July 7, 1 Roll: Sherlock Holmes
July 7, 2 Rolls: Travelers Checks
July 7, 3 Rolls: Boulder Dam

July 11

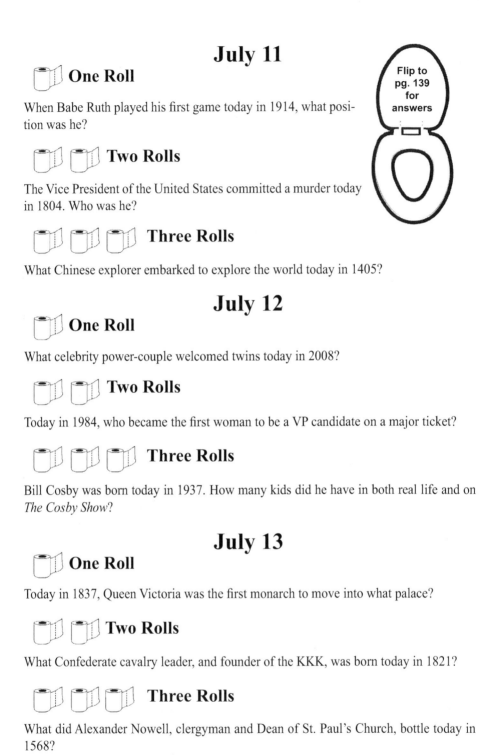

One Roll

Flip to pg. 139 for answers

When Babe Ruth played his first game today in 1914, what position was he?

Two Rolls

The Vice President of the United States committed a murder today in 1804. Who was he?

Three Rolls

What Chinese explorer embarked to explore the world today in 1405?

July 12

One Roll

What celebrity power-couple welcomed twins today in 2008?

Two Rolls

Today in 1984, who became the first woman to be a VP candidate on a major ticket?

Three Rolls

Bill Cosby was born today in 1937. How many kids did he have in both real life and on *The Cosby Show*?

July 13

One Roll

Today in 1837, Queen Victoria was the first monarch to move into what palace?

Two Rolls

What Confederate cavalry leader, and founder of the KKK, was born today in 1821?

Three Rolls

What did Alexander Nowell, clergyman and Dean of St. Paul's Church, bottle today in 1568?

Answer Sheet | Answer Sheet | Answer Sheet

Name_____ | Name_____ | Name_____

| July 11 | July 11 | July 11 |

July 11	July 11	July 11
1 Roll	1 Roll	1 Roll
2 Rolls	2 Rolls	2 Rolls
3 Rolls	3 Rolls	3 Rolls

July 12	July 12	July 12
1 Roll	1 Roll	1 Roll
2 Rolls	2 Rolls	2 Rolls
3 Rolls	3 Rolls	3 Rolls

July 13	July 13	July 13
1 Roll	1 Roll	1 Roll
2 Rolls	2 Rolls	2 Rolls
3 Rolls	3 Rolls	3 Rolls

After you have filled out the sheet, fold your column underneath along the dashed line so the next restroom user won't see your answers. *The first player uses the far right column.*

Answers - July 8-10
July 8, 1 Roll: Lebron James
July 8, 2 Rolls: Kevin Bacon
July 8, 3 Rolls: John Pass and John Stow were local workers who recast the bell after it supposedly cracked on its first ring

July 9, 1 Roll: Wimbledon
July 9, 2 Rolls: Zachary Taylor. Forensic testing confirmed that he was not poisoned.
July 9, 3 Rolls: Jupiter. It was the closest distance from the giant planet ever recorded.

July 10, 1 Roll: Boris Yeltsin
July 10, 2 Rolls: Mel Blanc. He was also Daffy Duck, Tweety Bird, Porky Pig, and a host of other characters.
July 10, 3 Rolls: Wyoming. The 19th Amendment would be redundant for Wyoming, as well as some other states that would eventually allow women to vote. Wyoming was the first.

July 14

One Roll

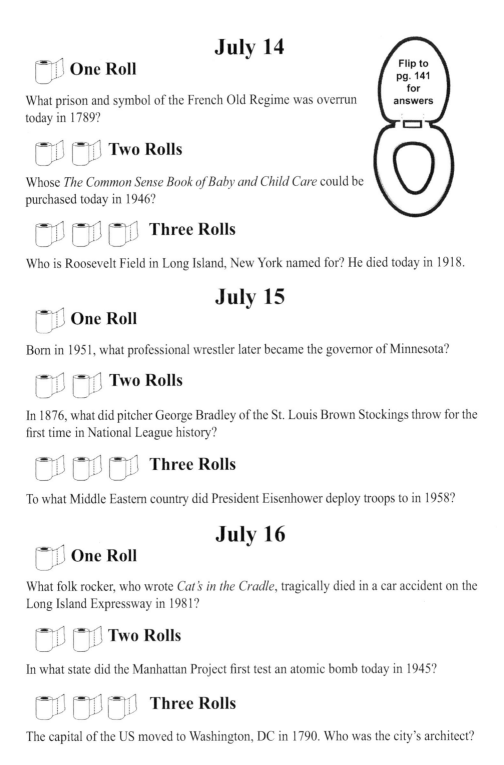

Flip to pg. 141 for answers

What prison and symbol of the French Old Regime was overrun today in 1789?

Two Rolls

Whose *The Common Sense Book of Baby and Child Care* could be purchased today in 1946?

Three Rolls

Who is Roosevelt Field in Long Island, New York named for? He died today in 1918.

July 15

One Roll

Born in 1951, what professional wrestler later became the governor of Minnesota?

Two Rolls

In 1876, what did pitcher George Bradley of the St. Louis Brown Stockings throw for the first time in National League history?

Three Rolls

To what Middle Eastern country did President Eisenhower deploy troops to in 1958?

July 16

One Roll

What folk rocker, who wrote *Cat's in the Cradle*, tragically died in a car accident on the Long Island Expressway in 1981?

Two Rolls

In what state did the Manhattan Project first test an atomic bomb today in 1945?

Three Rolls

The capital of the US moved to Washington, DC in 1790. Who was the city's architect?

Answer Sheet

Name_____

July 14

1 Roll
2 Rolls
3 Rolls

July 15

1 Roll
2 Rolls
3 Rolls

July 16

1 Roll
2 Rolls
3 Rolls

Answer Sheet

Name_____

July 14

1 Roll
2 Rolls
3 Rolls

July 15

1 Roll
2 Rolls
3 Rolls

July 16

1 Roll
2 Rolls
3 Rolls

Answer Sheet

Name_____

July 14

1 Roll
2 Rolls
3 Rolls

July 15

1 Roll
2 Rolls
3 Rolls

July 16

1 Roll
2 Rolls
3 Rolls

After you have filled out the sheet, fold your column underneath along the dashed line so the next restroom user won't see your answers. *The first player uses the far right column.*

Answers - July 11-13

July 11, 1 Roll: Pitcher for the Boston Red Sox
July 11, 2 Rolls: Aaron Burr. He and Alexander Hamilton paddled out to Weehawken, New Jersey for a duel. Hamilton wasted his shot. Burr returned fire and wounded the former Secretary of the Treasury. Hamilton died the next day.
July 11, 3 Rolls: Zheng He

July 12, 1 Roll: Brad Pitt and Angelina Jolie
July 12, 2 Rolls: Geraldine Ferraro was chosen to run with Walter Mondale. They lost to Ronald Reagan.
July 12, 3 Rolls: Five. On *The Cosby Show* it was: Sondra, Denise, Theo, Vanessa, and Rudy.

July 13, 1 Roll: Buckingham Palace. Today, it continues to be the official royal address.
July 13, 2 Rolls: Nathan Bedford Forrest. The KKK was founded in Pulaski, Tennessee. *Forrest Gump* was named after Forrest.
July 13, 3 Rolls: Beer. It was the first bottled beer.

July 17

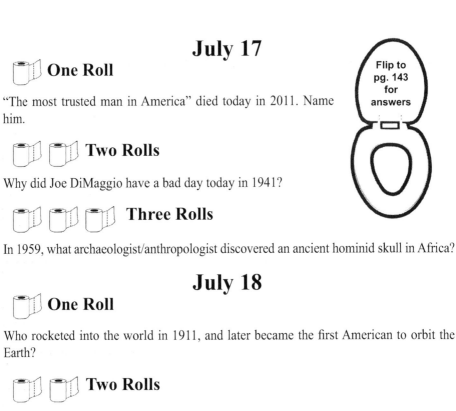

One Roll

"The most trusted man in America" died today in 2011. Name him.

Flip to pg. 143 for answers

Two Rolls

Why did Joe DiMaggio have a bad day today in 1941?

Three Rolls

In 1959, what archaeologist/anthropologist discovered an ancient hominid skull in Africa?

July 18

One Roll

Who rocketed into the world in 1911, and later became the first American to orbit the Earth?

Two Rolls

Hitler published *Mein Kampf* today in 1925. What does it translate to in English?

Three Rolls

In 1940, Franklin Roosevelt was nominated for an unprecedented third term. What Amendment prevents that today?

July 19

One Roll

What missing link for interpreting hieroglyphics was found by a French soldier in 1799?

Two Rolls

Today in 1993, what four word policy was established regarding sexual orientation and serving in the US military?

Three Rolls

The first President of South Korea died today in 1965. Name him.

Answer Sheet

Name_____

July 17

1 Roll
2 Rolls
3 Rolls

July 18

1 Roll
2 Rolls
3 Rolls

July 19

1 Roll
2 Rolls
3 Rolls

Answer Sheet

Name_____

July 17

1 Roll
2 Rolls
3 Rolls

July 18

1 Roll
2 Rolls
3 Rolls

July 19

1 Roll
2 Rolls
3 Rolls

Answer Sheet

Name_____

July 17

1 Roll
2 Rolls
3 Rolls

July 18

1 Roll
2 Rolls
3 Rolls

July 19

1 Roll
2 Rolls
3 Rolls

After you have filled out the sheet, fold your column underneath along the dashed line so the next restroom user won't see your answers. *The first player uses the far right column.*

Answers - July 14-16

July 14, 1 Roll: The Bastille. Though there's a marker in Paris for where the Bastille used to be, some rubble of the prison can be found in a park about a quarter of a mile away.

July 14, 2 Rolls: Dr. Benjamin Spock. New editions of this parenting book were printed into the 1990s.

July 14, 3 Rolls: Quentin Roosevelt, Theodore's youngest son. He was shot down during World War I, and today he is buried next to Teddy Roosevelt, Jr. in the World War II cemetery in Normandy, France.

July 15, 1 Roll: Jesse Ventura

July 15, 2 Rolls: A no hitter. Note that a year before, Joe Borden (aka Joe Josephs) hurled a no hitter for Philadelphia against Chicago in the National Association, which preceded the National League. Some historians consider the National Association to be the beginning of Major League Baseball.

July 15, 3 Rolls: Lebanon. Operation Blue Bat looked to support a Western government in the region.

July 16, 1 Roll: Harry Chapin

July 16, 2 Rolls: New Mexico. In a place called Trinity.

July 16, 3 Rolls: Pierre Charles L'Enfant. The capital was moved after a "Dinner Compromise" between Alexander Hamilton, James Madison, and Thomas Jefferson. The Southerners agreed to assume the national debt, and the Northerners shifted the capital south from New York.

July 20

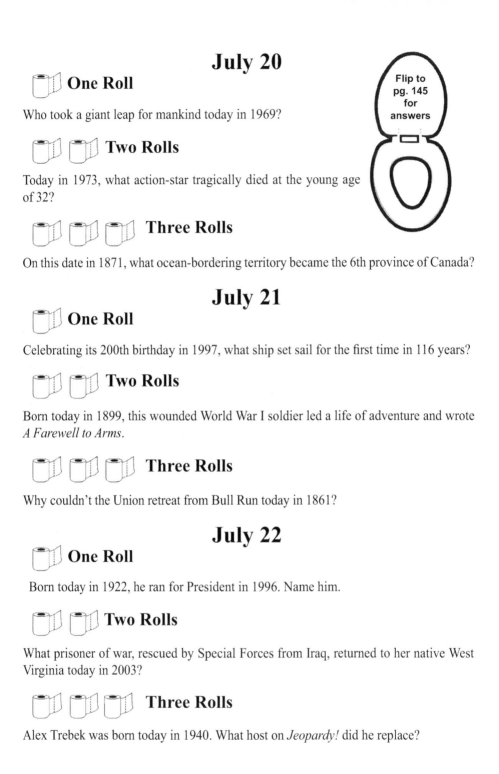

🧻 One Roll

Who took a giant leap for mankind today in 1969?

🧻 🧻 Two Rolls

Today in 1973, what action-star tragically died at the young age of 32?

🧻 🧻 🧻 Three Rolls

On this date in 1871, what ocean-bordering territory became the 6th province of Canada?

Flip to pg. 145 for answers

July 21

🧻 One Roll

Celebrating its 200th birthday in 1997, what ship set sail for the first time in 116 years?

🧻 🧻 Two Rolls

Born today in 1899, this wounded World War I soldier led a life of adventure and wrote *A Farewell to Arms*.

🧻 🧻 🧻 Three Rolls

Why couldn't the Union retreat from Bull Run today in 1861?

July 22

🧻 One Roll

Born today in 1922, he ran for President in 1996. Name him.

🧻 🧻 Two Rolls

What prisoner of war, rescued by Special Forces from Iraq, returned to her native West Virginia today in 2003?

🧻 🧻 🧻 Three Rolls

Alex Trebek was born today in 1940. What host on *Jeopardy!* did he replace?

Answer Sheet | Answer Sheet | Answer Sheet

Name_____ | Name_____ | Name_____

<table>
<tr><td colspan="3" align="center">July 20</td></tr>
<tr><td>1 Roll</td><td>1 Roll</td><td>1 Roll</td></tr>
<tr><td>2 Rolls</td><td>2 Rolls</td><td>2 Rolls</td></tr>
<tr><td>3 Rolls</td><td>3 Rolls</td><td>3 Rolls</td></tr>
</table>

<table>
<tr><td colspan="3" align="center">July 21</td></tr>
<tr><td>1 Roll</td><td>1 Roll</td><td>1 Roll</td></tr>
<tr><td>2 Rolls</td><td>2 Rolls</td><td>2 Rolls</td></tr>
<tr><td>3 Rolls</td><td>3 Rolls</td><td>3 Rolls</td></tr>
</table>

<table>
<tr><td colspan="3" align="center">July 22</td></tr>
<tr><td>1 Roll</td><td>1 Roll</td><td>1 Roll</td></tr>
<tr><td>2 Rolls</td><td>2 Rolls</td><td>2 Rolls</td></tr>
<tr><td>3 Rolls</td><td>3 Rolls</td><td>3 Rolls</td></tr>
</table>

After you have filled out the sheet, fold your column underneath along the dashed line so the next restroom user won't see your answers. *The first player uses the far right column.*

Answers - July 17-19
July 17, 1 Roll: Walter Cronkite
July 17, 2 Rolls: His 56-game hitting streak came to an end
July 17, 3 Rolls: Mary Leakey

July 18, 1 Roll: John Glenn
July 18, 2 Rolls: My Struggle, or My Battle
July 18, 3 Rolls: 22nd Amendment

July 19, 1 Roll: The Rosetta Stone. Some also point to the 15th as the day of its discovery.
July 19, 2 Rolls: "Don't ask, don't tell." This was repealed by President Obama in 2011. Soldiers are now permitted to be open about their sexuality.
July 19, 3 Rolls: Syngman Rhee

July 23

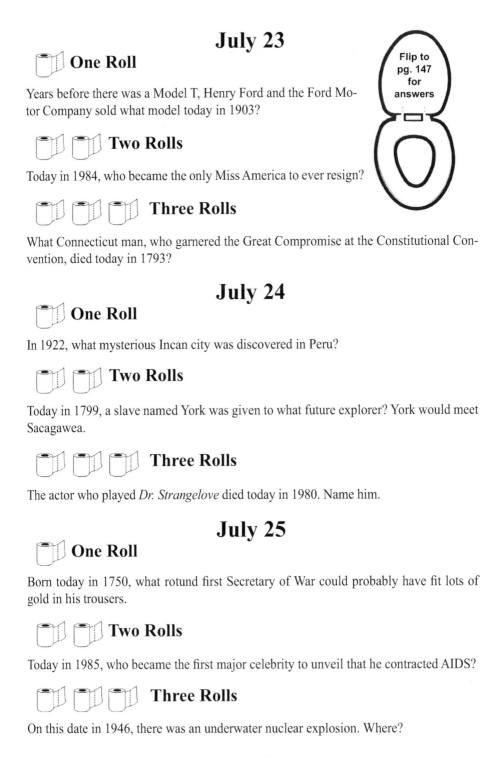

One Roll

Flip to pg. 147 for answers

Years before there was a Model T, Henry Ford and the Ford Motor Company sold what model today in 1903?

Two Rolls

Today in 1984, who became the only Miss America to ever resign?

Three Rolls

What Connecticut man, who garnered the Great Compromise at the Constitutional Convention, died today in 1793?

July 24

One Roll

In 1922, what mysterious Incan city was discovered in Peru?

Two Rolls

Today in 1799, a slave named York was given to what future explorer? York would meet Sacagawea.

Three Rolls

The actor who played *Dr. Strangelove* died today in 1980. Name him.

July 25

One Roll

Born today in 1750, what rotund first Secretary of War could probably have fit lots of gold in his trousers.

Two Rolls

Today in 1985, who became the first major celebrity to unveil that he contracted AIDS?

Three Rolls

On this date in 1946, there was an underwater nuclear explosion. Where?

Answer Sheet

Name_____

July 23

1 Roll
2 Rolls
3 Rolls

July 24

1 Roll
2 Rolls
3 Rolls

July 25

1 Roll
2 Rolls
3 Rolls

Answer Sheet

Name_____

July 23

1 Roll
2 Rolls
3 Rolls

July 24

1 Roll
2 Rolls
3 Rolls

July 25

1 Roll
2 Rolls
3 Rolls

Answer Sheet

Name_____

July 23

1 Roll
2 Rolls
3 Rolls

July 24

1 Roll
2 Rolls
3 Rolls

July 25

1 Roll
2 Rolls
3 Rolls

After you have filled out the sheet, fold your column underneath along the dashed line so the next restroom user won't see your answers. *The first player uses the far right column.*

Answers - July 20-22
July 20, 1 Roll: Neil Armstrong walked on the moon. As did Buzz Aldrin.
July 20, 2 Rolls: Bruce Lee
July 20, 3 Rolls: British Columbia

July 21, 1 Roll: The USS *Constitution*, or "Old Ironsides"
July 21, 2 Rolls: Ernest Hemingway
July 21, 3 Rolls: The roads were clogged with picnickers. Many Washingtonians felt that the battle would be "entertainment," and traveled out to watch the war. Needless to say, they left in a panic.

July 22, 1 Roll: Bob Dole. He lost, and Bill Clinton was reelected.
July 22, 2 Rolls: Jessica Lynch
July 22, 3 Rolls: Art Fleming

July 26

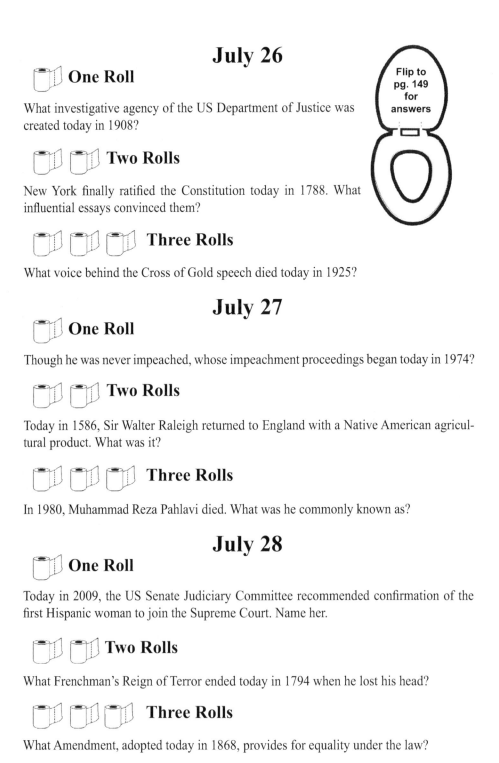

One Roll

What investigative agency of the US Department of Justice was created today in 1908?

Two Rolls

New York finally ratified the Constitution today in 1788. What influential essays convinced them?

Three Rolls

What voice behind the Cross of Gold speech died today in 1925?

Flip to pg. 149 for answers

July 27

One Roll

Though he was never impeached, whose impeachment proceedings began today in 1974?

Two Rolls

Today in 1586, Sir Walter Raleigh returned to England with a Native American agricultural product. What was it?

Three Rolls

In 1980, Muhammad Reza Pahlavi died. What was he commonly known as?

July 28

One Roll

Today in 2009, the US Senate Judiciary Committee recommended confirmation of the first Hispanic woman to join the Supreme Court. Name her.

Two Rolls

What Frenchman's Reign of Terror ended today in 1794 when he lost his head?

Three Rolls

What Amendment, adopted today in 1868, provides for equality under the law?

Answer Sheet | Answer Sheet | Answer Sheet

Name_____ | Name_____ | Name_____

July 26 | July 26 | July 26

1 Roll	1 Roll	1 Roll
2 Rolls	2 Rolls	2 Rolls
3 Rolls	3 Rolls	3 Rolls

July 27 | July 27 | July 27

1 Roll	1 Roll	1 Roll
2 Rolls	2 Rolls	2 Rolls
3 Rolls	3 Rolls	3 Rolls

July 28 | July 28 | July 28

1 Roll	1 Roll	1 Roll
2 Rolls	2 Rolls	2 Rolls
3 Rolls	3 Rolls	3 Rolls

After you have filled out the sheet, fold your column underneath along the dashed line so the next restroom user won't see your answers. *The first player uses the far right column.*

Answers - July 23-25
July 23, 1 Roll: Model A
July 23, 2 Rolls: Vanessa Williams. She resigned amid the publishing of scandalous pictures.
July 23, 3 Rolls: Roger Sherman. The Great Compromise established the two-house system of the US Legislative Branch. The House of Representatives is based on population, whereas the Senate has equal representation.

July 24, 1 Roll: Machu Picchu was discovered by archaeologist Hiram Bingham. Today, one of the trains that depart Cusco for Machu Picchu bears his name.
July 24, 2 Rolls: William Clark
July 24, 3 Rolls: Peter Sellers

July 25, 1 Roll: Henry Knox
July 25, 2 Rolls: Rock Hudson
July 25, 3 Rolls: Bikini Atoll. Over twenty nuclear tests occurred in the area within a decade.

July 29

One Roll

If this Civil War documentary filmmaker ever did a special on himself, it would begin on this date in 1953.

Flip to pg. 151 for answers

Two Rolls

If England didn't defeat this country's fleet of ships today in 1588, the thirteen colonies may not have spoken English.

Three Rolls

What pope who called for the First Crusade died today in 1099?

July 30

One Roll

Born today in 1947, who won the California gubernatorial recall election in 2003?

Two Rolls

What owner was banned from baseball on this date in 1990?

Three Rolls

What legislative body of Virginia met for the first time today in 1619?

July 31

One Roll

Born in England today in 1965, she has turned a new generation of kids onto reading. Name her.

Two Rolls

Rumored to be buried in Giants Stadium, what labor leader disappeared today in 1975?

Three Rolls

In 1961, Israel welcomed its one millionth "oleh." What's an "oleh"?

Answer Sheet | Answer Sheet | Answer Sheet

Name_____ | Name_____ | Name_____

July 29 | July 29 | July 29

1 Roll	1 Roll	1 Roll
2 Rolls	2 Rolls	2 Rolls
3 Rolls	3 Rolls	3 Rolls

July 30 | July 30 | July 30

1 Roll	1 Roll	1 Roll
2 Rolls	2 Rolls	2 Rolls
3 Rolls	3 Rolls	3 Rolls

July 31 | July 31 | July 31

1 Roll	1 Roll	1 Roll
2 Rolls	2 Rolls	2 Rolls
3 Rolls	3 Rolls	3 Rolls

After you have filled out the sheet, fold your column underneath along the dashed line so the next restroom user won't see your answers. *The first player uses the far right column.*

Answers - July 26-28

July 26, 1 Roll: Federal Bureau of Investigation (FBI)

July 26, 2 Rolls: *The Federalist Papers*, or the *Federalist*. Written by Alexander Hamilton, James Madison, and John Jay, the published essays looked to convince doubters in New York and elsewhere to ratify the constitution.

July 26, 3 Rolls: William Jennings Bryan. *The Wizard of Oz* was an allegory of Populism and the Election of 1896 between Republican William McKinley and Democrat William Jennings Bryan. McKinley stood for gold. Bryan stood for silver. Both are measured in ounces (oz). The Cowardly Lion was Bryan, the heartless Tin Man stood for the industrialists, and the Scarecrow represented the farmers. The Yellow Brick Road, of course, was gold.

July 27, 1 Roll: Richard Nixon. On August 8, he became the first president to resign the office.

July 27, 2 Rolls: Tobacco

July 27, 3 Rolls: The Shah of Iran

July 28, 1 Roll: Sonia Sotomayor

July 28, 2 Rolls: Maximilien Robespierre

July 28, 3 Rolls: 14th Amendment. This is one of the three "Civil War Amendments."

August 1

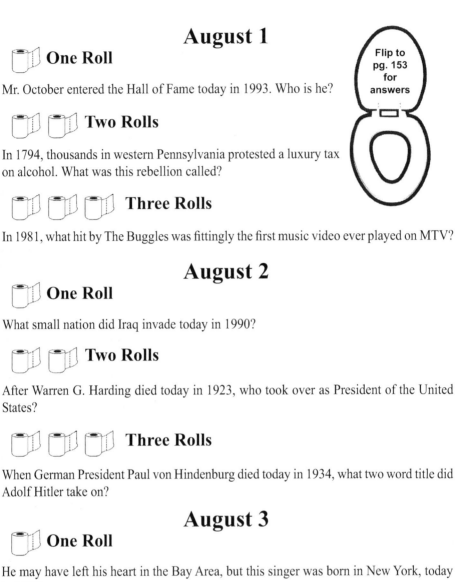

One Roll

Mr. October entered the Hall of Fame today in 1993. Who is he?

Flip to pg. 153 for answers

Two Rolls

In 1794, thousands in western Pennsylvania protested a luxury tax on alcohol. What was this rebellion called?

Three Rolls

In 1981, what hit by The Buggles was fittingly the first music video ever played on MTV?

August 2

One Roll

What small nation did Iraq invade today in 1990?

Two Rolls

After Warren G. Harding died today in 1923, who took over as President of the United States?

Three Rolls

When German President Paul von Hindenburg died today in 1934, what two word title did Adolf Hitler take on?

August 3

One Roll

He may have left his heart in the Bay Area, but this singer was born in New York, today in 1926.

Two Rolls

In 1936, whose hand would Adolf Hitler refuse to shake after he won the 100-meter dash?

Three Rolls

What State Department official, and Presidential advisor, was accused of being a communist today in 1948?

Answer Sheet

Name_____

August 1

| 1 Roll |
| 2 Rolls |
| 3 Rolls |

August 2

| 1 Roll |
| 2 Rolls |
| 3 Rolls |

August 3

| 1 Roll |
| 2 Rolls |
| 3 Rolls |

Answer Sheet

Name_____

August 1

| 1 Roll |
| 2 Rolls |
| 3 Rolls |

August 2

| 1 Roll |
| 2 Rolls |
| 3 Rolls |

August 3

| 1 Roll |
| 2 Rolls |
| 3 Rolls |

Answer Sheet

Name_____

August 1

| 1 Roll |
| 2 Rolls |
| 3 Rolls |

August 2

| 1 Roll |
| 2 Rolls |
| 3 Rolls |

August 3

| 1 Roll |
| 2 Rolls |
| 3 Rolls |

After you have filled out the sheet, fold your column underneath along the dashed line so the next restroom user won't see your answers. *The first player uses the far right column.*

Answers - July 29-31
July 29, 1 Roll: Ken Burns
July 29, 2 Rolls: Spain. The English navy established its dominance after defeating the Spanish Armada.
July 29, 3 Rolls: Pope Urban II called for the holy war in 1096

July 30, 1 Roll: Arnold Schwarzenegger
July 30, 2 Rolls: George Steinbrenner of the New York Yankees
July 30, 3 Rolls: House of Burgesses

July 31, 1 Roll: J.K. Rowling, author of *Harry Potter*
July 31, 2 Rolls: Jimmy Hoffa. He was president of the Teamsters Union. He was declared legally dead in 1982, and his remains have never been found.
July 31, 3 Rolls: Immigrant

August 4

One Roll

Barack Obama silenced most doubters when he presented his birth certificate, confirming he was born today in what state?

Flip to pg. 155 for answers

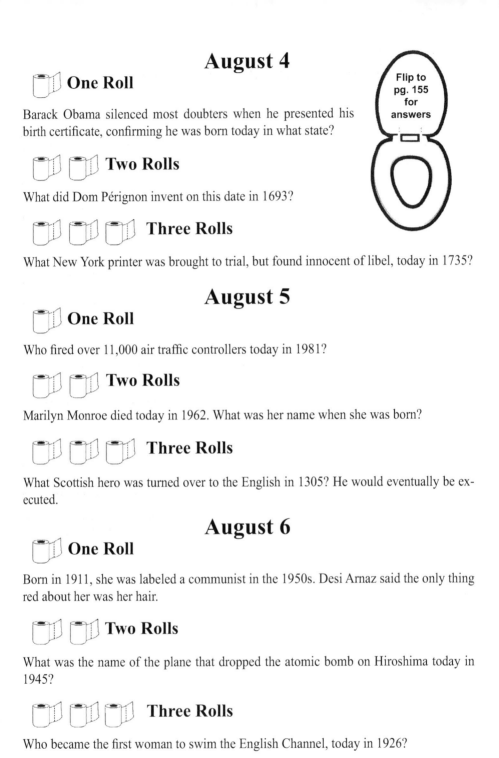

Two Rolls

What did Dom Pérignon invent on this date in 1693?

Three Rolls

What New York printer was brought to trial, but found innocent of libel, today in 1735?

August 5

One Roll

Who fired over 11,000 air traffic controllers today in 1981?

Two Rolls

Marilyn Monroe died today in 1962. What was her name when she was born?

Three Rolls

What Scottish hero was turned over to the English in 1305? He would eventually be executed.

August 6

One Roll

Born in 1911, she was labeled a communist in the 1950s. Desi Arnaz said the only thing red about her was her hair.

Two Rolls

What was the name of the plane that dropped the atomic bomb on Hiroshima today in 1945?

Three Rolls

Who became the first woman to swim the English Channel, today in 1926?

Answer Sheet | Answer Sheet | Answer Sheet

Name_____ Name_____ Name_____

August 4 | August 4 | August 4

1 Roll	1 Roll	1 Roll
2 Rolls	2 Rolls	2 Rolls
3 Rolls	3 Rolls	3 Rolls

August 5 | August 5 | August 5

1 Roll	1 Roll	1 Roll
2 Rolls	2 Rolls	2 Rolls
3 Rolls	3 Rolls	3 Rolls

August 6 | August 6 | August 6

1 Roll	1 Roll	1 Roll
2 Rolls	2 Rolls	2 Rolls
3 Rolls	3 Rolls	3 Rolls

After you have filled out the sheet, fold your column underneath along the dashed line so the next restroom user won't see your answers. *The first player uses the far right column.*

Answers - August 1-3

Aug. 1, 1 Roll: Reggie Jackson
Aug. 1, 2 Rolls: Whiskey Rebellion. It was put down by the federal army.
Aug. 1, 3 Rolls: *Video Killed the Radio Star* debuted just after midnight

Aug. 2, 1 Roll: Kuwait. The invasion led to eventual American intervention and the Persian Gulf War.
Aug. 2, 2 Rolls: Calvin Coolidge
Aug. 2, 3 Rolls: Der Führer (the leader)

Aug. 3, 1 Roll: Tony Bennett
Aug. 3, 2 Rolls: Jesse Owens, at the Olympics in Berlin. As an African American, he would not have fit into the Nazi definition of the "master race."
Aug. 3, 3 Rolls: Alger Hiss

August 7

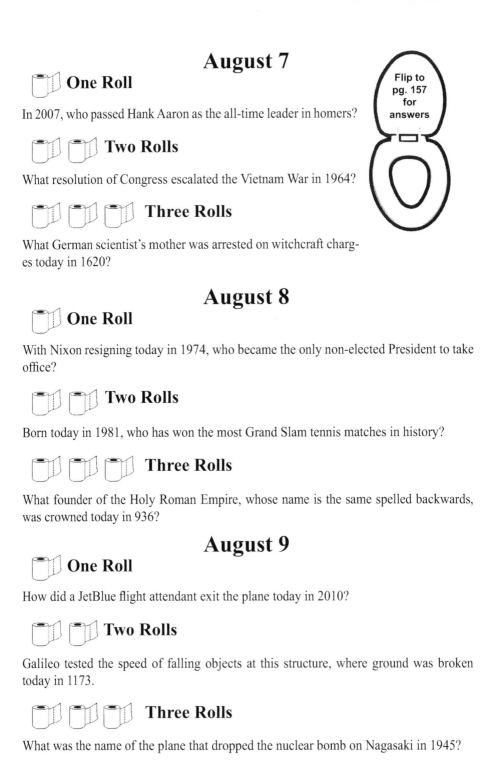

One Roll

In 2007, who passed Hank Aaron as the all-time leader in homers?

Flip to pg. 157 for answers

Two Rolls

What resolution of Congress escalated the Vietnam War in 1964?

Three Rolls

What German scientist's mother was arrested on witchcraft charges today in 1620?

August 8

One Roll

With Nixon resigning today in 1974, who became the only non-elected President to take office?

Two Rolls

Born today in 1981, who has won the most Grand Slam tennis matches in history?

Three Rolls

What founder of the Holy Roman Empire, whose name is the same spelled backwards, was crowned today in 936?

August 9

One Roll

How did a JetBlue flight attendant exit the plane today in 2010?

Two Rolls

Galileo tested the speed of falling objects at this structure, where ground was broken today in 1173.

Three Rolls

What was the name of the plane that dropped the nuclear bomb on Nagasaki in 1945?

Answer Sheet | Answer Sheet | Answer Sheet

Name_____ | Name_____ | Name_____

| August 7 | August 7 | August 7 |

1 Roll	1 Roll	1 Roll
2 Rolls	2 Rolls	2 Rolls
3 Rolls	3 Rolls	3 Rolls

| August 8 | August 8 | August 8 |

1 Roll	1 Roll	1 Roll
2 Rolls	2 Rolls	2 Rolls
3 Rolls	3 Rolls	3 Rolls

| August 9 | August 9 | August 9 |

1 Roll	1 Roll	1 Roll
2 Rolls	2 Rolls	2 Rolls
3 Rolls	3 Rolls	3 Rolls

After you have filled out the sheet, fold your column underneath along the dashed line so the next restroom user won't see your answers. *The first player uses the far right column.*

Answers - August 4-6

Aug. 4, 1 Roll: Hawaii, in 1961
Aug. 4, 2 Rolls: Champagne
Aug. 4, 3 Rolls: John Peter Zenger. After being defended by Andrew (no relation to Alexander) Hamilton, it was found that though Zenger printed negatively towards Governor William Cosby, his actions were not libel. The case established a foundation for freedom of the press.

Aug. 5, 1 Roll: President Ronald Reagan did, amid a strike
Aug. 5, 2 Rolls: Norma Jeane Mortensen at birth, changed to Norma Jeane Baker. If you just said Norma Jeane, count it.
Aug. 5, 3 Rolls: William Wallace, the protagonist of the movie *Braveheart*

Aug. 6, 1 Roll: Lucille Ball
Aug. 6, 2 Rolls: *Enola Gay*. The bomb was code named *Little Boy*.
Aug. 6, 3 Rolls: Gertrude Ederle

August 10

One Roll

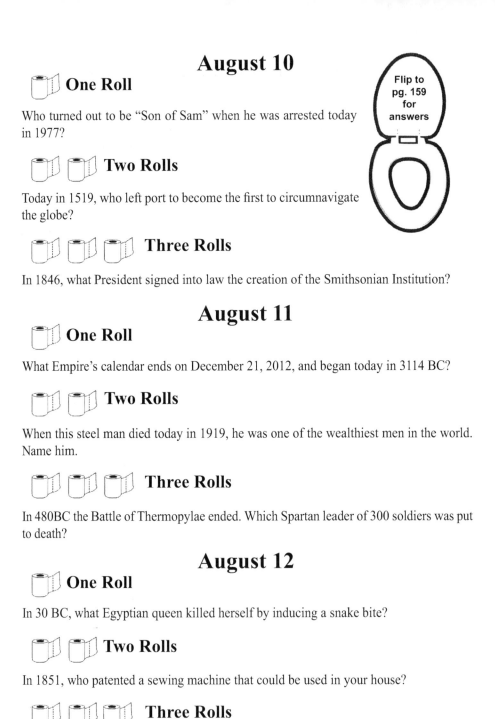

Flip to pg. 159 for answers

Who turned out to be "Son of Sam" when he was arrested today in 1977?

Two Rolls

Today in 1519, who left port to become the first to circumnavigate the globe?

Three Rolls

In 1846, what President signed into law the creation of the Smithsonian Institution?

August 11

One Roll

What Empire's calendar ends on December 21, 2012, and began today in 3114 BC?

Two Rolls

When this steel man died today in 1919, he was one of the wealthiest men in the world. Name him.

Three Rolls

In 480BC the Battle of Thermopylae ended. Which Spartan leader of 300 soldiers was put to death?

August 12

One Roll

In 30 BC, what Egyptian queen killed herself by inducing a snake bite?

Two Rolls

In 1851, who patented a sewing machine that could be used in your house?

Three Rolls

This great all-around female athlete won the LPGA Championship today in 1951.

Answer Sheet　Answer Sheet　Answer Sheet

Name_____　Name_____　Name_____

August 10　August 10　August 10

1 Roll	1 Roll	1 Roll
2 Rolls	2 Rolls	2 Rolls
3 Rolls	3 Rolls	3 Rolls

August 11　August 11　August 11

1 Roll	1 Roll	1 Roll
2 Rolls	2 Rolls	2 Rolls
3 Rolls	3 Rolls	3 Rolls

August 12　August 12　August 12

1 Roll	1 Roll	1 Roll
2 Rolls	2 Rolls	2 Rolls
3 Rolls	3 Rolls	3 Rolls

After you have filled out the sheet, fold your column underneath along the dashed line so the next restroom user won't see your answers. *The first player uses the far right column.*

Answers - August 7-9

Aug. 7, 1 Roll: Barry Bonds
Aug. 7, 2 Rolls: Gulf of Tonkin Resolution. It was so named after an attack on US forces in the Gulf of Tonkin. It was later learned that the news of the attack was embellished.
Aug. 7, 3 Rolls: Johannes Kepler

Aug. 8, 1 Roll: Gerald Ford. After Spiro Agnew resigned, Ford became the Vice President prior to Nixon's resignation. When Nixon resigned, he became the first non-elected President (that is, not elected as a President or VP).
Aug. 8, 2 Rolls: Roger Federer - 17. 5 US Open Titles, 7 Wimbledon Titles, 1 French Open Title, and 4 Australian Open Titles.
Aug. 8, 3 Rolls: Otto I

Aug. 9, 1 Roll: After a tirade, he grabbed a beer and slid down the emergency chute
Aug. 9, 2 Rolls: Leaning Tower of Pisa
Aug. 9, 3 Rolls: *Bockscar*. The bomb was code named *Fat Man*.

August 13

One Roll

What American-born French chef, who died today in 2004, was part of a World War II spy network before she was famous?

Two Rolls

Who conquered the Aztecs today in 1521?

Three Rolls

New York City has over 13,000 of these today. But the first one saw action today in 1907. What is it?

Flip to pg. 161 for answers

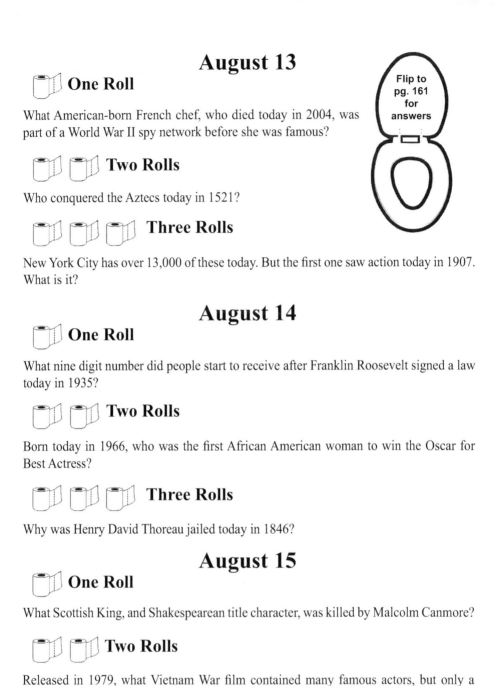

August 14

One Roll

What nine digit number did people start to receive after Franklin Roosevelt signed a law today in 1935?

Two Rolls

Born today in 1966, who was the first African American woman to win the Oscar for Best Actress?

Three Rolls

Why was Henry David Thoreau jailed today in 1846?

August 15

One Roll

What Scottish King, and Shakespearean title character, was killed by Malcolm Canmore?

Two Rolls

Released in 1979, what Vietnam War film contained many famous actors, but only a small part for Harrison Ford?

Three Rolls

What two countries were partitioned out of the British Empire at midnight in 1947?

Answer Sheet | # Answer Sheet | # Answer Sheet

Name_____ | Name_____ | Name_____

August 13 | ### August 13 | ### August 13

1 Roll	1 Roll	1 Roll
2 Rolls	2 Rolls	2 Rolls
3 Rolls	3 Rolls	3 Rolls

August 14 | ### August 14 | ### August 14

1 Roll	1 Roll	1 Roll
2 Rolls	2 Rolls	2 Rolls
3 Rolls	3 Rolls	3 Rolls

August 15 | ### August 15 | ### August 15

1 Roll	1 Roll	1 Roll
2 Rolls	2 Rolls	2 Rolls
3 Rolls	3 Rolls	3 Rolls

After you have filled out the sheet, fold your column underneath along the dashed line so the next restroom user won't see your answers. *The first player uses the far right column.*

Answers - August 10-12
Aug. 10, 1 Roll: David Berkowitz, a postal employee in New York
Aug. 10, 2 Rolls: Ferdinand Magellan
Aug. 10, 3 Rolls: James K. Polk

Aug. 11, 1 Roll: The Mayan Calendar
Aug. 11, 2 Rolls: Andrew Carnegie
Aug. 11, 3 Rolls: Leonidas

Aug. 12, 1 Roll: Cleopatra
Aug. 12, 2 Rolls: Isaac Singer
Aug. 12, 3 Rolls: Mildred "Babe" Didrikson Zaharias. She was also a basketball All-American, track and field star, and an expert baseball and softball player, diver, and bowler. She said she earned the nickname "Babe" after hitting five home runs in a children's baseball game, although her mother had called her that for years.

August 16

One Roll

Flip to pg. 163 for answers

Probably the most famous baseball player, and the most famous '50s-'70s rocker died on the same day 29 years apart. Name both.

Two Rolls

Today in 1983, Paul Simon married the actress who played Princess Leia in *Star Wars*. Name her.

Three Rolls

Who did Ringo Starr replace as drummer of the Beatles today in 1962?

August 17

One Roll

Francis Scott Key may not have approved of the way this man jammed the *Star Spangled Banner* at Woodstock today in 1969.

Two Rolls

Robert De Niro was born today in 1943. Who did he play in the 1980 film *Raging Bull*?

Three Rolls

Born today in 1929, what U-2 spy plane pilot was shot out of the Soviet sky in 1960?

August 18

One Roll

What "natural" actor was born today in 1936? Don't get "stung" by this question.

Two Rolls

Today can be considered to be the end of communism in the Soviet Union. Why?

Three Rolls

Dying today in 1227, whose Y chromosome lives on in millions of people throughout Asia?

Answer Sheet

Name_____

August 16

1 Roll
2 Rolls
3 Rolls

August 17

1 Roll
2 Rolls
3 Rolls

August 18

1 Roll
2 Rolls
3 Rolls

Answer Sheet

Name_____

August 16

1 Roll
2 Rolls
3 Rolls

August 17

1 Roll
2 Rolls
3 Rolls

August 18

1 Roll
2 Rolls
3 Rolls

Answer Sheet

Name_____

August 16

1 Roll
2 Rolls
3 Rolls

August 17

1 Roll
2 Rolls
3 Rolls

August 18

1 Roll
2 Rolls
3 Rolls

After you have filled out the sheet, fold your column underneath along the dashed line so the next restroom user won't see your answers. *The first player uses the far right column.*

Answers - August 13-15
Aug. 13, 1 Roll: Julia Child. She was part of the Office of Secret Services, the forerunner of the CIA. Mostly she did clerical work.
Aug. 13, 2 Rolls: Hernando Cortés. The capital of Tenochtitlan fell today.
Aug. 13, 3 Rolls: Taxi cab

Aug. 14, 1 Roll: Social Security Number. The Social Security Act became law today.
Aug. 14, 2 Rolls: Halle Berry won for *Monster's Ball* in 2002
Aug. 14, 3 Rolls: He refused to pay his taxes

Aug. 15, 1 Roll: Macbeth. It happened in 1057.
Aug. 15, 2 Rolls: *Apocalypse Now*. Marlon Brando, Martin Sheen, Robert Duvall, Laurence Fishburne, and Dennis Hopper were also in the cast. The masterpiece was directed by Francis Ford Coppola.
Aug. 15, 3 Rolls: India and Pakistan

August 19

One Roll

Who's the only president to be born in Arkansas?

Two Rolls

What actress did Alec Baldwin wed today in 1993?

Three Rolls

In 1951, what 3 foot 7 inch baseball player walked today in his only Major League at bat?

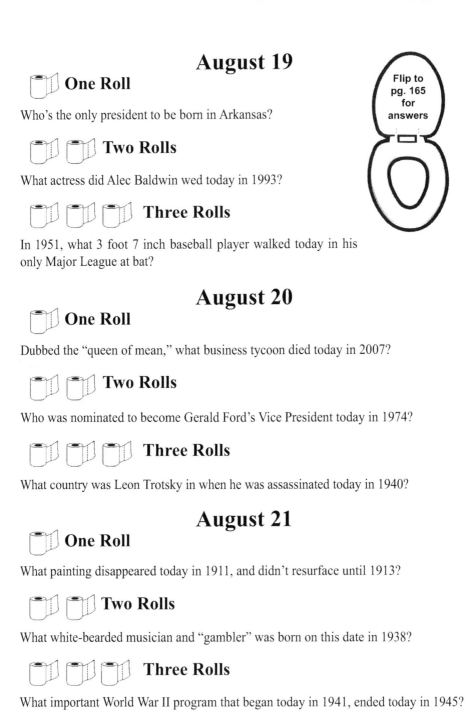

Flip to
pg. 165
for
answers

August 20

One Roll

Dubbed the "queen of mean," what business tycoon died today in 2007?

Two Rolls

Who was nominated to become Gerald Ford's Vice President today in 1974?

Three Rolls

What country was Leon Trotsky in when he was assassinated today in 1940?

August 21

One Roll

What painting disappeared today in 1911, and didn't resurface until 1913?

Two Rolls

What white-bearded musician and "gambler" was born on this date in 1938?

Three Rolls

What important World War II program that began today in 1941, ended today in 1945?

Answer Sheet | Answer Sheet | Answer Sheet

Name_____ Name_____ Name_____

August 19 | August 19 | August 19

1 Roll	1 Roll	1 Roll
2 Rolls	2 Rolls	2 Rolls
3 Rolls	3 Rolls	3 Rolls

August 20 | August 20 | August 20

1 Roll	1 Roll	1 Roll
2 Rolls	2 Rolls	2 Rolls
3 Rolls	3 Rolls	3 Rolls

August 21 | August 21 | August 21

1 Roll	1 Roll	1 Roll
2 Rolls	2 Rolls	2 Rolls
3 Rolls	3 Rolls	3 Rolls

After you have filled out the sheet, fold your column underneath along the dashed line so the next restroom user won't see your answers. *The first player uses the far right column.*

Answers - August 16-18
Aug. 16, 1 Roll: Babe Ruth (1948) and Elvis Presley (1977). But good news! Madonna was born today in 1958.
Aug. 16, 2 Rolls: Carrie Fisher
Aug. 16, 3 Rolls: Pete Best

Aug. 17, 1 Roll: Jimi Hendrix. By the way, Key never wrote the music in the first place. *The Anacreontic Song* was later added to Key's poem, *Defence of Fort McHenry*, to create the National Anthem.
Aug. 17, 2 Rolls: Jake LaMotta, a former Middleweight Champion
Aug. 17, 3 Rolls: Francis Gary Powers

Aug. 18, 1 Roll: Robert Redford of *The Natural* and *The Sting*
Aug. 18, 2 Rolls: It's the date of the August Coup, the failed attempt by old guard communists to retain power
Aug. 18, 3 Rolls: Genghis Khan. He impregnated countless women during his reign.

August 22

🧻 **One Roll**

Flip to pg. 167 for answers

Today in 1989, what pitcher struck out Rickey Henderson to become the first to reach 5,000 strikeouts in a career?

🧻🧻 **Two Rolls**

The first president of Kenya died in 1978. Name him.

🧻🧻🧻 **Three Rolls**

The world's oldest annually distributed sporting trophy was competed for today in 1851. What trophy?

August 23

🧻 **One Roll**

The Sheik was probably the most famous actor of his day. He died today in 1926 at only 31 years of age.

🧻🧻 **Two Rolls**

What Italian duo was executed for murder today in 1927?

🧻🧻🧻 **Three Rolls**

In 1924, radio broadcasters sent out messages to Mars. Why tonight?

August 24

🧻 **One Roll**

What baseball player, born today in 1960, didn't miss a day of work for 2,632 games?

🧻🧻 **Two Rolls**

What did the British set fire to on this date in 1814?

🧻🧻🧻 **Three Rolls**

The St. Bartholomew's Day massacre occurred today in 1572. What group of French Protestants was targeted?

Answer Sheet | Answer Sheet | Answer Sheet

Name_____ | Name_____ | Name_____

August 22 | August 22 | August 22

1 Roll	1 Roll	1 Roll
2 Rolls	2 Rolls	2 Rolls
3 Rolls	3 Rolls	3 Rolls

August 23 | August 23 | August 23

1 Roll	1 Roll	1 Roll
2 Rolls	2 Rolls	2 Rolls
3 Rolls	3 Rolls	3 Rolls

August 24 | August 24 | August 24

1 Roll	1 Roll	1 Roll
2 Rolls	2 Rolls	2 Rolls
3 Rolls	3 Rolls	3 Rolls

After you have filled out the sheet, fold your column underneath along the dashed line so the next restroom user won't see your answers. *The first player uses the far right column.*

Answers - August 19-21
Aug. 19, 1 Roll: Bill Clinton, born today in 1946
Aug. 19, 2 Rolls: Kim Basinger
Aug. 19, 3 Rolls: Eddie Gaedel of the St. Louis Browns

Aug. 20, 1 Roll: Leona Helmsley
Aug. 20, 2 Rolls: Nelson Rockefeller
Aug. 20, 3 Rolls: Mexico, near Mexico City. After he was exiled by Stalin, he lived in many countries before coming to Mexico City.

Aug. 21, 1 Roll: The Mona Lisa. Some believe the theft made the painting the landmark it is today.
Aug. 21, 2 Rolls: Kenny Rogers
Aug. 21, 3 Rolls: Lend-Lease. The program led to over $50 Billion in supplies being distributed to Allied nations.

August 25

One Roll

Flip to pg. 169 for answers

Born today in 1968, this delish daytime talk show host once worked the candy counter at Macy's.

Two Rolls

Opening in 1939, what movie had been rumored for decades to contain a suicide occurring in the background?

Three Rolls

Today in 1940, Ann Hayward and Arno Rudolphi got married on a famous Coney Island landmark. Which one?

August 26

One Roll

We hope this star wasn't "home alone" when he was born today in 1980.

Two Rolls

Today in 1939 was a good time for the Dodgers and Reds to comb their hair. Why?

Three Rolls

In 1346, what innovation did the English use to defeat the French at the Battle of Crécy?

August 27

One Roll

What 1883 volcanic eruption released more energy than thousands of atomic bombs?

Two Rolls

The man who plays Pee-wee Herman was born today in 1952. What's his real name?

Three Rolls

What document, approved by the National Assembly of France today in 1789, defined rights and liberty?

Answer Sheet | Answer Sheet | Answer Sheet

Name_____ | Name_____ | Name_____

August 25 | August 25 | August 25

August 25	August 25	August 25
1 Roll	1 Roll	1 Roll
2 Rolls	2 Rolls	2 Rolls
3 Rolls	3 Rolls	3 Rolls

August 26 | August 26 | August 26

August 26	August 26	August 26
1 Roll	1 Roll	1 Roll
2 Rolls	2 Rolls	2 Rolls
3 Rolls	3 Rolls	3 Rolls

August 27 | August 27 | August 27

August 27	August 27	August 27
1 Roll	1 Roll	1 Roll
2 Rolls	2 Rolls	2 Rolls
3 Rolls	3 Rolls	3 Rolls

After you have filled out the sheet, fold your column underneath along the dashed line so the next restroom user won't see your answers. ***The first player uses the far right column.***

Answers - August 22-24
Aug. 22, 1 Roll: Nolan Ryan. He finished with 5,714 K's. He is still well ahead of the other leaders.
Aug. 22, 2 Rolls: Jomo Kenyatta
Aug. 22, 3 Rolls: America's Cup, for yachting

Aug. 23, 1 Roll: Rudolph Valentino
Aug. 23, 2 Rolls: Sacco and Vanzetti. Skeptics believe they were innocent.
Aug. 23, 3 Rolls: Mars was closer to Earth than it had been in centuries. It was only 34,630,000 miles away.

Aug. 24, 1 Roll: Cal Ripken, Jr.
Aug. 24, 2 Rolls: The White House. The President escaped before it was destroyed during the War of 1812.
Aug. 24, 3 Rolls: Huguenots

August 28

One Roll

Flip to pg. 171 for answers

Today in 1963, at what memorial did Martin Luther King, Jr. deliver his *I Have a Dream* speech?

Two Rolls

UPS was founded today in 1907. What does UPS stand for?

Three Rolls

Almost seven years to the day Hurricane Katrina hit New Orleans, what hurricane landed in 2012?

August 29

One Roll

What big announcement did John McCain make on his 72nd birthday in 2008?

Two Rolls

In what town was Michael Jackson born on this date in 1958?

Three Rolls

What actress, who played George Jefferson's wife, was born today in 1917?

August 30

One Roll

What rather wealthy "Sage of Omaha" was born today in 1930?

Two Rolls

Who was confirmed today in 1967, becoming the first African American Supreme Court justice?

Three Rolls

Retiring today from the New York Mets in 1965, what manager, who wore #37, won five World Series rings with the Yankees?

Answer Sheet | Answer Sheet | Answer Sheet

Name_____ | Name_____ | Name_____

August 28 | August 28 | August 28

1 Roll	1 Roll	1 Roll
2 Rolls	2 Rolls	2 Rolls
3 Rolls	3 Rolls	3 Rolls

August 29 | August 29 | August 29

1 Roll	1 Roll	1 Roll
2 Rolls	2 Rolls	2 Rolls
3 Rolls	3 Rolls	3 Rolls

August 30 | August 30 | August 30

1 Roll	1 Roll	1 Roll
2 Rolls	2 Rolls	2 Rolls
3 Rolls	3 Rolls	3 Rolls

After you have filled out the sheet, fold your column underneath along the dashed line so the next restroom user won't see your answers. *The first player uses the far right column.*

Answers - August 25-27
Aug. 25, 1 Roll: Rachael Ray
Aug. 25, 2 Rolls: *The Wizard of Oz.* This rumor has been debunked recently, as examining the film reveals an exotic bird spreading its wings, not a Munchkin hanging himself. The Munchkins were not even on the set yet, as the movie was filmed out of chronological order.
Aug. 25, 3 Rolls: The Parachute Jump. You might say, they took the plunge.

Aug. 26, 1 Roll: Macaulay Culkin
Aug. 26, 2 Rolls: It was the first televised baseball game
Aug. 26, 3 Rolls: Longbows. It was one of the most important battles of the Hundred Years' War.

Aug. 27, 1 Roll: Krakatoa
Aug. 27, 2 Rolls: Paul Reubens
Aug. 27, 3 Rolls: *Declaration of the Rights of Man and of the Citizen*

August 31

One Roll

In 1888, who killed a prostitute to begin a murder-spree in England?

Two Rolls

In 2006, what famous painting, which had been stolen, was recovered in Norway?

Three Rolls

Today in 1897, Thomas Edison patented his kinetograph. What is a kinetograph?

Flip to pg. 173 for answers

September 1

One Roll

What country did Germany invade today in 1939 to start World War II in Europe?

Two Rolls

What American won the World Chess Championship today in 1972?

Three Rolls

What was spotted at the bottom of the Atlantic Ocean today in 1985?

September 2

One Roll

Better known as Gilligan, what actor died today in 2005?

Two Rolls

Today in 1969, the first ATM was installed. What does ATM stand for?

Three Rolls

In 1901, what famous seven-word foreign policy phrase was uttered in a speech by VP Theodore Roosevelt?

Answer Sheet

Name_____

August 31

1 Roll
2 Rolls
3 Rolls

September 1

1 Roll
2 Rolls
3 Rolls

September 2

1 Roll
2 Rolls
3 Rolls

Answer Sheet

Name_____

August 31

1 Roll
2 Rolls
3 Rolls

September 1

1 Roll
2 Rolls
3 Rolls

September 2

1 Roll
2 Rolls
3 Rolls

Answer Sheet

Name_____

August 31

1 Roll
2 Rolls
3 Rolls

September 1

1 Roll
2 Rolls
3 Rolls

September 2

1 Roll
2 Rolls
3 Rolls

After you have filled out the sheet, fold your column underneath along the dashed line so the next restroom user won't see your answers. *The first player uses the far right column.*

Answers - August 28-30

Aug. 28, 1 Roll: Lincoln Memorial
Aug. 28, 2 Rolls: United Parcel Service
Aug. 28, 3 Rolls: Hurricane Isaac. Hurricane Katrina arrived on August 29, 2005.

Aug. 29, 1 Roll: He announced his running-mate, Sarah Palin
Aug. 29, 2 Rolls: Gary, Indiana
Aug. 29, 3 Rolls: Isabel Sanford played Louise "Weezy" Jefferson

Aug. 30, 1 Roll: Warren Buffett
Aug. 30, 2 Rolls: Thurgood Marshall, who years earlier argued against segregation in the *Brown* v. *Board of Education* case
Aug. 30, 3 Rolls: Casey Stengel

September 3

One Roll

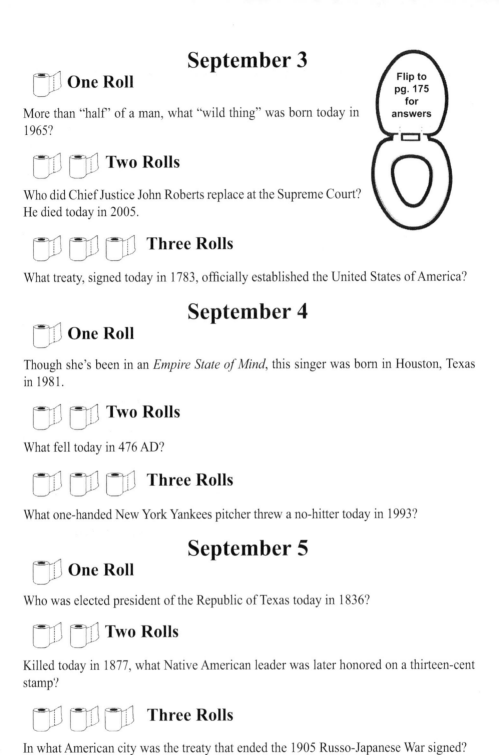

Flip to pg. 175 for answers

More than "half" of a man, what "wild thing" was born today in 1965?

Two Rolls

Who did Chief Justice John Roberts replace at the Supreme Court? He died today in 2005.

Three Rolls

What treaty, signed today in 1783, officially established the United States of America?

September 4

One Roll

Though she's been in an *Empire State of Mind*, this singer was born in Houston, Texas in 1981.

Two Rolls

What fell today in 476 AD?

Three Rolls

What one-handed New York Yankees pitcher threw a no-hitter today in 1993?

September 5

One Roll

Who was elected president of the Republic of Texas today in 1836?

Two Rolls

Killed today in 1877, what Native American leader was later honored on a thirteen-cent stamp?

Three Rolls

In what American city was the treaty that ended the 1905 Russo-Japanese War signed?

Answer Sheet

Name_____

September 3

1 Roll
2 Rolls
3 Rolls

September 4

1 Roll
2 Rolls
3 Rolls

September 5

1 Roll
2 Rolls
3 Rolls

Answer Sheet

Name_____

September 3

1 Roll
2 Rolls
3 Rolls

September 4

1 Roll
2 Rolls
3 Rolls

September 5

1 Roll
2 Rolls
3 Rolls

Answer Sheet

Name_____

September 3

1 Roll
2 Rolls
3 Rolls

September 4

1 Roll
2 Rolls
3 Rolls

September 5

1 Roll
2 Rolls
3 Rolls

After you have filled out the sheet, fold your column underneath along the dashed line so the next restroom user won't see your answers. *The first player uses the far right column.*

Answers - August 31-September 2
Aug. 31, 1 Roll: Jack the Ripper
Aug. 31, 2 Rolls: *The Scream*
Aug. 31, 3 Rolls: Motion picture camera

Sept. 1, 1 Roll: Poland
Sept. 1, 2 Rolls: Bobby Fischer
Sept. 1, 3 Rolls: The *Titanic*

Sept. 2, 1 Roll: Bob Denver
Sept. 2, 2 Rolls: Automated Teller Machine. It found a home at Chemical Bank in Rockville Centre, New York.
Sept. 2, 3 Rolls: "Speak softly and carry a big stick"

September 6

One Roll

Flip to pg. 177 for answers

Who sang *Candle in the Wind* at Princess Diana's funeral on this date in 1997?

Two Rolls

Today in 1920, who beat Billy Miske in the first ever championship fight to be heard on the radio?

Three Rolls

On this date in 1911, President McKinley was shot in Buffalo. Who shot him?

September 7

One Roll

What country was promised control over their own canal today in 1977?

Two Rolls

What country declared its independence from Portugal today in 1822?

Three Rolls

Today in 1533, Queen Elizabeth was born. Who were her parents?

September 8

One Roll

In 1998, who hit his 62nd home run of the season to break a record held by Roger Maris?

Two Rolls

Alecia Beth Moore was born today in 1979. What "colorful" singer is she better known as?

Three Rolls

On this date in 1954, the SEATO alliance was formed in Manila. What does SEATO stand for?

Answer Sheet | Answer Sheet | Answer Sheet

Name_____ Name_____ Name_____

September 6	September 6	September 6
1 Roll	1 Roll	1 Roll
2 Rolls	2 Rolls	2 Rolls
3 Rolls	3 Rolls	3 Rolls

September 7	September 7	September 7
1 Roll	1 Roll	1 Roll
2 Rolls	2 Rolls	2 Rolls
3 Rolls	3 Rolls	3 Rolls

September 8	September 8	September 8
1 Roll	1 Roll	1 Roll
2 Rolls	2 Rolls	2 Rolls
3 Rolls	3 Rolls	3 Rolls

After you have filled out the sheet, fold your column underneath along the dashed line so the next restroom user won't see your answers. *The first player uses the far right column.*

Answers - September 3-5
Sept. 3, 1 Roll: Charlie Sheen
Sept. 3, 2 Rolls: William Rehnquist
Sept. 3, 3 Rolls: The Treaty of Paris ended the Revolutionary War

Sept. 4, 1 Roll: Beyoncé Knowles
Sept. 4, 2 Rolls: The Roman Empire. Though, the eastern part of the Empire lived on as the Byzantines.
Sept. 4, 3 Rolls: Jim Abbott. He no-hit the Cleveland Indians.

Sept. 5, 1 Roll: Sam Houston
Sept. 5, 2 Rolls: Crazy Horse
Sept. 5, 3 Rolls: Portsmouth, New Hampshire. Theodore Roosevelt later won the Nobel Peace Prize for brokering the peace.

September 9

One Roll

What Asian leader died today in 1976, yet his body is still visible on Earth?

Flip to pg. 179 for answers

Two Rolls

Adam Sandler was born today in 1966. What is the name of his production company?

Three Rolls

What mainland US state was the only one to be directly attacked in World War II? It happened today in 1942.

September 10

One Roll

It's not a spin to say that this political talk show host was born today in 1949.

Two Rolls

What company introduced TV Dinners today in 1953?

Three Rolls

Within twenty years, when was the last use of the guillotine in France? It happened today in...

September 11

One Roll

On this date in 2011, what opened in New York City?

Two Rolls

Whose hit record did Pete Rose break today in 1985?

Three Rolls

In 1972, BART became mass transit for the San Francisco region. What does BART stand for?

Answer Sheet   Answer Sheet   Answer Sheet

Name_____   Name_____   Name_____

September 9   September 9   September 9

1 Roll	1 Roll	1 Roll
2 Rolls	2 Rolls	2 Rolls
3 Rolls	3 Rolls	3 Rolls

September 10   September 10   September 10

1 Roll	1 Roll	1 Roll
2 Rolls	2 Rolls	2 Rolls
3 Rolls	3 Rolls	3 Rolls

September 11   September 11   September 11

1 Roll	1 Roll	1 Roll
2 Rolls	2 Rolls	2 Rolls
3 Rolls	3 Rolls	3 Rolls

After you have filled out the sheet, fold your column underneath along the dashed line so the next restroom user won't see your answers. *The first player uses the far right column.*

Answers - September 6-8
Sept. 6, 1 Roll: Elton John
Sept. 6, 2 Rolls: Jack Dempsey
Sept. 6, 3 Rolls: Leon Czolgosz. McKinley died days later and Vice President Theodore Roosevelt took over. At age 42 he became the youngest man to ever serve in the White House.

Sept. 7, 1 Roll: Panama. A treaty with the United States promised the transfer of control. It took until the last day of the twentieth century to change hands.
Sept. 7, 2 Rolls: Brazil
Sept. 7, 3 Rolls: Henry VIII and Anne Boleyn

Sept. 8, 1 Roll: Mark McGwire. He hit it off of Steve Trachsel.
Sept. 8, 2 Rolls: Pink
Sept. 8, 3 Rolls: Southeast Asia Treaty Organization

September 12

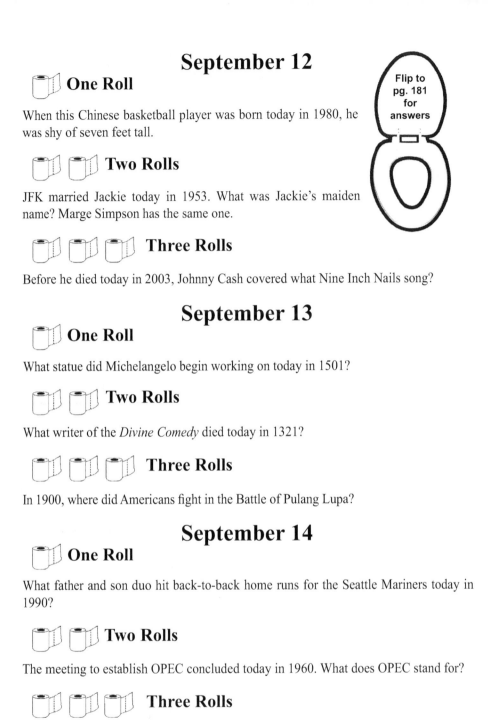

One Roll

When this Chinese basketball player was born today in 1980, he was shy of seven feet tall.

Flip to pg. 181 for answers

Two Rolls

JFK married Jackie today in 1953. What was Jackie's maiden name? Marge Simpson has the same one.

Three Rolls

Before he died today in 2003, Johnny Cash covered what Nine Inch Nails song?

September 13

One Roll

What statue did Michelangelo begin working on today in 1501?

Two Rolls

What writer of the *Divine Comedy* died today in 1321?

Three Rolls

In 1900, where did Americans fight in the Battle of Pulang Lupa?

September 14

One Roll

What father and son duo hit back-to-back home runs for the Seattle Mariners today in 1990?

Two Rolls

The meeting to establish OPEC concluded today in 1960. What does OPEC stand for?

Three Rolls

Though a famous advocate for birth control, she was born today in 1879.

Answer Sheet   Answer Sheet   Answer Sheet

Name_____   Name_____   Name_____

September 12   September 12   September 12

1 Roll	1 Roll	1 Roll
2 Rolls	2 Rolls	2 Rolls
3 Rolls	3 Rolls	3 Rolls

September 13   September 13   September 13

1 Roll	1 Roll	1 Roll
2 Rolls	2 Rolls	2 Rolls
3 Rolls	3 Rolls	3 Rolls

September 14   September 14   September 14

1 Roll	1 Roll	1 Roll
2 Rolls	2 Rolls	2 Rolls
3 Rolls	3 Rolls	3 Rolls

After you have filled out the sheet, fold your column underneath along the dashed line so the next restroom user won't see your answers. *The first player uses the far right column.*

Answers - September 9-11
Sept. 9, 1 Roll: Mao Zedong. His body at the mausoleum in Tiananmen Square is visited daily by locals and tourists.
Sept. 9, 2 Rolls: Happy Madison Productions
Sept. 9, 3 Rolls: Oregon. Nobuo Fujita flew a plane and started some forest fires with incendiary bombs. Then he flew away.

Sept. 10, 1 Roll: Bill O'Reilly
Sept. 10, 2 Rolls: Swanson
Sept. 10, 3 Rolls: 1977. Yes, 1977. Then, France did away with capital punishment.

Sept. 11, 1 Roll: The 9/11 Memorial opened to mark the ten year anniversary of the attacks on the United States.
Sept. 11, 2 Rolls: Ty Cobb. Rose singled off of San Diego pitcher Eric Show for hit number 4,192. Outspoken owner Marge Schott presented him with a new Corvette with the license plate PR 4192.
Sept. 11, 3 Rolls: Bay Area Rapid Transit

September 15

One Roll

No mask was needed for radio. But what Western hero donned one for his debut on television in 1949?

Flip to pg. 183 for answers

Two Rolls

Which President, who once got stuck in the White House bathtub, was born today in 1857?

Three Rolls

What comedienne who sat next to Charles Nelson Reilly on *Match Game* died today in 2007?

September 16

One Roll

Who began a six-day fast in 1932 to protest the British electoral format?

Two Rolls

On this date, what war led to the first US draft in a time of peace?

Three Rolls

As part of the scorched-earth policy, what czar ordered the burning of Moscow? The streets around the Kremlin blazed today in 1812.

September 17

One Roll

The bloodiest single day in American warfare happened at this battle in 1862.

Two Rolls

How many delegates (within ten) signed the Constitution today in 1787?

Three Rolls

Name two of the signers of the 1978 Camp David Accords.

Answer Sheet | Answer Sheet | Answer Sheet

Name_____ | Name_____ | Name_____

September 15 | September 15 | September 15

1 Roll	1 Roll	1 Roll
2 Rolls	2 Rolls	2 Rolls
3 Rolls	3 Rolls	3 Rolls

September 16 | September 16 | September 16

1 Roll	1 Roll	1 Roll
2 Rolls	2 Rolls	2 Rolls
3 Rolls	3 Rolls	3 Rolls

September 17 | September 17 | September 17

1 Roll	1 Roll	1 Roll
2 Rolls	2 Rolls	2 Rolls
3 Rolls	3 Rolls	3 Rolls

After you have filled out the sheet, fold your column underneath along the dashed line so the next restroom user won't see your answers. *The first player uses the far right column.*

Answers - September 12-14
Sept. 12, 1 Roll: Yao Ming
Sept. 12, 2 Rolls: Bouvier
Sept. 12, 3 Rolls: *Hurt*

Sept. 13, 1 Roll: *David*
Sept. 13, 2 Rolls: Dante Alighieri
Sept. 13, 3 Rolls: The Philippines. It was part of the Phillipine-American War (1899-1902).

Sept. 14, 1 Roll: Ken Griffey Sr. and Jr.
Sept. 14, 2 Rolls: Organization of the Petroleum Exporting Countries
Sept. 14, 3 Rolls: Margaret Sanger

September 18

One Roll

Flip to pg. 185 for answers

As part of a Masonic ritual, who laid the cornerstone of the Capitol today in 1793?

Two Rolls

In 1996, who became the only pitcher to strike out 20 batters twice in a career?

Three Rolls

What upstate New York fort, first utilized by the French today in 1755, was abandoned decades later by the British?

September 19

One Roll

What cartoon character debuted on screen with *Steamboat Willie* in 1928?

Two Rolls

What popcorn guru died today in 1995 at the age of 88?

Three Rolls

Printed today in 1796, there was a famous speech that was never spoken. Which one?

September 20

One Roll

What muckraking author of *The Jungle* was born today in 1878?

Two Rolls

In 1187, what Muslim leader laid siege to Jerusalem during the Crusades?

Three Rolls

After an assassination claimed the President, who was sworn into office today in 1881?

Answer Sheet | Answer Sheet | Answer Sheet

Name_____ | Name_____ | Name_____

September 18 | September 18 | September 18

1 Roll	1 Roll	1 Roll
2 Rolls	2 Rolls	2 Rolls
3 Rolls	3 Rolls	3 Rolls

September 19 | September 19 | September 19

1 Roll	1 Roll	1 Roll
2 Rolls	2 Rolls	2 Rolls
3 Rolls	3 Rolls	3 Rolls

September 20 | September 20 | September 20

1 Roll	1 Roll	1 Roll
2 Rolls	2 Rolls	2 Rolls
3 Rolls	3 Rolls	3 Rolls

After you have filled out the sheet, fold your column underneath along the dashed line so the next restroom user won't see your answers. *The first player uses the far right column.*

Answers - September 15-17

Sept. 15, 1 Roll: *The Lone Ranger.* The show lasted until 1957.

Sept. 15, 2 Rolls: William Howard Taft. He was the largest US President, tipping the scales at over 300 pounds.

Sept. 15, 3 Rolls: Brett Sommers. Reilly also died in 2007.

Sept. 16, 1 Roll: Mohandas K. Gandhi. He was upset how the British were segregating untouchables from representation.

Sept. 16, 2 Rolls: World War II. The draft law was passed today in 1940.

Sept. 16, 3 Rolls: Czar Alexander I. The idea was to prevent Napoleon from obtaining the supplies and riches of the city. Ultimately, Napoleon's army would starve.

Sept. 17, 1 Roll: Antietam, or Sharpsburg. There were over 23,000 casualties.

Sept. 17, 2 Rolls: Thirty-nine. Or, thirty-eight if you believe that George Read signed twice. He allegedly signed for John Dickinson, who couldn't make it. There were originally 55 delegates.

Sept. 17, 3 Rolls: Menachem Begin of Israel, President Jimmy Carter of the United States, and Anwar Sadat of Egypt

September 21

One Roll

Born in 1947, Stephen King's first bestseller was inspired by John Lennon's *Instant Karma*? Name it.

Two Rolls

George Clooney took the good and the bad when he guest-starred on this show in 1985.

Three Rolls

Arrested today in 1776, who claimed he had "but one life to give for my country"?

Flip to pg. 187 for answers

September 22

One Roll

Jennifer Aniston and Lisa Kudrow were unknowns until what TV show debuted in 1994?

Two Rolls

Born today in 1960, what *Happy Days* actor was later "in charge"?

Three Rolls

What immigrant composer of *God Bless America* and *White Christmas* died at the age of 101 in 1989?

September 23

One Roll

Music legends "The Boss" and "Ray" were born 19 years apart today. Name both.

Two Rolls

In 1913, what pilot, who has a tennis tournament named for him, flew across the Mediterranean?

Three Rolls

In 2010, what star's performance on Sesame Street was censored because of her skimpy attire?

Answer Sheet | Answer Sheet | Answer Sheet

Name_____ | Name_____ | Name_____

September 21 | September 21 | September 21

1 Roll	1 Roll	1 Roll
2 Rolls	2 Rolls	2 Rolls
3 Rolls	3 Rolls	3 Rolls

September 22 | September 22 | September 22

1 Roll	1 Roll	1 Roll
2 Rolls	2 Rolls	2 Rolls
3 Rolls	3 Rolls	3 Rolls

September 23 | September 23 | September 23

1 Roll	1 Roll	1 Roll
2 Rolls	2 Rolls	2 Rolls
3 Rolls	3 Rolls	3 Rolls

After you have filled out the sheet, fold your column underneath along the dashed line so the next restroom user won't see your answers. *The first player uses the far right column.*

Answers - September 18-20

Sept. 18, 1 Roll: George Washington. Washington, DC was a desolate area back then.
Sept. 18, 2 Rolls: Roger Clemens of the Boston Red Sox. He did it this time against the Tigers. In 1986, he struck out 20 Mariners.
Sept. 18, 3 Rolls: Fort Ticonderoga

Sept. 19, 1 Roll: Mickey Mouse
Sept. 19, 2 Rolls: Orville Redenbacher
Sept. 19, 3 Rolls: George Washington's Farewell Address was published in a newspaper, not spoken to the world. In the address, Washington warned to stay free from permanent alliances and avoid political parties. The speech was influenced by Alexander Hamilton and James Madison.

Sept. 20, 1 Roll: Upton Sinclair. The book detailed the repugnant hazards of the meatpacking industry.
Sept. 20, 2 Rolls: Saladin
Sept. 20, 3 Rolls: Chester A. Arthur took over for the late President Garfield, who died of the gunshot wound he received months earlier.

September 24

🧻 **One Roll**

The original voice of Kermit the Frog was born today in 1936. Name him.

🧻🧻 **Two Rolls**

What Canadian sprinter, who won gold at the Olympics today in 1988, would later have to cough up the medal?

🧻🧻🧻 **Three Rolls**

What meeting center and current marketplace on Boston's Freedom Trail opened today in 1742?

Flip to pg. 189 for answers

September 25

🧻 **One Roll**

What Presidential brother, who died today in 1988, had his own line of beer?

🧻🧻 **Two Rolls**

What group of Arkansas students came to school today in 1958 with military escorts?

🧻🧻🧻 **Three Rolls**

Married in 2000, what star-couple was both born on the 25th, yet are 25 years apart in age?

September 26

🧻 **One Roll**

What candidates took part in the first ever Presidential television debate today in 1960?

🧻🧻 **Two Rolls**

The Brady Bunch debuted today in 1969. Traditionally on the opening, who would be the center square at the end?

🧻🧻🧻 **Three Rolls**

Passing in 2006, Iva Tuguri was a Japanese-American radio personality. What was her nickname?

Answer Sheet   Answer Sheet   Answer Sheet

Name_____   Name_____   Name_____

September 24   September 24   September 24

1 Roll	1 Roll	1 Roll
2 Rolls	2 Rolls	2 Rolls
3 Rolls	3 Rolls	3 Rolls

September 25   September 25   September 25

1 Roll	1 Roll	1 Roll
2 Rolls	2 Rolls	2 Rolls
3 Rolls	3 Rolls	3 Rolls

September 26   September 26   September 26

1 Roll	1 Roll	1 Roll
2 Rolls	2 Rolls	2 Rolls
3 Rolls	3 Rolls	3 Rolls

After you have filled out the sheet, fold your column underneath along the dashed line so the next restroom user won't see your answers. *The first player uses the far right column.*

Answers - September 21-23
Sept. 21, 1 Roll: *The Shining*
Sept. 21, 2 Rolls: *The Facts of Life*
Sept. 21, 3 Rolls: Nathan Hale. He was executed the next day. His last words are legendary, but uncertain. The quote might very well have been taken from a 1713 play called *Cato*.

Sept. 22, 1 Roll: *Friends*
Sept. 22, 2 Rolls: Scott Baio
Sept. 22, 3 Rolls: Irving Berlin

Sept. 23, 1 Roll: Bruce Springsteen (1949), and Ray Charles (1930)
Sept. 23, 2 Rolls: Roland Garros, the namesake of the French Open
Sept. 23, 3 Rolls: Katy Perry. You can still get the performance online.

September 27

One Roll

On this date in 1940, the Axis Powers officially formed. Name its three countries.

Two Rolls

Singer Marvin Lee Aday was born today in 1947. What high protein nickname does he use?

Three Rolls

What company was born today in 1998? You might need it to cheat on this question.

Flip to pg. 191 for answers

September 28

One Roll

When he died today in 1895, the milk was already safe to drink.

Two Rolls

Carl Sagan's documentary on the universe debuted today in 1980. What was it called?

Three Rolls

A World War I legend holds that British soldier Henry Tandey spared the life of a wounded man today in 1918. Whose life did he spare?

September 29

One Roll

In 1954, who made the memorable over-the-shoulder catch in centerfield during Game 1 of the World Series?

Two Rolls

What British hero of the Battle of Trafalgar was born today in 1758?

Three Rolls

Lech Walesa was born in 1943. His union helped topple communism in Poland. Name it.

Answer Sheet | # Answer Sheet | # Answer Sheet

Name_____ | Name_____ | Name_____

September 27 | September 27 | September 27

1 Roll		1 Roll		1 Roll
2 Rolls		2 Rolls		2 Rolls
3 Rolls		3 Rolls		3 Rolls

September 28 | September 28 | September 28

1 Roll		1 Roll		1 Roll
2 Rolls		2 Rolls		2 Rolls
3 Rolls		3 Rolls		3 Rolls

September 29 | September 29 | September 29

1 Roll		1 Roll		1 Roll
2 Rolls		2 Rolls		2 Rolls
3 Rolls		3 Rolls		3 Rolls

After you have filled out the sheet, fold your column underneath along the dashed line so the next restroom user won't see your answers. *The first player uses the far right column.*

Answers - September 24-26
Sept. 24, 1 Roll: Jim Henson
Sept. 24, 2 Rolls: Ben Johnson. He was exposed for steroid usage.
Sept. 24, 3 Rolls: Faneuil Hall

Sept. 25, 1 Roll: Billy Carter. Billy Beer didn't last too long, but it's hard to forget it.
Sept. 25, 2 Rolls: The Little Rock Nine. Governor Orval Faubus had prevented the nine students from entering the school. But, President Eisenhower used the 101st Airborne to enforce desegregation laws.
Sept. 25, 3 Rolls: Michael Douglas (1944) and Catherine Zeta-Jones (1969)

Sept. 26, 1 Roll: John F. Kennedy and Richard M. Nixon. People who listened to the radio believed Nixon won, but the younger Kennedy appeared to have more charisma on television.
Sept. 26, 2 Rolls: Alice, the housekeeper
Sept. 26, 3 Rolls: Tokyo Rose. She was in Japan when the war began, and was forced to do propaganda radio shows to decrease the morale of any Americans picking up the signal. Only problem was, the men fell in love with her sultry voice. She was acquitted of any wrongdoing after the war.

September 30

One Roll

Flip to pg. 193 for answers

What teenage heartthrob, and *Rebel Without a Cause*, had his life cut short today in 1955?

Two Rolls

Ellie Wiesel was born today in 1928. What book did he pen detailing the horrors of the Holocaust?

Three Rolls

In 1791, what Mozart opera debuted in Vienna, just a few months before his death?

October 1

One Roll

Ford unveiled this car in 1908, and it became an affordable ride for the middle class.

Two Rolls

The first World Series began today in 1903. What two cities played?

Three Rolls

In 1888, what science magazine was published for the first time?

October 2

One Roll

It wasn't over until it was over the fence in 1947. Who hit the first pinch-hit home run in a World Series?

Two Rolls

Woodrow Wilson suffered a stroke today in 1919. At the time, what was he trying to get the Senate to ratify?

Three Rolls

What photographer, born in 1949, took the famous picture of a naked John Lennon with a fully clothed Yoko Ono?

Answer Sheet

Name_____

September 30

1 Roll
2 Rolls
3 Rolls

October 1

1 Roll
2 Rolls
3 Rolls

October 2

1 Roll
2 Rolls
3 Rolls

Answer Sheet

Name_____

September 30

1 Roll
2 Rolls
3 Rolls

October 1

1 Roll
2 Rolls
3 Rolls

October 2

1 Roll
2 Rolls
3 Rolls

Answer Sheet

Name_____

September 30

1 Roll
2 Rolls
3 Rolls

October 1

1 Roll
2 Rolls
3 Rolls

October 2

1 Roll
2 Rolls
3 Rolls

After you have filled out the sheet, fold your column underneath along the dashed line so the next restroom user won't see your answers. *The first player uses the far right column.*

Answers - September 27-29
Sept. 27, 1 Roll: Germany, Italy, and Japan
Sept. 27, 2 Rolls: Meat Loaf
Sept. 27, 3 Rolls: Google

Sept. 28, 1 Roll: Louis Pasteur
Sept. 28, 2 Rolls: *Cosmos: A Personal Voyage*
Sept. 28, 3 Rolls: Adolf Hitler. Tandey, a decorated soldier, came across a wounded Hitler near Marcoing. He let him pass. Of course, this could all just be legend.

Sept. 29, 1 Roll: Willie Mays
Sept. 29, 2 Rolls: Horatio Nelson. The loss was devastating to Napoleon, who never could dominate Britain. The main square in London is named for this important battle. Nelson's statue is high atop a column in the square, as he died in the 1805 battle.
Sept. 29, 3 Rolls: Solidarity. The union was ultimately recognized by the communists, and free elections occurred in Poland.

October 3

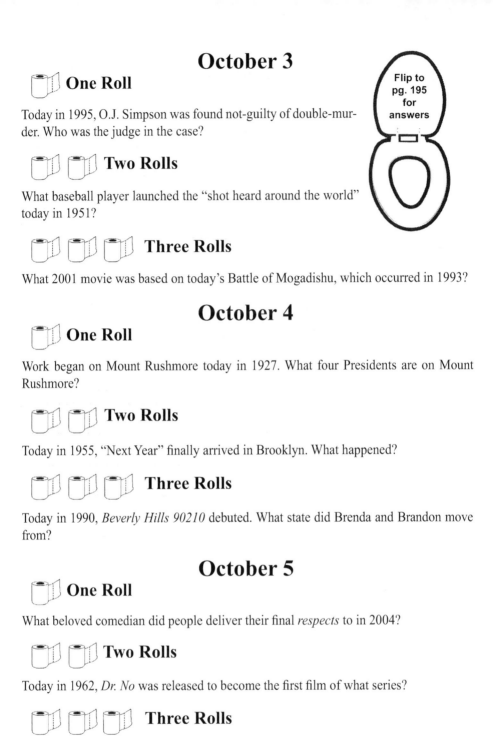

One Roll

Today in 1995, O.J. Simpson was found not-guilty of double-murder. Who was the judge in the case?

Flip to pg. 195 for answers

Two Rolls

What baseball player launched the "shot heard around the world" today in 1951?

Three Rolls

What 2001 movie was based on today's Battle of Mogadishu, which occurred in 1993?

October 4

One Roll

Work began on Mount Rushmore today in 1927. What four Presidents are on Mount Rushmore?

Two Rolls

Today in 1955, "Next Year" finally arrived in Brooklyn. What happened?

Three Rolls

Today in 1990, *Beverly Hills 90210* debuted. What state did Brenda and Brandon move from?

October 5

One Roll

What beloved comedian did people deliver their final *respects* to in 2004?

Two Rolls

Today in 1962, *Dr. No* was released to become the first film of what series?

Three Rolls

What US government scandal was made known today in 1986?

Answer Sheet | Answer Sheet | Answer Sheet

Name_____ | Name_____ | Name_____

October 3	October 3	October 3
1 Roll	1 Roll	1 Roll
2 Rolls	2 Rolls	2 Rolls
3 Rolls	3 Rolls	3 Rolls

October 4	October 4	October 4
1 Roll	1 Roll	1 Roll
2 Rolls	2 Rolls	2 Rolls
3 Rolls	3 Rolls	3 Rolls

October 5	October 5	October 5
1 Roll	1 Roll	1 Roll
2 Rolls	2 Rolls	2 Rolls
3 Rolls	3 Rolls	3 Rolls

After you have filled out the sheet, fold your column underneath along the dashed line so the next restroom user won't see your answers. *The first player uses the far right column.*

Answers - September 30-October 2

Sept. 30, 1 Roll: James Dean. He died in a car accident. Though he was only acting for a few years, his image and name have become immortal.
Sept. 30, 2 Rolls: *Night*
Sept. 30, 3 Rolls: *The Magic Flute*

Oct. 1, 1 Roll: Model T. It cost $825.
Oct. 1, 2 Rolls: Boston (AL) and Pittsburgh (NL). Pittsburgh won the first game 7-3, but Boston won the series.
Oct. 1, 3 Rolls: *National Geographic*

Oct. 2, 1 Roll: Yogi Berra
Oct. 2, 2 Rolls: The Treaty of Versailles
Oct. 2, 3 Rolls: Annie Leibovitz. The picture graced the cover of *Rolling Stone*. The photograph was

October 6

🧻 **One Roll**

Flip to pg. 197 for answers

What Philadelphia Phillies pitcher threw the second no-hit game in Major League Baseball post-season history today in 2010?

🧻🧻 **Two Rolls**

Today in 1927, Al Jolson's *The Jazz Singer* became the first movie to contain what?

🧻🧻🧻 **Three Rolls**

Passing in 1989, what iconic actress was the quickest to receive ten Oscar nominations?

October 7

🧻 **One Roll**

What communist country entered the world today in 1949?

🧻🧻 **Two Rolls**

Born today in 1931, what Archbishop and Nobel Peace Prize winner was an outspoken voice against apartheid?

🧻🧻🧻 **Three Rolls**

The man who drafted the Bill of Rights died today in 1792. Name him.

October 8

🧻 **One Roll**

What city's 1871 fire began when Mrs. O'Leary's cow allegedly knocked over a lantern?

🧻🧻 **Two Rolls**

Which founding father, who died today in 1793, had the largest signature on the Declaration of Independence?

🧻🧻🧻 **Three Rolls**

What did Don Larsen do in 1956 which has never been done again?

Answer Sheet | Answer Sheet | Answer Sheet

Name_____ | Name_____ | Name_____

October 6	October 6	October 6
1 Roll	1 Roll	1 Roll
2 Rolls	2 Rolls	2 Rolls
3 Rolls	3 Rolls	3 Rolls

October 7	October 7	October 7
1 Roll	1 Roll	1 Roll
2 Rolls	2 Rolls	2 Rolls
3 Rolls	3 Rolls	3 Rolls

October 8	October 8	October 8
1 Roll	1 Roll	1 Roll
2 Rolls	2 Rolls	2 Rolls
3 Rolls	3 Rolls	3 Rolls

After you have filled out the sheet, fold your column underneath along the dashed line so the next restroom user won't see your answers. *The first player uses the far right column.*

Answers - October 3-5
Oct. 3, 1 Roll: Judge Lance Ito
Oct. 3, 2 Rolls: Bobby Thomson of the New York Giants hit a home run off of Ralph Branca of the Brooklyn Dodgers to win the pennant
Oct. 3, 3 Rolls: *Black Hawk Down*

Oct. 4, 1 Roll: From left to right: George Washington, Thomas Jefferson, Theodore Roosevelt, and Abraham Lincoln
Oct. 4, 2 Rolls: The Dodgers won their only World Series in Brooklyn. They defeated the Yankees 2-0 at Yankee Stadium to take the series, 4 games to 3. After every disappointing season, the Dodger faithful would proclaim, "Wait 'til next year."
Oct. 4, 3 Rolls: Minnesota

Oct. 5, 1 Roll: Rodney Dangerfield
Oct. 5, 2 Rolls: *James Bond*
Oct. 5, 3 Rolls: Iran-Contra Scandal. In the scandal, weapons were secretly being sold to Iranians, and the money was being used to support Nicaraguan rebels.

October 9

One Roll

What Latin American military leader was executed on this date in 1967?

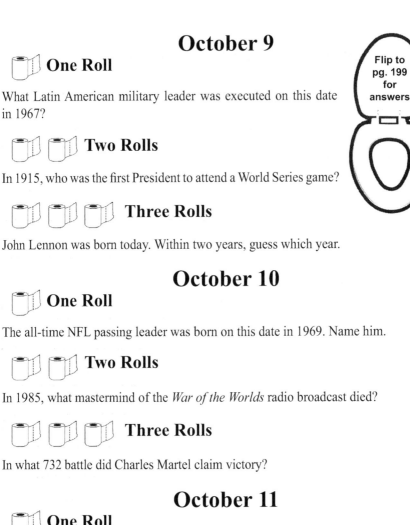

Flip to pg. 199 for answers

Two Rolls

In 1915, who was the first President to attend a World Series game?

Three Rolls

John Lennon was born today. Within two years, guess which year.

October 10

One Roll

The all-time NFL passing leader was born on this date in 1969. Name him.

Two Rolls

In 1985, what mastermind of the *War of the Worlds* radio broadcast died?

Three Rolls

In what 732 battle did Charles Martel claim victory?

October 11

One Roll

What show debuted live on this date in 1975? If we gave you the day of the week, it might give away the answer.

Two Rolls

What comedian died on this date in 1991? His last words might have been that he was coming to join Elizabeth.

Three Rolls

What war, fought between British and Dutch descendants in South Africa, began on this date in 1899?

Answer Sheet | Answer Sheet | Answer Sheet

Name_____ | Name_____ | Name_____

October 9 | October 9 | October 9

October 9	October 9	October 9
1 Roll	1 Roll	1 Roll
2 Rolls	2 Rolls	2 Rolls
3 Rolls	3 Rolls	3 Rolls

October 10 | October 10 | October 10

October 10	October 10	October 10
1 Roll	1 Roll	1 Roll
2 Rolls	2 Rolls	2 Rolls
3 Rolls	3 Rolls	3 Rolls

October 11 | October 11 | October 11

October 11	October 11	October 11
1 Roll	1 Roll	1 Roll
2 Rolls	2 Rolls	2 Rolls
3 Rolls	3 Rolls	3 Rolls

After you have filled out the sheet, fold your column underneath along the dashed line so the next restroom user won't see your answers. *The first player uses the far right column.*

Answers - October 6-8
Oct. 6, 1 Roll: Roy Halladay. He no-hit the Cincinnati Reds in the National League Division Series.
Oct. 6, 2 Rolls: Spoken words
Oct. 6, 3 Rolls: Bette Davis

Oct. 7, 1 Roll: East Germany
Oct. 7, 2 Rolls: Desmond Tutu
Oct. 7, 3 Rolls: George Mason

Oct. 8, 1 Roll: Chicago
Oct. 8, 2 Rolls: John Hancock. Legend has it he wanted to make sure the King didn't have to use his reading glasses to see it. Note that there is no evidence that these words were ever spoken.
Oct. 8, 3 Rolls: He threw a perfect game in the World Series

October 12

One Roll

What holiday was celebrated for the first time ever in 1792? It must have been the anniversary of something.

Two Rolls

This Confederate General died today in 1870, five years after he surrendered at Appomattox Court House.

Three Rolls

Today in 1960, what did Nikita Khrushchev do with his shoe at the United Nations?

Flip to pg. 201 for answers

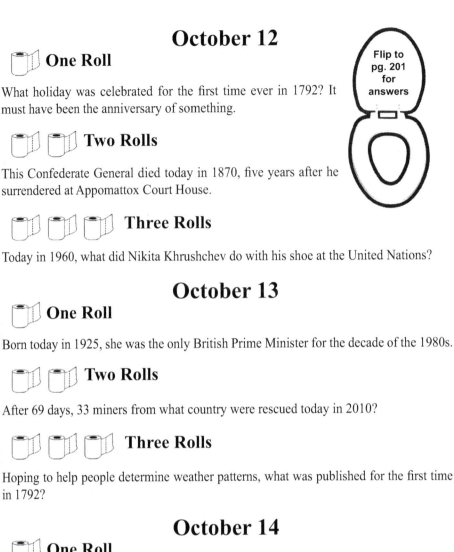

October 13

One Roll

Born today in 1925, she was the only British Prime Minister for the decade of the 1980s.

Two Rolls

After 69 days, 33 miners from what country were rescued today in 2010?

Three Rolls

Hoping to help people determine weather patterns, what was published for the first time in 1792?

October 14

One Roll

What international stand-off began today in 1962? It was the closest the world ever came to World War III during the Cold War.

Two Rolls

Who won the Battle of Hastings in 1066?

Three Rolls

Who was shot today in 1912 while campaigning for the Bull Moose Party?

Answer Sheet

Name_____

October 12

1 Roll
2 Rolls
3 Rolls

October 13

1 Roll
2 Rolls
3 Rolls

October 14

1 Roll
2 Rolls
3 Rolls

Answer Sheet

Name_____

October 12

1 Roll
2 Rolls
3 Rolls

October 13

1 Roll
2 Rolls
3 Rolls

October 14

1 Roll
2 Rolls
3 Rolls

Answer Sheet

Name_____

October 12

1 Roll
2 Rolls
3 Rolls

October 13

1 Roll
2 Rolls
3 Rolls

October 14

1 Roll
2 Rolls
3 Rolls

After you have filled out the sheet, fold your column underneath along the dashed line so the next restroom user won't see your answers. *The first player uses the far right column.*

Answers - October 9-11
Oct. 9, 1 Roll: Che Guevera
Oct. 9, 2 Rolls: Woodrow Wilson
Oct. 9, 3 Rolls: 1940

Oct. 10, 1 Roll: Brett Favre. He threw for 71,838 yards in his career.
Oct. 10, 2 Rolls: Orson Welles. Though there was a disclaimer, some New York and New Jersey residents were fooled into thinking Martians were attacking on October 30, 1938. Some even pointed their guns at water towers believing they were aliens. Even when this broadcast was parodied years later in Ecuador and Buffalo, some people were still duped.
Oct. 10, 3 Rolls: Battle of Tours

Oct. 11, 1 Roll: *Saturday Night Live*
Oct. 11, 2 Rolls: Redd Foxx
Oct. 11, 3 Rolls: Boer War, or Second Boer War

October 15

One Roll

In 1989, who broke Gordie Howe's all-time scoring record in hockey? The record was broken in Edmonton.

Two Rolls

In 1939, what airport opened its doors in New York?

Three Rolls

In 1940, *The Great Dictator* debuted. What mustached-comedian starred in it?

Flip to pg. 203 for answers

October 16

One Roll

Today in 1793, what French queen lost her head? Her last words were an apology for stepping on the executioner's foot.

Two Rolls

Who began a "Long March" in China today in 1934? The 6,000 mile trip lasted a year.

Three Rolls

Where did abolitionist John Brown lead a violent raid today in 1859?

October 17

One Roll

Al Capone went to prison today in 1931. After spending some time in Atlanta, where was he moved to next?

Two Rolls

Today in 1979, Mother Teresa was awarded the Nobel Peace Prize. In what Indian city did she do much of her humanitarian work?

Three Rolls

Eminem was born today in 1972. What name is on his birth certificate?

Answer Sheet   Answer Sheet   Answer Sheet

Name_____   Name_____   Name_____

October 15   October 15   October 15

1 Roll	1 Roll	1 Roll
2 Rolls	2 Rolls	2 Rolls
3 Rolls	3 Rolls	3 Rolls

October 16   October 16   October 16

1 Roll	1 Roll	1 Roll
2 Rolls	2 Rolls	2 Rolls
3 Rolls	3 Rolls	3 Rolls

October 17   October 17   October 17

1 Roll	1 Roll	1 Roll
2 Rolls	2 Rolls	2 Rolls
3 Rolls	3 Rolls	3 Rolls

After you have filled out the sheet, fold your column underneath along the dashed line so the next restroom user won't see your answers. *The first player uses the far right column.*

Answers - October 12-14
Oct. 12, 1 Roll: Columbus Day…300 years after 1492
Oct. 12, 2 Rolls: Robert E. Lee
Oct. 12, 3 Rolls: Enraged, he banged it on a desk after a delegate from the Philippines said that the USSR had swallowed up Eastern Europe

Oct. 13, 1 Roll: Margaret Thatcher
Oct. 13, 2 Rolls: Chile
Oct. 13, 3 Rolls: *Old Farmer's Almanac*

Oct. 14, 1 Roll: Cuban Missile Crisis
Oct. 14, 2 Rolls: William the Conqueror
Oct. 14, 3 Rolls: Teddy Roosevelt. He was shot on his way to deliver a speech in Milwaukee. He refused to go to the hospital until he finished giving his speech, which went on for about an hour. But it was perhaps the length of the speech that saved his life. The bullet's impact was slowed down considerably by the eyeglass case and folded speech he had in his shirt pocket. He said after speaking, "it takes more than that to kill a Bull Moose."

October 18

One Roll

Flip to pg. 205 for answers

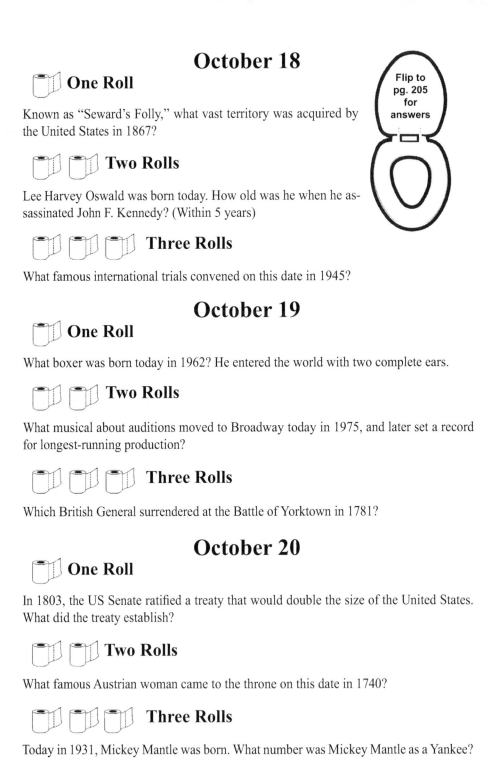

Known as "Seward's Folly," what vast territory was acquired by the United States in 1867?

Two Rolls

Lee Harvey Oswald was born today. How old was he when he assassinated John F. Kennedy? (Within 5 years)

Three Rolls

What famous international trials convened on this date in 1945?

October 19

One Roll

What boxer was born today in 1962? He entered the world with two complete ears.

Two Rolls

What musical about auditions moved to Broadway today in 1975, and later set a record for longest-running production?

Three Rolls

Which British General surrendered at the Battle of Yorktown in 1781?

October 20

One Roll

In 1803, the US Senate ratified a treaty that would double the size of the United States. What did the treaty establish?

Two Rolls

What famous Austrian woman came to the throne on this date in 1740?

Three Rolls

Today in 1931, Mickey Mantle was born. What number was Mickey Mantle as a Yankee?

Answer Sheet | Answer Sheet | Answer Sheet

Name_____ | Name_____ | Name_____

October 18 | October 18 | October 18

1 Roll	1 Roll	1 Roll
2 Rolls	2 Rolls	2 Rolls
3 Rolls	3 Rolls	3 Rolls

October 19 | October 19 | October 19

1 Roll	1 Roll	1 Roll
2 Rolls	2 Rolls	2 Rolls
3 Rolls	3 Rolls	3 Rolls

October 20 | October 20 | October 20

1 Roll	1 Roll	1 Roll
2 Rolls	2 Rolls	2 Rolls
3 Rolls	3 Rolls	3 Rolls

After you have filled out the sheet, fold your column underneath along the dashed line so the next restroom user won't see your answers. *The first player uses the far right column.*

Answers - October 15-17
Oct. 15, 1 Roll: Wayne Gretzky, who had been a member of the Edmonton Oilers, broke the record as a Los Angeles King
Oct. 15, 2 Rolls: LaGuardia Airport
Oct. 15, 3 Rolls: Charlie Chaplin. The film was a satire on Hitler.

Oct. 16, 1 Roll: Marie Antoinette
Oct. 16, 2 Rolls: Mao Zedong
Oct. 16, 3 Rolls: The federal arsenal in Harper's Ferry, West Virginia (then, just plain Virginia)

Oct. 17, 1 Roll: Alcatraz
Oct. 17, 2 Rolls: Calcutta (Kolkata)
Oct. 17, 3 Rolls: Marshall Bruce Mathers III

October 21

One Roll

Flip to pg. 207 for answers

What Boston Red Sox catcher waved a game-winning home run fair in Game 6 of the 1975 World Series?

Two Rolls

Kim Kardashian was born today in 1980. Who is her oldest sister?

Three Rolls

What famous biology teacher, who taught evolution, died at the age of 70 in 1970?

October 22

One Roll

Maybe it's not such a small world. What Florida destination recorded its 100 millionth guest today in 1979?

Two Rolls

What Pope's inauguration was today in 1978?

Three Rolls

What Romanov was declared Emperor of All Russia on this date in 1721?

October 23

One Roll

Perhaps the greatest soccer player of all time was born in Brazil on this date in 1940. Name him.

Two Rolls

Whose walk-off home run gave Canada their second World Series in 1993?

Three Rolls

What international war, named for a body part, began on this date in 1739?

Answer Sheet | Answer Sheet | Answer Sheet

Name_____ | Name_____ | Name_____

October 21	October 21	October 21
1 Roll	1 Roll	1 Roll
2 Rolls	2 Rolls	2 Rolls
3 Rolls	3 Rolls	3 Rolls

October 22	October 22	October 22
1 Roll	1 Roll	1 Roll
2 Rolls	2 Rolls	2 Rolls
3 Rolls	3 Rolls	3 Rolls

October 23	October 23	October 23
1 Roll	1 Roll	1 Roll
2 Rolls	2 Rolls	2 Rolls
3 Rolls	3 Rolls	3 Rolls

After you have filled out the sheet, fold your column underneath along the dashed line so the next restroom user won't see your answers. *The first player uses the far right column.*

Answers - October 18-20

Oct. 18, 1 Roll: Alaska
Oct. 18, 2 Rolls: Only 24 years old. He was born in 1939.
Oct. 18, 3 Rolls: Nuremberg Trials. This was an opening session, and the indictments were read on November 20.

Oct. 19, 1 Roll: Evander Holyfield…the champion who Mike Tyson took a bite out of
Oct. 19, 2 Rolls: *A Chorus Line* performed 6,137 shows. Its 1997 record was eventually broken by several shows, including the current leader, *Phantom of the Opera*.
Oct. 19, 3 Rolls: General Charles Cornwallis. The defeat was the deciding battle in the Revolutionary War.

Oct. 20, 1 Roll: The Louisiana Purchase. The area was bought from France in exchange for about $15 million.
Oct. 20, 2 Rolls: Maria Theresa…the mother of Marie Antoinette
Oct. 20, 3 Rolls: After a bad start wearing number 6, he switched to number 7. Count either as correct.

October 24

One Roll

Fifty years after she rode the bus, what civil rights icon died at the age of 92 in 2005?

Flip to pg. 209 for answers

Two Rolls

What international organization approved its charter on this date in 1945?

Three Rolls

What Middle Eastern war ended in 1973?

October 25

One Roll

What small nation did the United States invade today in 1983?

Two Rolls

What tennis personality, known for his challenge to Billie Jean King, died in 1995?

Three Rolls

What version of Microsoft Windows was released on this date in 2001?

October 26

One Roll

Where did Wyatt Earp and the Clantons have the most famous shootout of the Old West?

Two Rolls

What act, signed into law by President Bush in 2001, gave authorities more leverage when dealing with domestic terrorism?

Three Rolls

What legendary women's reformer, who was a powerful voice at the Seneca Falls Convention, died in 1902?

Answer Sheet | Answer Sheet | Answer Sheet

Name_____ | Name_____ | Name_____

October 24 | October 24 | October 24

1 Roll	1 Roll	1 Roll
2 Rolls	2 Rolls	2 Rolls
3 Rolls	3 Rolls	3 Rolls

October 25 | October 25 | October 25

1 Roll	1 Roll	1 Roll
2 Rolls	2 Rolls	2 Rolls
3 Rolls	3 Rolls	3 Rolls

October 26 | October 26 | October 26

1 Roll	1 Roll	1 Roll
2 Rolls	2 Rolls	2 Rolls
3 Rolls	3 Rolls	3 Rolls

After you have filled out the sheet, fold your column underneath along the dashed line so the next restroom user won't see your answers. *The first player uses the far right column.*

Answers - October 21-23
Oct. 21, 1 Roll: Carlton Fisk
Oct. 21, 2 Rolls: Kourtney Kardashian was born a year-and-a-half prior, in 1979
Oct. 21, 3 Rolls: John Scopes. He was the focus of the 1925 Scopes Trial which concerned the teaching of evolution in the classroom.

Oct. 22, 1 Roll: Walt Disney World. The guest was 8 year-old Kurt Miller of Baltimore.
Oct. 22, 2 Rolls: Pope John Paul II
Oct. 22, 3 Rolls: Pyotr Alexeyevich Romanov, or Peter the Great

Oct. 23, 1 Roll: Edson Arantes do Nascimento, or Pelé
Oct. 23, 2 Rolls: Joe Carter of the Toronto Blue Jays
Oct. 23, 3 Rolls: War of Jenkins' Ear

October 27

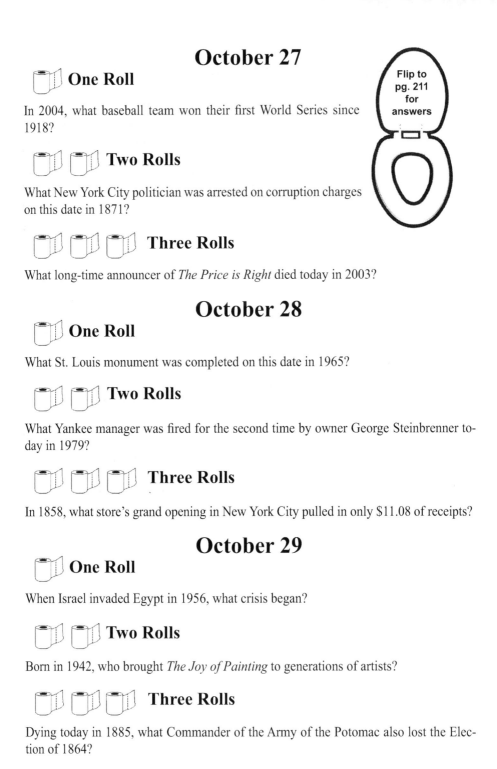

One Roll

Flip to pg. 211 for answers

In 2004, what baseball team won their first World Series since 1918?

Two Rolls

What New York City politician was arrested on corruption charges on this date in 1871?

Three Rolls

What long-time announcer of *The Price is Right* died today in 2003?

October 28

One Roll

What St. Louis monument was completed on this date in 1965?

Two Rolls

What Yankee manager was fired for the second time by owner George Steinbrenner today in 1979?

Three Rolls

In 1858, what store's grand opening in New York City pulled in only $11.08 of receipts?

October 29

One Roll

When Israel invaded Egypt in 1956, what crisis began?

Two Rolls

Born in 1942, who brought *The Joy of Painting* to generations of artists?

Three Rolls

Dying today in 1885, what Commander of the Army of the Potomac also lost the Election of 1864?

Answer Sheet | Answer Sheet | Answer Sheet

Name_____ | Name_____ | Name_____

October 27	October 27	October 27
1 Roll	1 Roll	1 Roll
2 Rolls	2 Rolls	2 Rolls
3 Rolls	3 Rolls	3 Rolls

October 28	October 28	October 28
1 Roll	1 Roll	1 Roll
2 Rolls	2 Rolls	2 Rolls
3 Rolls	3 Rolls	3 Rolls

October 29	October 29	October 29
1 Roll	1 Roll	1 Roll
2 Rolls	2 Rolls	2 Rolls
3 Rolls	3 Rolls	3 Rolls

After you have filled out the sheet, fold your column underneath along the dashed line so the next restroom user won't see your answers. *The first player uses the far right column.*

Answers - October 24-26
Oct. 24, 1 Roll: Rosa Parks
Oct. 24, 2 Rolls: The United Nations
Oct. 24, 3 Rolls: Yom Kippur War

Oct. 25, 1 Roll: Grenada
Oct. 25, 2 Rolls: Bobby Riggs. He lost to King in the famed "Battle of the Sexes."
Oct. 25, 3 Rolls: Windows XP

Oct. 26, 1 Roll: At the O.K. Corral in 1881
Oct. 26, 2 Rolls: The Patriot Act
Oct. 26, 3 Rolls: Elizabeth Cady Stanton

October 30

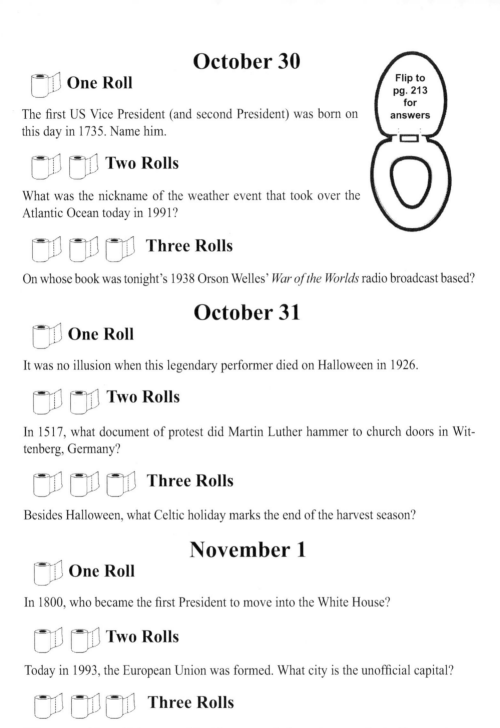

One Roll

The first US Vice President (and second President) was born on this day in 1735. Name him.

Two Rolls

What was the nickname of the weather event that took over the Atlantic Ocean today in 1991?

Three Rolls

On whose book was tonight's 1938 Orson Welles' *War of the Worlds* radio broadcast based?

Flip to pg. 213 for answers

October 31

One Roll

It was no illusion when this legendary performer died on Halloween in 1926.

Two Rolls

In 1517, what document of protest did Martin Luther hammer to church doors in Wittenberg, Germany?

Three Rolls

Besides Halloween, what Celtic holiday marks the end of the harvest season?

November 1

One Roll

In 1800, who became the first President to move into the White House?

Two Rolls

Today in 1993, the European Union was formed. What city is the unofficial capital?

Three Rolls

What assembly, which restored legitimacy to dethroned monarchs in Europe, began meeting today in 1814?

Answer Sheet | Answer Sheet | Answer Sheet

Name_____ | Name_____ | Name_____

October 30 | October 30 | October 30

1 Roll	1 Roll	1 Roll
2 Rolls	2 Rolls	2 Rolls
3 Rolls	3 Rolls	3 Rolls

October 31 | October 31 | October 31

1 Roll	1 Roll	1 Roll
2 Rolls	2 Rolls	2 Rolls
3 Rolls	3 Rolls	3 Rolls

November 1 | November 1 | November 1

1 Roll	1 Roll	1 Roll
2 Rolls	2 Rolls	2 Rolls
3 Rolls	3 Rolls	3 Rolls

After you have filled out the sheet, fold your column underneath along the dashed line so the next restroom user won't see your answers. *The first player uses the far right column.*

Answers - October 27-29
Oct. 27, 1 Roll: Boston Red Sox
Oct. 27, 2 Rolls: Boss Tweed
Oct. 27, 3 Rolls: Rod Roddy

Oct. 28, 1 Roll: The Gateway Arch
Oct. 28, 2 Rolls: Billy Martin
Oct. 28, 3 Rolls: Macy's

Oct. 29, 1 Roll: The Suez Crisis
Oct. 29, 2 Rolls: Bob Ross
Oct. 29, 3 Rolls: George B. McClellan. Abraham Lincoln was re-elected in 1864.

November 2

One Roll
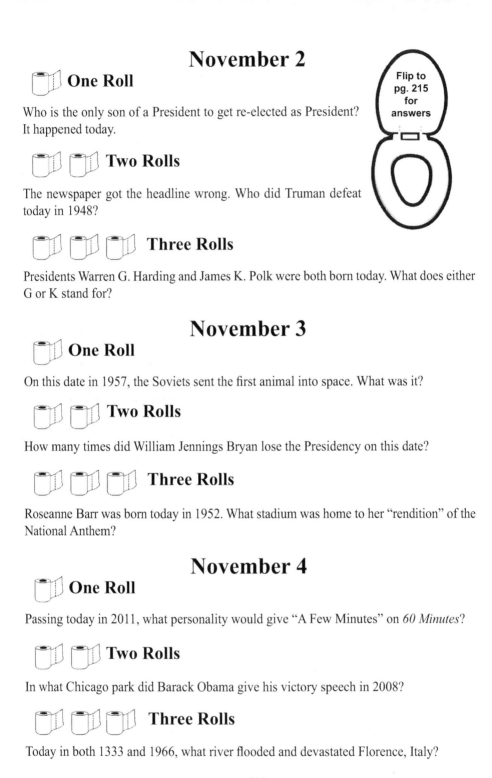

Who is the only son of a President to get re-elected as President? It happened today.

Flip to pg. 215 for answers

Two Rolls

The newspaper got the headline wrong. Who did Truman defeat today in 1948?

Three Rolls

Presidents Warren G. Harding and James K. Polk were both born today. What does either G or K stand for?

November 3

One Roll

On this date in 1957, the Soviets sent the first animal into space. What was it?

Two Rolls

How many times did William Jennings Bryan lose the Presidency on this date?

Three Rolls

Roseanne Barr was born today in 1952. What stadium was home to her "rendition" of the National Anthem?

November 4

One Roll

Passing today in 2011, what personality would give "A Few Minutes" on *60 Minutes*?

Two Rolls

In what Chicago park did Barack Obama give his victory speech in 2008?

Three Rolls

Today in both 1333 and 1966, what river flooded and devastated Florence, Italy?

Answer Sheet | Answer Sheet | Answer Sheet

Name_____ Name_____ Name_____

November 2 | November 2 | November 2

1 Roll	1 Roll	1 Roll
2 Rolls	2 Rolls	2 Rolls
3 Rolls	3 Rolls	3 Rolls

November 3 | November 3 | November 3

1 Roll	1 Roll	1 Roll
2 Rolls	2 Rolls	2 Rolls
3 Rolls	3 Rolls	3 Rolls

November 4 | November 4 | November 4

1 Roll	1 Roll	1 Roll
2 Rolls	2 Rolls	2 Rolls
3 Rolls	3 Rolls	3 Rolls

After you have filled out the sheet, fold your column underneath along the dashed line so the next restroom user won't see your answers. *The first player uses the far right column.*

Answers - October 30-November 1
Oct. 30, 1 Roll: John Adams
Oct. 30, 2 Rolls: The Perfect Storm
Oct. 30, 3 Rolls: H.G. Wells wrote the book which was modified for radio. For more on the broadcast, see October 10th, 2 Rolls.

Oct. 31, 1 Roll: Harry Houdini
Oct. 31, 2 Rolls: The 95 Theses
Oct. 31, 3 Rolls: Samhain

Nov. 1, 1 Roll: John Adams
Nov. 1, 2 Rolls: Brussels, Belgium. Many of the important government offices are there. The EU has no official capital.
Nov. 1, 3 Rolls: The Congress of Vienna

November 5

Flip to pg. 217 for answers

One Roll

Democratic candidate John F. Kennedy was elected to his first national office today in 1946. What office?

Two Rolls

What two political parties did President Woodrow Wilson defeat today in 1912?

Three Rolls

What colony set up the first American postal service today in 1639?

November 6

One Roll

A year to the day Abraham Lincoln was elected President of the US, who was elected President of the Confederacy in 1861?

Two Rolls

What Hollywood actress was convicted of shoplifting today in 2002?

Three Rolls

What tag-team of bank robbers was killed in Bolivia today in 1908?

November 7

One Roll

Born in 1867, what female scientist was known for her work with radioactivity?

Two Rolls

On this date in 1991, who announced to the world that he was HIV Positive?

Three Rolls

Today in what year did Franklin Delano Roosevelt win his fourth Presidential Election?

Answer Sheet | Answer Sheet | Answer Sheet

Name_____ | Name_____ | Name_____

November 5	November 5	November 5
1 Roll	1 Roll	1 Roll
2 Rolls	2 Rolls	2 Rolls
3 Rolls	3 Rolls	3 Rolls

November 6	November 6	November 6
1 Roll	1 Roll	1 Roll
2 Rolls	2 Rolls	2 Rolls
3 Rolls	3 Rolls	3 Rolls

November 7	November 7	November 7
1 Roll	1 Roll	1 Roll
2 Rolls	2 Rolls	2 Rolls
3 Rolls	3 Rolls	3 Rolls

After you have filled out the sheet, fold your column underneath along the dashed line so the next restroom user won't see your answers. *The first player uses the far right column.*

Answers - November 2-4

Nov. 2, 1 Roll: George W. Bush in 2004. John Quincy Adams was a one term President, and the only other son of a President to become Commander-in-Chief.

Nov. 2, 2 Rolls: Thomas Dewey. The next day, the *Chicago Tribune* famously misprinted the headline *Dewey Defeats Truman*.

Nov. 2, 3 Rolls: Gamaliel and Knox

Nov. 3, 1 Roll: A dog named Laika. The dog most likely died within hours, circled the Earth a few thousand times, and then vaporized in the atmosphere.

Nov. 3, 2 Rolls: Twice. 1896 (to William McKinley) and 1908 (to William Taft). He also lost in 1900 (again to McKinley).

Nov. 3, 3 Rolls: San Diego's Jack Murphy Stadium. She screamed the lyrics, then grabbed her crotch and spit.

Nov. 4, 1 Roll: Andy Rooney
Nov. 4, 2 Rolls: Grant Park
Nov. 4, 3 Rolls: The Arno River

November 8

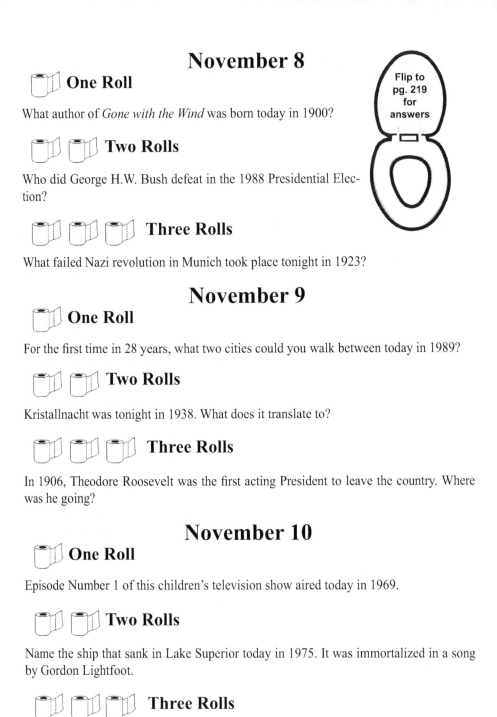

🧻 One Roll

What author of *Gone with the Wind* was born today in 1900?

Flip to pg. 219 for answers

🧻 🧻 Two Rolls

Who did George H.W. Bush defeat in the 1988 Presidential Election?

🧻 🧻 🧻 Three Rolls

What failed Nazi revolution in Munich took place tonight in 1923?

November 9

🧻 One Roll

For the first time in 28 years, what two cities could you walk between today in 1989?

🧻 🧻 Two Rolls

Kristallnacht was tonight in 1938. What does it translate to?

🧻 🧻 🧻 Three Rolls

In 1906, Theodore Roosevelt was the first acting President to leave the country. Where was he going?

November 10

🧻 One Roll

Episode Number 1 of this children's television show aired today in 1969.

🧻 🧻 Two Rolls

Name the ship that sank in Lake Superior today in 1975. It was immortalized in a song by Gordon Lightfoot.

🧻 🧻 🧻 Three Rolls

A decade before passing today in 2006, this senior citizen was doing pushups at the Oscars. Name him.

Answer Sheet   Answer Sheet   Answer Sheet

Name_____   Name_____   Name_____

November 8   November 8   November 8

1 Roll	1 Roll	1 Roll
2 Rolls	2 Rolls	2 Rolls
3 Rolls	3 Rolls	3 Rolls

November 9   November 9   November 9

1 Roll	1 Roll	1 Roll
2 Rolls	2 Rolls	2 Rolls
3 Rolls	3 Rolls	3 Rolls

November 10   November 10   November 10

1 Roll	1 Roll	1 Roll
2 Rolls	2 Rolls	2 Rolls
3 Rolls	3 Rolls	3 Rolls

After you have filled out the sheet, fold your column underneath along the dashed line so the next restroom user won't see your answers. *The first player uses the far right column.*

Answers - November 5-7
Nov. 5, 1 Roll: He was elected to the House of Representatives
Nov. 5, 2 Rolls: Republicans (William Taft) and Bull-Moose/Progressive Party (Theodore Roosevelt). Wilson was the Democratic candidate.
Nov. 5, 3 Rolls: Massachusetts

Nov. 6, 1 Roll: Jefferson Davis
Nov. 6, 2 Rolls: Winona Ryder
Nov. 6, 3 Rolls: Butch Cassidy and the Sundance Kid. Though, there were no remains. Some claimed the two survived and lived for another thirty years.

Nov. 7, 1 Roll: Marie Curie
Nov. 7, 2 Rolls: Magic Johnson
Nov. 7, 3 Rolls: 1944. It was the last time a President won more than a second term.

November 11

One Roll

What war ended today on the 11th day, in the 11th month, in the 11th hour?

Flip to pg. 221 for answers

Two Rolls

Fernandomania hit a fever pitch when this Dodgers rookie won the Cy Young Award today in 1981.

Three Rolls

Route 66 was established today in 1926. What two cities are the end points?

November 12

One Roll

What immigrant processing area closed today in 1954?

Two Rolls

Not as golden, but what California bridge opened today in 1936?

Three Rolls

What sculptor of *The Thinker* was born today in 1840?

November 13

One Roll

Born in 1955, who was an original host on *Comic Relief* alongside Robin Williams and Billy Crystal?

Two Rolls

What memorial was dedicated today in 1982, less than 10 years after the conflict it honors?

Three Rolls

In a letter dated today in 1789, what did Benjamin Franklin tell M. Le. Roy he was certain about?

Answer Sheet   Answer Sheet   Answer Sheet

Name_____   Name_____   Name_____

November 11   November 11   November 11

1 Roll	1 Roll	1 Roll
2 Rolls	2 Rolls	2 Rolls
3 Rolls	3 Rolls	3 Rolls

November 12   November 12   November 12

1 Roll	1 Roll	1 Roll
2 Rolls	2 Rolls	2 Rolls
3 Rolls	3 Rolls	3 Rolls

November 13   November 13   November 13

1 Roll	1 Roll	1 Roll
2 Rolls	2 Rolls	2 Rolls
3 Rolls	3 Rolls	3 Rolls

After you have filled out the sheet, fold your column underneath along the dashed line so the next restroom user won't see your answers. *The first player uses the far right column.*

Answers - November 8-10
Nov. 8, 1 Roll: Margaret Mitchell
Nov. 8, 2 Rolls: Michael Dukakis
Nov. 8, 3 Rolls: Beer Hall Putsch

Nov. 9, 1 Roll: East and West Berlin. Within hours, the Berlin wall would come down.
Nov. 9, 2 Rolls: Night of Broken Glass. The organized violence against European Jews coincided with the beginning of the Holocaust.
Nov. 9, 3 Rolls: Panama…to oversee canal construction. He then went to Puerto Rico before heading home.

Nov. 10, 1 Roll: Sesame Street. There are currently well over 4,000 episodes.
Nov. 10, 2 Rolls: The *Edmund Fitzgerald*
Nov. 10, 3 Rolls: Jack Palance. He costarred with Billy Crystal in *City Slickers*. Palance was 73 when he did one-handed pushups after winning the 1991 Oscar for Best Supporting Actor.

November 14

One Roll

In a 1993 plebiscite, what commonwealth voted against becoming the 51st United State?

Flip to pg. 223 for answers

Two Rolls

What civil rights leader and founder of the Tuskegee Institute died today in 1915?

Three Rolls

Moby-Dick was published today in 1851. What coffee company is named for the first mate?

November 15

One Roll

What hamburger chain founded by Dave Thomas opened its doors today in 1969?

Two Rolls

What Union General began a "march to the sea" from Atlanta to Savannah in 1864?

Three Rolls

The Articles of Confederation were adopted in 1777. Who drafted them?

November 16

One Roll

The first Harry Potter movie opened today in 2001. What was it called?

Two Rolls

What President became the first to visit Vietnam after the war ended. He did so today.

Three Rolls

UNESCO was founded today in 1945. What does it stand for?

Answer Sheet

Name_____

November 14

1 Roll
2 Rolls
3 Rolls

November 15

1 Roll
2 Rolls
3 Rolls

November 16

1 Roll
2 Rolls
3 Rolls

Answer Sheet

Name_____

November 14

1 Roll
2 Rolls
3 Rolls

November 15

1 Roll
2 Rolls
3 Rolls

November 16

1 Roll
2 Rolls
3 Rolls

Answer Sheet

Name_____

November 14

1 Roll
2 Rolls
3 Rolls

November 15

1 Roll
2 Rolls
3 Rolls

November 16

1 Roll
2 Rolls
3 Rolls

After you have filled out the sheet, fold your column underneath along the dashed line so the next restroom user won't see your answers. *The first player uses the far right column.*

Answers - November 11-13
Nov. 11, 1 Roll: World War I. An armistice ended the fighting.
Nov. 11, 2 Rolls: Fernando Valenzuela. He was also the Rookie-of-the-Year.
Nov. 11, 3 Rolls: Chicago, Illinois and Santa Monica/Los Angeles, California

Nov. 12, 1 Roll: Ellis Island. It is still open as a tourist attraction.
Nov. 12, 2 Rolls: Bay Bridge. It links San Francisco to Oakland.
Nov. 12, 3 Rolls: Auguste Rodin

Nov. 13, 1 Roll: Whoopi Goldberg
Nov. 13, 2 Rolls: The Vietnam War Memorial in Washington, DC
Nov. 13, 3 Rolls: Death and Taxes. He stated that, "Our new Constitution is now established, and has an appearance that promises permanency; but in the world nothing can be said to be certain except death and taxes."

221

November 17

One Roll

He wasn't born in a taxi, but what voice of *The Lorax* was born today in 1944?

Flip to pg. 225 for answers

Two Rolls

SALT began today in 1969. What did SALT stand for?

Three Rolls

For those watching at home, what children's TV-movie interrupted the closing moments of a Jets-Raiders game in 1968?

November 18

One Roll

What skill did William Tell display today in 1307?

Two Rolls

On this date in 1497, what African geographic feature did explorer Vasco de Gama sail around?

Three Rolls

Where did the 1978 mass suicide led by cult leader Jim Jones take place?

November 19

One Roll

Born in 1938, what television mogul founded CNN, the first cable news network?

Two Rolls

What US-British treaty, rather unpopular amongst Americans, was signed today in 1794?

Three Rolls

Delivered today in 1863, how many words were in Lincoln's Gettysburg Address? (Within 50)

Answer Sheet

Name_____

November 17

1 Roll
2 Rolls
3 Rolls

November 18

1 Roll
2 Rolls
3 Rolls

November 19

1 Roll
2 Rolls
3 Rolls

Answer Sheet

Name_____

November 17

1 Roll
2 Rolls
3 Rolls

November 18

1 Roll
2 Rolls
3 Rolls

November 19

1 Roll
2 Rolls
3 Rolls

Answer Sheet

Name_____

November 17

1 Roll
2 Rolls
3 Rolls

November 18

1 Roll
2 Rolls
3 Rolls

November 19

1 Roll
2 Rolls
3 Rolls

After you have filled out the sheet, fold your column underneath along the dashed line so the next restroom user won't see your answers. *The first player uses the far right column.*

Answers - November 14-16
Nov. 14, 1 Roll: Puerto Rico
Nov. 14, 2 Rolls: Booker T. Washington
Nov. 14, 3 Rolls: Starbucks. The company was almost named Pequod, for the ship. Ultimately the store was named after the first mate of the ship, Starbuck.

Nov. 15, 1 Roll: Wendy's, or Wendy's Old Fashioned Hamburgers. The first store opened in Columbus, Ohio. The franchise is named for Dave Thomas' daughter.
Nov. 15, 2 Rolls: William Tecumseh Sherman
Nov. 15, 3 Rolls: John Dickinson chaired the committee. Benjamin Franklin also gets an honorable mention for helping him out. The Articles would not be ratified until 1781.

Nov. 16, 1 Roll: *Harry Potter and the Sorcerer's Stone*
Nov. 16, 2 Rolls: Bill Clinton. He visited in 2000.
Nov. 16, 3 Rolls: United Nations Educational, Scientific and Cultural Organization

November 20

One Roll

Born in 1942, what former Delaware Senator, and Vice President, commuted to Washington via Amtrak?

Flip to pg. 227 for answers

Two Rolls

Though he died in 1975, which Fascist Spanish leader is "still dead" according to *Saturday Night Live*?

Three Rolls

In 1982, which college band went onto the field before the football game was over?

November 21

One Roll

The "Galloping Ghost" finished his collegiate career today in 1925. Who was he?

Two Rolls

What did Pilgrims sign today in 1620 that promoted a direct democracy?

Three Rolls

François-Marie Arouet was born today in 1694. What was he better known as?

November 22

One Roll

In 1963, what city was home to what would become the greatest conspiracy theory in American History?

Two Rolls

English pirate Edward Teach died today in 1718. What was his colorful nickname?

Three Rolls

In 1990, George H. W. Bush surprised US troops for Thanksgiving. In what country did he greet them?

Answer Sheet   Answer Sheet   Answer Sheet

Name_____   Name_____   Name_____

November 20   November 20   November 20

1 Roll	1 Roll	1 Roll
2 Rolls	2 Rolls	2 Rolls
3 Rolls	3 Rolls	3 Rolls

November 21   November 21   November 21

1 Roll	1 Roll	1 Roll
2 Rolls	2 Rolls	2 Rolls
3 Rolls	3 Rolls	3 Rolls

November 22   November 22   November 22

1 Roll	1 Roll	1 Roll
2 Rolls	2 Rolls	2 Rolls
3 Rolls	3 Rolls	3 Rolls

After you have filled out the sheet, fold your column underneath along the dashed line so the next restroom user won't see your answers. *The first player uses the far right column.*

Answers - November 17-19
Nov. 17, 1 Roll: Danny DeVito
Nov. 17, 2 Rolls: Strategic Arms Limitation Talks
Nov. 17, 3 Rolls: *Heidi.* With the Jets leading by three points, fans in Eastern and Central time zones lost the feed to the game. As the Raiders came back to ultimately win 43-32, NBC was flooded with calls from angry football fans. Besides showing how popular football had become, the fiasco changed the way games would be subsequently televised.

Nov. 18, 1 Roll: Archery. He shot an apple off of his son's head with a crossbow.
Nov. 18, 2 Rolls: The Cape of Good Hope
Nov. 18, 3 Rolls: Jonestown, Guyana

Nov. 19, 1 Roll: Ted Turner
Nov. 19, 2 Rolls: The Jay Treaty. John Jay's treaty was ultimately ratified by the Senate, even though it did nothing to end impressment (British seizure of Americans who were *supposedly* in the British navy).
Nov. 19, 3 Rolls: 272 Words. Or, roughly 11 Tweets.

November 23

One Roll

The girl who played Hannah Montana was born in 1992. Who's her musical father?

Flip to pg. 229 for answers

Two Rolls

What Boston College quarterback threw a Hail Mary pass to defeat Miami on this date in 1984?

Three Rolls

Today in what year (within 10) did the stock market finally regain its losses from 1929?

November 24

One Roll

What controversial work did Charles Darwin publish today in 1859?

Two Rolls

Who shot Lee Harvey Oswald on live television today in 1963?

Three Rolls

In 1832, what three words did South Carolina declare the Tariffs of 1828 and 1832 to be?

November 25

One Roll

Where was John F. Kennedy buried today in 1963?

Two Rolls

Later known for writing a book on steroids, what Oakland A's star was named Rookie-of-the-Year today in 1986?

Three Rolls

Christina Applegate was born in 1971. How many touchdowns did her TV dad score in one high school game?

Answer Sheet | Answer Sheet | Answer Sheet

Name_____ | Name_____ | Name_____

November 23 | November 23 | November 23

1 Roll	1 Roll	1 Roll
2 Rolls	2 Rolls	2 Rolls
3 Rolls	3 Rolls	3 Rolls

November 24 | November 24 | November 24

1 Roll	1 Roll	1 Roll
2 Rolls	2 Rolls	2 Rolls
3 Rolls	3 Rolls	3 Rolls

November 25 | November 25 | November 25

1 Roll	1 Roll	1 Roll
2 Rolls	2 Rolls	2 Rolls
3 Rolls	3 Rolls	3 Rolls

After you have filled out the sheet, fold your column underneath along the dashed line so the next restroom user won't see your answers. *The first player uses the far right column.*

Answers - November 20-22

Nov. 20, 1 Roll: Joe Biden. He would commute roughly 250 miles a day when the Senate was in session.
Nov. 20, 2 Rolls: Francisco Franco
Nov. 20, 3 Rolls: Stanford. With the game clock counting down, the California Golden Bears used five laterals to score a touchdown on the final kickoff. Thinking the game was over, Stanford's band went onto the field prematurely. They became movable obstacles for California's kick-return team.

Nov. 21, 1 Roll: Red Grange
Nov. 21, 2 Rolls: The Mayflower Compact
Nov. 21, 3 Rolls: Voltaire

Nov. 22, 1 Roll: Dallas, Texas. Today was the day that President John F. Kennedy was assassinated.
Nov. 22, 2 Rolls: Blackbeard
Nov. 22, 3 Rolls: Saudi Arabia

November 26

 **One Roll**

What Dolphins quarterback broke the all-time touchdown record in 1995 with a pass to Keith Byers?

Flip to pg. 231 for answers

 **Two Rolls**

Born today in 1607, what clergyman's name would soon be associated with a rather smart school?

 **Three Rolls**

What music show, which premiered today in 1989, went all acoustic?

November 27

 **One Roll**

Jaleel White was born today in 1976. What thick-glasses wearing character on *Family Matters* did he play?

 **Two Rolls**

Assassinated today in 1978, what movie subject became the first openly gay person elected to office?

 **Three Rolls**

Today in 1582, who did William Shakespeare receive a license to marry?

November 28

 **One Roll**

What Comedy Central satire host was born on this *daily* in 1962?

 **Two Rolls**

What city was named capital of the Washington Territory today in 1853?

 **Three Rolls**

What World War II conference held in the Middle East began today in 1943?

Answer Sheet   Answer Sheet   Answer Sheet

Name_____   Name_____   Name_____

November 26   November 26   November 26

November 26	November 26	November 26
1 Roll	1 Roll	1 Roll
2 Rolls	2 Rolls	2 Rolls
3 Rolls	3 Rolls	3 Rolls

November 27   November 27   November 27

November 27	November 27	November 27
1 Roll	1 Roll	1 Roll
2 Rolls	2 Rolls	2 Rolls
3 Rolls	3 Rolls	3 Rolls

November 28   November 28   November 28

November 28	November 28	November 28
1 Roll	1 Roll	1 Roll
2 Rolls	2 Rolls	2 Rolls
3 Rolls	3 Rolls	3 Rolls

After you have filled out the sheet, fold your column underneath along the dashed line so the next restroom user won't see your answers. *The first player uses the far right column.*

Answers - November 23-25

Nov. 23, 1 Roll: Country singer Billy Ray Cyrus is Miley's dad
Nov. 23, 2 Rolls: Doug Flutie
Nov. 23, 3 Rolls: 1954. The Dow Jones hit 381, the pre-crash high.

Nov. 24, 1 Roll: *The Origin of Species*, or *On the Origin of Species*
Nov. 24, 2 Rolls: Jack Ruby
Nov. 24, 3 Rolls: "Null and Void." The Ordinance of Nullification was a threat to Civil War. But, Henry Clay compromised a solution, and the can of civil war was kicked to another generation.

Nov. 25, 1 Roll: Arlington National Cemetery
Nov. 25, 2 Rolls: Jose Canseco
Nov. 25, 3 Rolls: Al Bundy scored 4 touchdowns for Polk High School. Applegate played his daughter, Kelly.

November 29

🧻 One Roll

Flip to pg. 233 for answers

To celebrate the 600th anniversary of this Korean city, a time capsule was buried in 1994. What city?

🧻🧻 Two Rolls

George Harrison of the Beatles died today in 2001. What celestial song did he write?

🧻🧻🧻 Three Rolls

What famous college football rivalry began way back on this date in 1890?

November 30

🧻 One Roll

Born in 1929, he hosted *American Bandstand* for thirty years.

🧻🧻 Two Rolls

Whose automobile exposé, *Unsafe at Any Speed*, went on sale today in 1965?

🧻🧻🧻 Three Rolls

Who presided over the Senate in the 1804-1805 impeachment trial of Justice Samuel Chase?

December 1

🧻 One Roll

How did Henry Ford change production forever today in 1913?

🧻🧻 Two Rolls

What comedic mind, born in 1940, starred in live stand-up, *Brewster's Millions*, and *See No Evil, Hear No Evil*?

🧻🧻🧻 Three Rolls

In 1990, European workers from what two countries rejoiced as they saw each other for the first time?

Answer Sheet | Answer Sheet | Answer Sheet

Name_____ Name_____ Name_____

November 29	November 29	November 29
1 Roll	1 Roll	1 Roll
2 Rolls	2 Rolls	2 Rolls
3 Rolls	3 Rolls	3 Rolls

November 30	November 30	November 30
1 Roll	1 Roll	1 Roll
2 Rolls	2 Rolls	2 Rolls
3 Rolls	3 Rolls	3 Rolls

December 1	December 1	December 1
1 Roll	1 Roll	1 Roll
2 Rolls	2 Rolls	2 Rolls
3 Rolls	3 Rolls	3 Rolls

After you have filled out the sheet, fold your column underneath along the dashed line so the next restroom user won't see your answers. *The first player uses the far right column.*

Answers - November 26-28

Nov. 26, 1 Roll: Dan Marino. Brett Favre is the current all-time leader in touchdowns with 508.
Nov. 26, 2 Rolls: Harvard University is named for John Harvard
Nov. 26, 3 Rolls: *MTV Unplugged*

Nov. 27, 1 Roll: Steve Urkel
Nov. 27, 2 Rolls: Harvey Milk. He was elected to the San Francisco Board of Supervisors, and was portrayed by Sean Penn in the movie *Milk*.
Nov. 27, 3 Rolls: Anne Hathaway. They married the next day.

Nov. 28, 1 Roll: Jon Stewart, host of *The Daily Show*
Nov. 28, 2 Rolls: Olympia
Nov. 28, 3 Rolls: Tehran Conference. It was attended by Joseph Stalin, Winston Churchill, and Franklin Roosevelt. It was the first conference held by "The Big Three."

December 2

One Roll

Flip to pg. 235 for answers

Born in 1981, on what children's show did Britney Spears become a household name?

Two Rolls

What Houston-based energy company went bankrupt in 2001?

Three Rolls

What 1823 US statement, that attempted to end colonization in the Western Hemisphere, was issued today?

December 3

One Roll

What actress, and significant other of John F. Kennedy, Jr., splashed into the world today in 1960?

Two Rolls

What did Louis Washkansky get transplanted with today in 1967?

Three Rolls

In 1621, who announced to the world that he perfected a telescope?

December 4

One Roll

In 1969, what borough of New York City was Jay-Z born in?

Two Rolls

Today in 1997, the NBA dished out a stiff sentence to what player who choked his coach?

Three Rolls

What state claims that they had the first Thanksgiving today in 1619...well before the Pilgrims celebrated it?

Answer Sheet   Answer Sheet   Answer Sheet

Name_____   Name_____   Name_____

December 2   December 2   December 2

December 2	December 2	December 2
1 Roll	1 Roll	1 Roll
2 Rolls	2 Rolls	2 Rolls
3 Rolls	3 Rolls	3 Rolls

December 3   December 3   December 3

December 3	December 3	December 3
1 Roll	1 Roll	1 Roll
2 Rolls	2 Rolls	2 Rolls
3 Rolls	3 Rolls	3 Rolls

December 4   December 4   December 4

December 4	December 4	December 4
1 Roll	1 Roll	1 Roll
2 Rolls	2 Rolls	2 Rolls
3 Rolls	3 Rolls	3 Rolls

After you have filled out the sheet, fold your column underneath along the dashed line so the next restroom user won't see your answers. ***The first player uses the far right column.***

Answers - November 29-December 1

Nov. 29, 1 Roll: Seoul. The capsule is slated to be opened in 2394…for the 1000th anniversary.
Nov. 29, 2 Rolls: *Here Comes the Sun*
Nov. 29, 3 Rolls: Army and Navy. At West Point, Navy won 24-0 in the first contest.

Nov. 30, 1 Roll: Dick Clark. He was also a game show host, and the celebrity who rang in New Year's Eve from Times Square.
Nov. 30, 2 Rolls: Ralph Nader
Nov. 30, 3 Rolls: Aaron Burr. He returned to Washington months after killing Alexander Hamilton in a duel. As Vice President, it was his job to preside over an impeachment trial in the Senate. The trial proceedings began today, and lasted until March 1, 1805. Chase was acquitted.

Dec. 1, 1 Roll: He turned out a moving assembly line for making cars
Dec. 1, 2 Rolls: Richard Pryor
Dec. 1, 3 Rolls: Britain and France. They were working on the Chunnel which connects both countries. Today, they finally saw daylight at the other end.

December 5

One Roll

Three Presidents, on bills smaller than 50, were re-elected by the Electoral College today (1792, 1804, 1832). Name two of them.

Flip to pg. 237 for answers

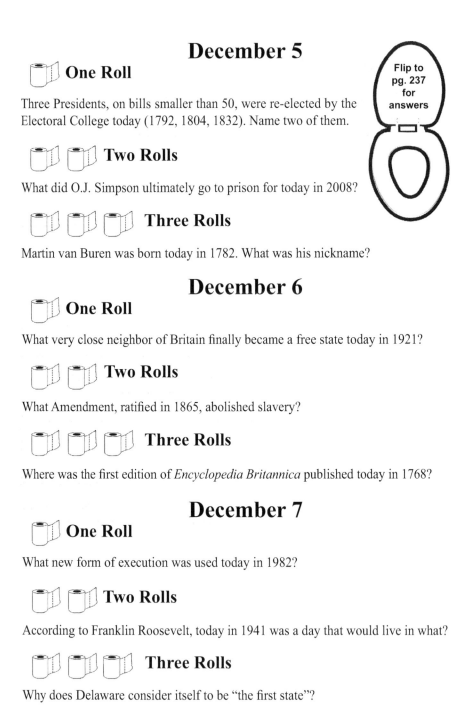

Two Rolls

What did O.J. Simpson ultimately go to prison for today in 2008?

Three Rolls

Martin van Buren was born today in 1782. What was his nickname?

December 6

One Roll

What very close neighbor of Britain finally became a free state today in 1921?

Two Rolls

What Amendment, ratified in 1865, abolished slavery?

Three Rolls

Where was the first edition of *Encyclopedia Britannica* published today in 1768?

December 7

One Roll

What new form of execution was used today in 1982?

Two Rolls

According to Franklin Roosevelt, today in 1941 was a day that would live in what?

Three Rolls

Why does Delaware consider itself to be "the first state"?

Answer Sheet | Answer Sheet | Answer Sheet

Name_____ Name_____ Name_____

December 5 | December 5 | December 5

1 Roll	1 Roll	1 Roll
2 Rolls	2 Rolls	2 Rolls
3 Rolls	3 Rolls	3 Rolls

December 6 | December 6 | December 6

1 Roll	1 Roll	1 Roll
2 Rolls	2 Rolls	2 Rolls
3 Rolls	3 Rolls	3 Rolls

December 7 | December 7 | December 7

1 Roll	1 Roll	1 Roll
2 Rolls	2 Rolls	2 Rolls
3 Rolls	3 Rolls	3 Rolls

After you have filled out the sheet, fold your column underneath along the dashed line so the next restroom user won't see your answers. *The first player uses the far right column.*

Answers - December 2-4
Dec. 2, 1 Roll: *The Mickey Mouse Club*
Dec. 2, 2 Rolls: Enron
Dec. 2, 3 Rolls: The Monroe Doctrine

Dec. 3, 1 Roll: Daryl Hannah, the mermaid in *Splash*
Dec. 3, 2 Rolls: He was the first to receive a human heart transplant. He lived another three weeks, but the surgery was championed a success. His death was not heart related.
Dec. 3, 3 Rolls: Galileo Galilei

Dec. 4, 1 Roll: Brooklyn. He was born Shawn Corey Carter.
Dec. 4, 2 Rolls: Latrell Sprewell. He choked Warrior coach P.J. Carlesimo and was suspended one year. It was the longest suspension in league history.
Dec. 4, 3 Rolls: Virginia. English settlers arrived near the James River and gave a day of thanksgiving to God.

December 8

🧻 **One Roll**

Born today in 1925, who was the only African American in the Rat Pack?

Flip to pg. 239 for answers

🧻🧻 **Two Rolls**

Who shot John Lennon on this date in 1980?

🧻🧻🧻 **Three Rolls**

What labor union led by Samuel Gompers was founded today in 1886?

December 9

🧻 **One Roll**

In 1992, what high profile couple announced their separation in England?

 **Two Rolls**

In 1967, what rock star was arrested on stage in New Haven and charged with disrupting the peace?

🧻🧻🧻 **Three Rolls**

What long-time Illinois politician, who shares a name with a long-time music star, died today in 2003?

December 10

 **One Roll**

What poet, born today in 1830, didn't become famous until after she died?

 **Two Rolls**

In 1688, King James II fled England amidst what bloodless revolution?

🧻🧻🧻 **Three Rolls**

Though he died today in 1896, what philanthropic inventor's obituary was published before he died?

Answer Sheet | Answer Sheet | Answer Sheet

Name_____ | Name_____ | Name_____

December 8 | December 8 | December 8

1 Roll	1 Roll	1 Roll
2 Rolls	2 Rolls	2 Rolls
3 Rolls	3 Rolls	3 Rolls

December 9 | December 9 | December 9

1 Roll	1 Roll	1 Roll
2 Rolls	2 Rolls	2 Rolls
3 Rolls	3 Rolls	3 Rolls

December 10 | December 10 | December 10

1 Roll	1 Roll	1 Roll
2 Rolls	2 Rolls	2 Rolls
3 Rolls	3 Rolls	3 Rolls

After you have filled out the sheet, fold your column underneath along the dashed line so the next restroom user won't see your answers. ***The first player uses the far right column.***

Answers - December 5-7

Dec. 5, 1 Roll: George Washington, Thomas Jefferson, and Andrew Jackson
Dec. 5, 2 Rolls: Armed robbery
Dec. 5, 3 Rolls: Old Kinderhook. His O.K. name helped to popularize the common phrase we use today (though the term was around before he was elected).

Dec. 6, 1 Roll: Ireland
Dec. 6, 2 Rolls: 13th Amendment
Dec. 6, 3 Rolls: Scotland

Dec. 7, 1 Roll: Lethal injection. It was done in Texas.
Dec. 7, 2 Rolls: Infamy. Today is the anniversary of the bombing of Pearl Harbor. The event drew the United States into World War II.
Dec. 7, 3 Rolls: Today in 1787 it became the first state to ratify the constitution

December 11

One Roll

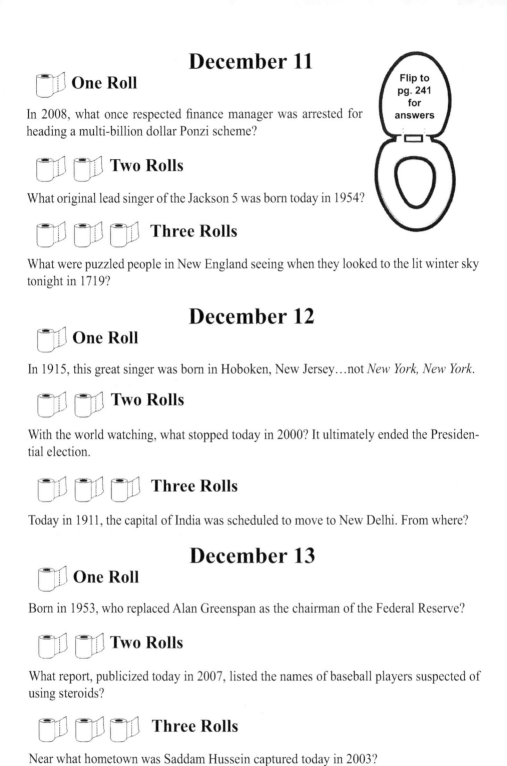

Flip to pg. 241 for answers

In 2008, what once respected finance manager was arrested for heading a multi-billion dollar Ponzi scheme?

Two Rolls

What original lead singer of the Jackson 5 was born today in 1954?

Three Rolls

What were puzzled people in New England seeing when they looked to the lit winter sky tonight in 1719?

December 12

One Roll

In 1915, this great singer was born in Hoboken, New Jersey…not *New York, New York.*

Two Rolls

With the world watching, what stopped today in 2000? It ultimately ended the Presidential election.

Three Rolls

Today in 1911, the capital of India was scheduled to move to New Delhi. From where?

December 13

One Roll

Born in 1953, who replaced Alan Greenspan as the chairman of the Federal Reserve?

Two Rolls

What report, publicized today in 2007, listed the names of baseball players suspected of using steroids?

Three Rolls

Near what hometown was Saddam Hussein captured today in 2003?

Answer Sheet | Answer Sheet | Answer Sheet

Name_____ | Name_____ | Name_____

December 11	December 11	December 11
1 Roll	1 Roll	1 Roll
2 Rolls	2 Rolls	2 Rolls
3 Rolls	3 Rolls	3 Rolls

December 12	December 12	December 12
1 Roll	1 Roll	1 Roll
2 Rolls	2 Rolls	2 Rolls
3 Rolls	3 Rolls	3 Rolls

December 13	December 13	December 13
1 Roll	1 Roll	1 Roll
2 Rolls	2 Rolls	2 Rolls
3 Rolls	3 Rolls	3 Rolls

After you have filled out the sheet, fold your column underneath along the dashed line so the next restroom user won't see your answers. *The first player uses the far right column.*

Answers - December 8-10

Dec. 8, 1 Roll: Sammy Davis, Jr.
Dec. 8, 2 Rolls: Mark David Chapman shot Lennon in New York City after asking for an autograph
Dec. 8, 3 Rolls: American Federation of Labor (AFL)

Dec. 9, 1 Roll: Prince Charles and Princess Diana
Dec. 9, 2 Rolls: Jim Morrison
Dec. 9, 3 Rolls: Paul Simon

Dec. 10, 1 Roll: Emily Dickinson. Most of her poems were hidden, and it was her sister who discovered them.
Dec. 10, 2 Rolls: The Glorious Revolution. It led to the crowning of William and Mary.
Dec. 10, 3 Rolls: Alfred Nobel. When Alfred's brother died, a French newspaper published the wrong obituary. It was of Alfred! They castigated him for the destructive invention of dynamite. Afterward, he came up with a better way to be remembered…the Nobel Prize.

December 14

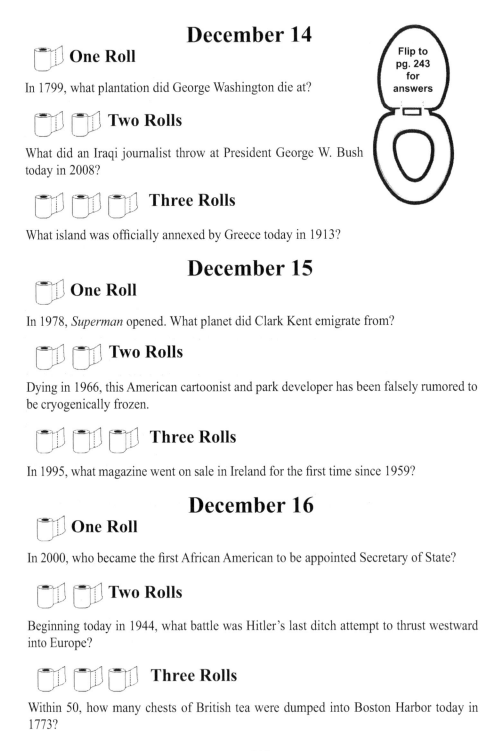

One Roll

In 1799, what plantation did George Washington die at?

Two Rolls

What did an Iraqi journalist throw at President George W. Bush today in 2008?

Three Rolls

What island was officially annexed by Greece today in 1913?

December 15

One Roll

In 1978, *Superman* opened. What planet did Clark Kent emigrate from?

Two Rolls

Dying in 1966, this American cartoonist and park developer has been falsely rumored to be cryogenically frozen.

Three Rolls

In 1995, what magazine went on sale in Ireland for the first time since 1959?

December 16

One Roll

In 2000, who became the first African American to be appointed Secretary of State?

Two Rolls

Beginning today in 1944, what battle was Hitler's last ditch attempt to thrust westward into Europe?

Three Rolls

Within 50, how many chests of British tea were dumped into Boston Harbor today in 1773?

Flip to pg. 243 for answers

Answer Sheet | Answer Sheet | Answer Sheet

Name_____ | Name_____ | Name_____

December 14 | December 14 | December 14

1 Roll	1 Roll	1 Roll
2 Rolls	2 Rolls	2 Rolls
3 Rolls	3 Rolls	3 Rolls

December 15 | December 15 | December 15

1 Roll	1 Roll	1 Roll
2 Rolls	2 Rolls	2 Rolls
3 Rolls	3 Rolls	3 Rolls

December 16 | December 16 | December 16

1 Roll	1 Roll	1 Roll
2 Rolls	2 Rolls	2 Rolls
3 Rolls	3 Rolls	3 Rolls

After you have filled out the sheet, fold your column underneath along the dashed line so the next restroom user won't see your answers. *The first player uses the far right column.*

Answers - December 11-13

Dec. 11, 1 Roll: Bernie Madoff
Dec. 11, 2 Rolls: Jermaine Jackson, the older brother of Michael. Michael eventually joined him on lead vocals.
Dec. 11, 3 Rolls: Aurora Borealis was seen for the first time by American colonists

Dec. 12, 1 Roll: Frank Sinatra
Dec. 12, 2 Rolls: The Florida recount. The Supreme Court ordered the recount to stop, thereby giving George W. Bush the Presidential Election over Al Gore. The name of the case was *Bush v. Gore*.
Dec. 12, 3 Rolls: Calcutta (Kolkata)

Dec. 13, 1 Roll: Ben Bernanke. He took over in 2006.
Dec. 13, 2 Rolls: The Mitchell Report (named for Senator George Mitchell of Maine)
Dec. 13, 3 Rolls: Tikrit. He was captured during Operation Red Dawn.

December 17

One Roll

Pitchers must have been *salivating* when the American League permitted them to use what pitch in 1920?

Flip to pg. 245 for answers

Two Rolls

What *Liberator* of South America died today in 1830?

Three Rolls

Today in 1903, the Wright Brothers experienced a short flight. Where did this first flight take place?

December 18

One Roll

For the first time on TV, what Dr. Seuss character tried to ruin the 1966 holiday season?

Two Rolls

Today in 1936, what import from China arrived at the National Zoo in Washington, DC?

Three Rolls

Brad Pitt was born today in 1963. In what outlaw film did he see his first big starring role in 1991?

December 19

One Roll

What Benjamin Franklin book of proverbs, weather patterns, and household hints was first published in 1732?

Two Rolls

Who's the Boss? Born today in 1972, her father was. Name her.

Three Rolls

According to Daniel Defoe, who left the island today in 1686?

Answer Sheet | Answer Sheet | Answer Sheet

Name_____ | Name_____ | Name_____

December 17 | December 17 | December 17

1 Roll	1 Roll	1 Roll
2 Rolls	2 Rolls	2 Rolls
3 Rolls	3 Rolls	3 Rolls

December 18 | December 18 | December 18

1 Roll	1 Roll	1 Roll
2 Rolls	2 Rolls	2 Rolls
3 Rolls	3 Rolls	3 Rolls

December 19 | December 19 | December 19

1 Roll	1 Roll	1 Roll
2 Rolls	2 Rolls	2 Rolls
3 Rolls	3 Rolls	3 Rolls

After you have filled out the sheet, fold your column underneath along the dashed line so the next restroom user won't see your answers. ***The first player uses the far right column.***

Answers - December 14-16
Dec. 14, 1 Roll: Mount Vernon
Dec. 14, 2 Rolls: His shoes. The President ducked them both.
Dec. 14, 3 Rolls: Crete

Dec. 15, 1 Roll: Krypton
Dec. 15, 2 Rolls: Walt Disney. The rumors are false, as he was cremated after his death.
Dec. 15, 3 Rolls: *Playboy*. The censorship had been lifted.

Dec. 16, 1 Roll: Colin Powell
Dec. 16, 2 Rolls: Battle of the Bulge. He was unsuccessful.
Dec. 16, 3 Rolls: 342 chests were tossed into the harbor during the Boston Tea Party

December 20

One Roll

Flip to pg. 247 for answers

What tire mogul was born today in 1868? Just the last name is fine.

Two Rolls

What annually aired Jimmy Stewart holiday tale debuted today in 1946?

Three Rolls

In 1989, what country did the US invade with hopes of removing Manuel Noriega from power?

December 21

One Roll

What is the scientific term to explain today/tomorrow in the Northern Hemisphere?

Two Rolls

At what structure in England do hundreds of people gather at on this date every year?

Three Rolls

Debuting in 1937, what was the first full-length animated film to be in color?

December 22

One Roll

What hair loss pill was approved by the FDA today in 1997?

Two Rolls

Born today in 1945, what female ABC journalist was an aide to President Nixon?

Three Rolls

In 1944, the Germans demanded a US surrender at Bastogne. What one word did an American General reply with?

Answer Sheet | Answer Sheet | Answer Sheet

Name_____ Name_____ Name_____

December 20 | **December 20** | **December 20**

1 Roll	1 Roll	1 Roll
2 Rolls	2 Rolls	2 Rolls
3 Rolls	3 Rolls	3 Rolls

December 21 | **December 21** | **December 21**

1 Roll	1 Roll	1 Roll
2 Rolls	2 Rolls	2 Rolls
3 Rolls	3 Rolls	3 Rolls

December 22 | **December 22** | **December 22**

1 Roll	1 Roll	1 Roll
2 Rolls	2 Rolls	2 Rolls
3 Rolls	3 Rolls	3 Rolls

After you have filled out the sheet, fold your column underneath along the dashed line so the next restroom user won't see your answers. *The first player uses the far right column.*

Answers - December 17-19
Dec. 17, 1 Roll: Spitballs
Dec. 17, 2 Rolls: Simón Bolívar
Dec. 17, 3 Rolls: Kitty Hawk, North Carolina

Dec. 18, 1 Roll: The Grinch. *How the Grinch Stole Christmas* hit the airwaves today.
Dec. 18, 2 Rolls: The Giant Panda
Dec. 18, 3 Rolls: *Thelma & Louise.* He played J.D.

Dec. 19, 1 Roll: *Poor Richard's Almanack*
Dec. 19, 2 Rolls: Alyssa Milano. She played Tony Danza's daughter on the show.
Dec. 19, 3 Rolls: *Robinson Crusoe*

December 23

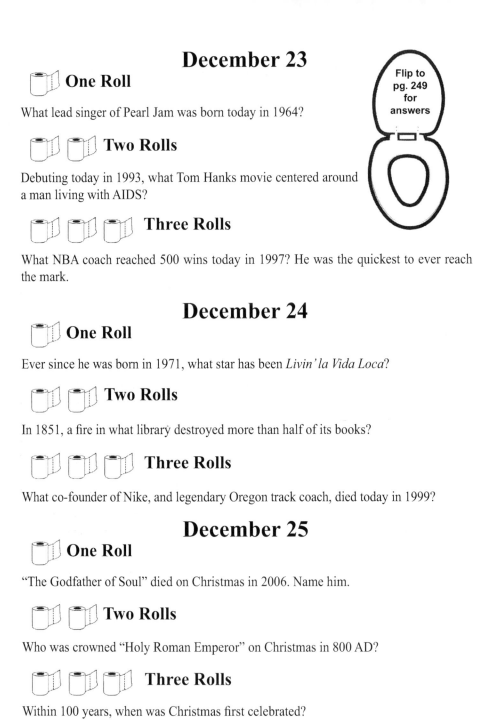

One Roll

What lead singer of Pearl Jam was born today in 1964?

Two Rolls

Debuting today in 1993, what Tom Hanks movie centered around a man living with AIDS?

Three Rolls

What NBA coach reached 500 wins today in 1997? He was the quickest to ever reach the mark.

Flip to pg. 249 for answers

December 24

One Roll

Ever since he was born in 1971, what star has been *Livin' la Vida Loca*?

Two Rolls

In 1851, a fire in what library destroyed more than half of its books?

Three Rolls

What co-founder of Nike, and legendary Oregon track coach, died today in 1999?

December 25

One Roll

"The Godfather of Soul" died on Christmas in 2006. Name him.

Two Rolls

Who was crowned "Holy Roman Emperor" on Christmas in 800 AD?

Three Rolls

Within 100 years, when was Christmas first celebrated?

Answer Sheet   Answer Sheet   Answer Sheet

Name_____   Name_____   Name_____

December 23   December 23   December 23

1 Roll	1 Roll	1 Roll
2 Rolls	2 Rolls	2 Rolls
3 Rolls	3 Rolls	3 Rolls

December 24   December 24   December 24

1 Roll	1 Roll	1 Roll
2 Rolls	2 Rolls	2 Rolls
3 Rolls	3 Rolls	3 Rolls

December 25   December 25   December 25

1 Roll	1 Roll	1 Roll
2 Rolls	2 Rolls	2 Rolls
3 Rolls	3 Rolls	3 Rolls

After you have filled out the sheet, fold your column underneath along the dashed line so the next restroom user won't see your answers. ***The first player uses the far right column.***

Answers - December 20-22
Dec. 20, 1 Roll: Harvey Firestone…not to be confused with actor Harvey Fierstein
Dec. 20, 2 Rolls: *It's a Wonderful Life*
Dec. 20, 3 Rolls: Panama

Dec. 21, 1 Roll: The winter solstice. The time fluctuates, but it is the shortest day of the year in the Northern Hemisphere.
Dec. 21, 2 Rolls: Stonehenge. Though a mystery, many believe it is astrologically aligned to coincide with the winter solstice.
Dec. 21, 3 Rolls: Disney's *Snow White and the Seven Dwarfs*. Cartoons were generally short. This one was nearly an hour and a half long.

Dec. 22, 1 Roll: Propecia
Dec. 22, 2 Rolls: Diane Sawyer
Dec. 22, 3 Rolls: "Nuts!" General Anthony McAuliffe summed up the anarchy of the battle. No surrender ever took place.

December 26

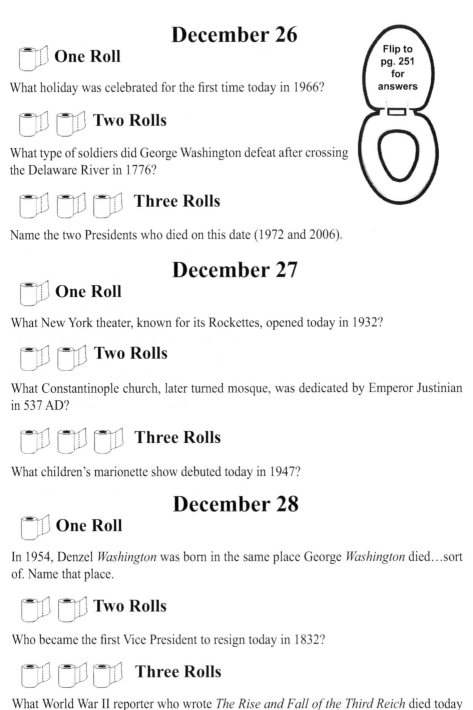

One Roll

What holiday was celebrated for the first time today in 1966?

Flip to pg. 251 for answers

Two Rolls

What type of soldiers did George Washington defeat after crossing the Delaware River in 1776?

Three Rolls

Name the two Presidents who died on this date (1972 and 2006).

December 27

One Roll

What New York theater, known for its Rockettes, opened today in 1932?

Two Rolls

What Constantinople church, later turned mosque, was dedicated by Emperor Justinian in 537 AD?

Three Rolls

What children's marionette show debuted today in 1947?

December 28

One Roll

In 1954, Denzel *Washington* was born in the same place George *Washington* died...sort of. Name that place.

Two Rolls

Who became the first Vice President to resign today in 1832?

Three Rolls

What World War II reporter who wrote *The Rise and Fall of the Third Reich* died today in 1993?

Answer Sheet | Answer Sheet | Answer Sheet

Name_____ | Name_____ | Name_____

December 26 | December 26 | December 26

1 Roll	1 Roll	1 Roll
2 Rolls	2 Rolls	2 Rolls
3 Rolls	3 Rolls	3 Rolls

December 27 | December 27 | December 27

1 Roll	1 Roll	1 Roll
2 Rolls	2 Rolls	2 Rolls
3 Rolls	3 Rolls	3 Rolls

December 28 | December 28 | December 28

1 Roll	1 Roll	1 Roll
2 Rolls	2 Rolls	2 Rolls
3 Rolls	3 Rolls	3 Rolls

After you have filled out the sheet, fold your column underneath along the dashed line so the next restroom user won't see your answers. *The first player uses the far right column.*

Answers - December 23-25
Dec. 23, 1 Roll: Eddie Vedder
Dec. 23, 2 Rolls: *Philadelphia*
Dec. 23, 3 Rolls: Phil Jackson did it in just 682 games

Dec. 24, 1 Roll: Ricky Martin…the song translates to *Livin' the Crazy Life*
Dec. 24, 2 Rolls: Library of Congress
Dec. 24, 3 Rolls: Bill Bowerman

Dec. 25, 1 Roll: James Brown
Dec. 25, 2 Rolls: Charlemagne
Dec. 25, 3 Rolls: 354 AD…some believe the accurate year is 336 AD because of a church record that indicated today as the birth of Jesus Christ. Count it if you got within 100 years of either date.

December 29

🧻 **One Roll**

What actor who played Sam Malone on *Cheers* was born today in 1947?

🧻🧻 **Two Rolls**

What 1890 massacre of the Sioux tribe became a symbol of Native American oppression?

🧻🧻🧻 **Three Rolls**

How did Rasputin finally die today in 1916?

Flip to pg. 252 for answers

December 30

🧻 **One Roll**

What legendary ship that fought the *Merrimack* sank during a storm today in 1862?

🧻🧻 **Two Rolls**

Born in 1865, what poet wrote *The White Man's Burden* as a criticism of imperialism?

🧻🧻🧻 **Three Rolls**

Today in 1852, Rutherford B. Hayes married Lucy. What was her juicy nickname as First Lady?

December 31

🧻 **One Roll**

The actor who played Hannibal Lecter was born today in 1937. Name him.

🧻🧻 **Two Rolls**

What New York subway rider turned himself into the police today in 1984?

🧻🧻🧻 **Three Rolls**

Of Tokyo, Seoul, Guam, Bangkok, Jakarta, Melbourne, or Beijing…who celebrates New Year's first?

Answer Sheet | Answer Sheet | Answer Sheet

Name_____ | Name_____ | Name_____

December 29 | December 29 | December 29

1 Roll	1 Roll	1 Roll
2 Rolls	2 Rolls	2 Rolls
3 Rolls	3 Rolls	3 Rolls

December 30 | December 30 | December 30

1 Roll	1 Roll	1 Roll
2 Rolls	2 Rolls	2 Rolls
3 Rolls	3 Rolls	3 Rolls

December 31 | December 31 | December 31

1 Roll	1 Roll	1 Roll
2 Rolls	2 Rolls	2 Rolls
3 Rolls	3 Rolls	3 Rolls

After you have filled out the sheet, fold your column underneath along the dashed line so the next restroom user won't see your answers. *The first player uses the far right column.*

Answers - December 26-28

Dec. 26, 1 Roll: Kwanzaa

Dec. 26, 2 Rolls: Mercenaries called Hessians…they were from Hesse, Germany. The Battle of Trenton was Washington's first battle victory of the war.

Dec. 26, 3 Rolls: Harry S Truman and Gerald Ford. Since George Washington, they were the only two presidents to die in December. Washington died on December 14, 1799.

Dec. 27, 1 Roll: Radio City Music Hall

Dec. 27, 2 Rolls: Hagia Sophia

Dec. 27, 3 Rolls: *Howdy Doody*

Dec. 28, 1 Roll: Mount Vernon…New York. George Washington died at his plantation called Mount Vernon…in Virginia.

Dec. 28, 2 Rolls: John C. Calhoun. He and President Andrew Jackson had political differences. Martin van Buren became the new Vice President, and eventually became the next President.

Dec. 28, 3 Rolls: William Shirer

Answers - December 29-31

Dec. 29, 1 Roll: Ted Danson

Dec. 29, 2 Rolls: Wounded Knee Massacre

Dec. 29, 3 Rolls: He ultimately drowned in the Neva River. Before, he was poisoned, stabbed, beat up, and even shot.

Dec. 30, 1 Roll: USS *Monitor*

Dec. 30, 2 Rolls: Rudyard Kipling

Dec. 30, 3 Rolls: Lemonade Lucy. She was an advocate of temperance, and wouldn't serve alcohol in the White House.

Dec. 31, 1 Roll: Anthony Hopkins

Dec. 31, 2 Rolls: Bernhard Goetz. He admitted to shooting four teenagers who threatened him. He was convicted of illegally carrying a firearm.

Dec. 31, 3 Rolls: Melbourne, Australia

Scorecard - Player 1   Name: _____

DIRECTIONS: For every month, add up the total number of questions you got right for each number of rolls. Place that number in the appropriate box in the "# Right" column and multiply accordingly to determine the Total Points you earned. Then compute your "Grand Total."

Month	# Right		Pts.		Tot. Pts.
Jan. - 1 Roll		x	1	=	
Jan. - 2 Rolls		x	2	=	
Jan. - 3 Rolls		x	3	=	
Feb. - 1 Roll		x	1	=	
Feb. - 2 Rolls		x	2	=	
Feb. - 3 Rolls		x	3	=	
Mar. - 1 Roll		x	1	=	
Mar. - 2 Rolls		x	2	=	
Mar. - 3 Rolls		x	3	=	
Apr. - 1 Roll		x	1	=	
Apr. - 2 Rolls		x	2	=	
Apr. - 3 Rolls		x	3	=	
May - 1 Roll		x	1	=	
May - 2 Rolls		x	2	=	
May - 3 Rolls		x	3	=	
June - 1 Roll		x	1	=	
June - 2 Rolls		x	2	=	
June - 3 Rolls		x	3	=	

Month	# Right		Pts.		Tot. Pts.
July - 1 Roll		x	1	=	
July - 2 Rolls		x	2	=	
July - 3 Rolls		x	3	=	
Aug. - 1 Roll		x	1	=	
Aug. - 2 Rolls		x	2	=	
Aug. - 3 Rolls		x	3	=	
Sept. - 1 Roll		x	1	=	
Sept. - 2 Rolls		x	2	=	
Sept. - 3 Rolls		x	3	=	
Oct. - 1 Roll		x	1	=	
Oct. - 2 Rolls		x	2	=	
Oct. - 3 Rolls		x	3	=	
Nov. - 1 Roll		x	1	=	
Nov. - 2 Rolls		x	2	=	
Nov. - 3 Rolls		x	3	=	
Dec. - 1 Roll		x	1	=	
Dec. - 2 Rolls		x	2	=	
Dec. - 3 Rolls		x	3	=	

Grand Total

Scorecard - Player 2   Name: _____

DIRECTIONS: For every month, add up the total number of questions you got right for each number of rolls. Place that number in the appropriate box in the "# Right" column and multiply accordingly to determine the Total Points you earned. Then compute your "Grand Total."

Month	# Right		Pts.		Tot. Pts.
Jan. - 1 Roll		x	1	=	
Jan. - 2 Rolls		x	2	=	
Jan. - 3 Rolls		x	3	=	
Feb. - 1 Roll		x	1	=	
Feb. - 2 Rolls		x	2	=	
Feb. - 3 Rolls		x	3	=	
Mar. - 1 Roll		x	1	=	
Mar. - 2 Rolls		x	2	=	
Mar. - 3 Rolls		x	3	=	
Apr. - 1 Roll		x	1	=	
Apr. - 2 Rolls		x	2	=	
Apr. - 3 Rolls		x	3	=	
May - 1 Roll		x	1	=	
May - 2 Rolls		x	2	=	
May - 3 Rolls		x	3	=	
June - 1 Roll		x	1	=	
June - 2 Rolls		x	2	=	
June - 3 Rolls		x	3	=	

Month	# Right		Pts.		Tot. Pts.
July - 1 Roll		x	1	=	
July - 2 Rolls		x	2	=	
July - 3 Rolls		x	3	=	
Aug. - 1 Roll		x	1	=	
Aug. - 2 Rolls		x	2	=	
Aug. - 3 Rolls		x	3	=	
Sept. - 1 Roll		x	1	=	
Sept. - 2 Rolls		x	2	=	
Sept. - 3 Rolls		x	3	=	
Oct. - 1 Roll		x	1	=	
Oct. - 2 Rolls		x	2	=	
Oct. - 3 Rolls		x	3	=	
Nov. - 1 Roll		x	1	=	
Nov. - 2 Rolls		x	2	=	
Nov. - 3 Rolls		x	3	=	
Dec. - 1 Roll		x	1	=	
Dec. - 2 Rolls		x	2	=	
Dec. - 3 Rolls		x	3	=	

Grand Total

Scorecard - Player 3   Name: _____

DIRECTIONS: For every month, add up the total number of questions you got right for each number of rolls. Place that number in the appropriate box in the "# Right" column and multiply accordingly to determine the Total Points you earned. Then compute your "Grand Total."

Month	# Right		Pts.		Tot. Pts.
Jan. - 1 Roll		x	1	=	
Jan. - 2 Rolls		x	2	=	
Jan. - 3 Rolls		x	3	=	
Feb. - 1 Roll		x	1	=	
Feb. - 2 Rolls		x	2	=	
Feb. - 3 Rolls		x	3	=	
Mar. - 1 Roll		x	1	=	
Mar. - 2 Rolls		x	2	=	
Mar. - 3 Rolls		x	3	=	
Apr. - 1 Roll		x	1	=	
Apr. - 2 Rolls		x	2	=	
Apr. - 3 Rolls		x	3	=	
May - 1 Roll		x	1	=	
May - 2 Rolls		x	2	=	
May - 3 Rolls		x	3	=	
June - 1 Roll		x	1	=	
June - 2 Rolls		x	2	=	
June - 3 Rolls		x	3	=	

Month	# Right		Pts.		Tot. Pts.
July - 1 Roll		x	1	=	
July - 2 Rolls		x	2	=	
July - 3 Rolls		x	3	=	
Aug. - 1 Roll		x	1	=	
Aug. - 2 Rolls		x	2	=	
Aug. - 3 Rolls		x	3	=	
Sept. - 1 Roll		x	1	=	
Sept. - 2 Rolls		x	2	=	
Sept. - 3 Rolls		x	3	=	
Oct. - 1 Roll		x	1	=	
Oct. - 2 Rolls		x	2	=	
Oct. - 3 Rolls		x	3	=	
Nov. - 1 Roll		x	1	=	
Nov. - 2 Rolls		x	2	=	
Nov. - 3 Rolls		x	3	=	
Dec. - 1 Roll		x	1	=	
Dec. - 2 Rolls		x	2	=	
Dec. - 3 Rolls		x	3	=	

Grand Total

How did you do?

1,800 + — King/Queen of the Throne

1,500-1,799 — Topper of the Hopper

1,300-1,499 — Porcelain Prince/Princess

1,100-1,299 — Toileterrific!

900-1,099 — Keep Flushing for the Stars

700-899 — Might Need a Plunger

500-699 — Gotta call the Plumber

Below 500 — Clogged
Try a different Toiletrivia Book!

Made in the USA
San Bernardino, CA
19 November 2015